Create Magic!

oH Katie!!

Life is meant to be Fun!

Here's to the JOYS of choosing to feel Good! AND Celebrating the FUN in our Hearts every moment!! HURRAY!!

Joan Marie

Joan Marie

Create Magic
Life is meant to be Fun!
Joan Marie
Joan Marie Art

Published by Joan Marie Art, St. Louis, MO

Artwork by Joan Marie
Book Design: www.DavisCreative.com

Publisher's Cataloging-In-Publication Data

(Prepared by The Donohue Group, Inc.)

Names: Marie, Joan, author, illustrator.
Title: Create magic! : life is meant to be fun! / Joan Marie.
Description: St. Louis, MO : Joan Marie Art, [2018]
Identifiers: ISBN 9780960080106 (hardback) | ISBN 9780960080113 (paperback) | ISBN 9780960080120 (ebook)
Subjects: LCSH: Happiness--Pictorial works. | Love--Pictorial works. | Gratitude--Pictorial works. | Spiritual healing--Pictorial works. | BISAC: SELF-HELP / Personal Growth / Happiness. | ART / General. | BODY, MIND & SPIRIT / Inspiration & Personal Growth Art.
Classification: LCC BF575.H27 M37 2018 (print) | LCC BF575.H27 (ebook) | DDC 158.1--dc23

2018

A Note from Joan Marie

Life is an ever-flowing journey of change and discovery for me. Hence, you will see the many styles of art I have explored, seeking answers and expressing different voices we all share inside.

From Ethereal…to Spiritual…to Essence Portraiture…to Whimsical… to Abstraction/Expressionism…to Happeee Girl…to Rainbow Whimsical…to Fantasy

…to my current life's passion: **Creating Higher Vision Portraits**, (example: The double-headed eagle in the beginning pages) …expressing ones' higher vision of oneself through your Spirit Animal, your favorite symbols, your face now or as a child, or a combination of all. More about this intuitive wisdom which has flowed into my life on my website. (:

How do you best use this book?

After the intro, you might want to open to any page to see what your message for the day is.

It is such fun to share my favorite art and photos beginning at age 36, in 1986, while living in Sedona. Starting on page 22, my art is presented chronologically. You can see the confidence and energy grow through the years as the colors shift from bright pastels, to pure black and white, to intense vibrancy, and back again with the freedom to choose whatever expresses the message strongest!

I am sharing a bit of the spiritual knowledge that has helped free me of that non-stop insulting voice in my head telling me I'm not good enough. As my spiritual wisdom increases, the more I twirl and smile in my mind as well as more and more physical twirling and jumping happens too!

I have learned to stop the resistance, self-doubt, and questioning. Learning to go with the flow and loving what is in this very moment, has opened a whole new experience of joy.

Thank you for entering my world of exploration to express happiness. Life is the meaning that we give it, and I believe it is Love.

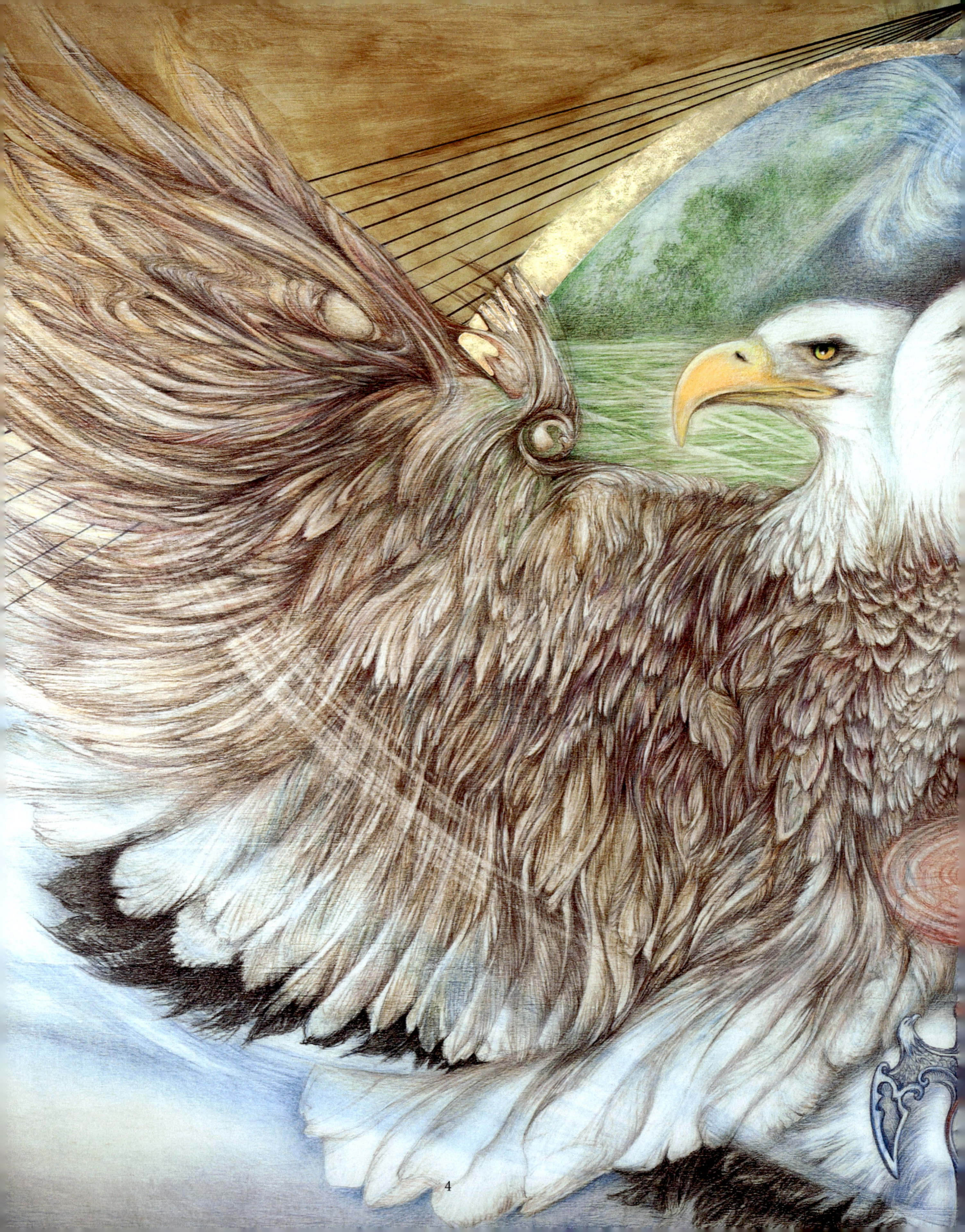

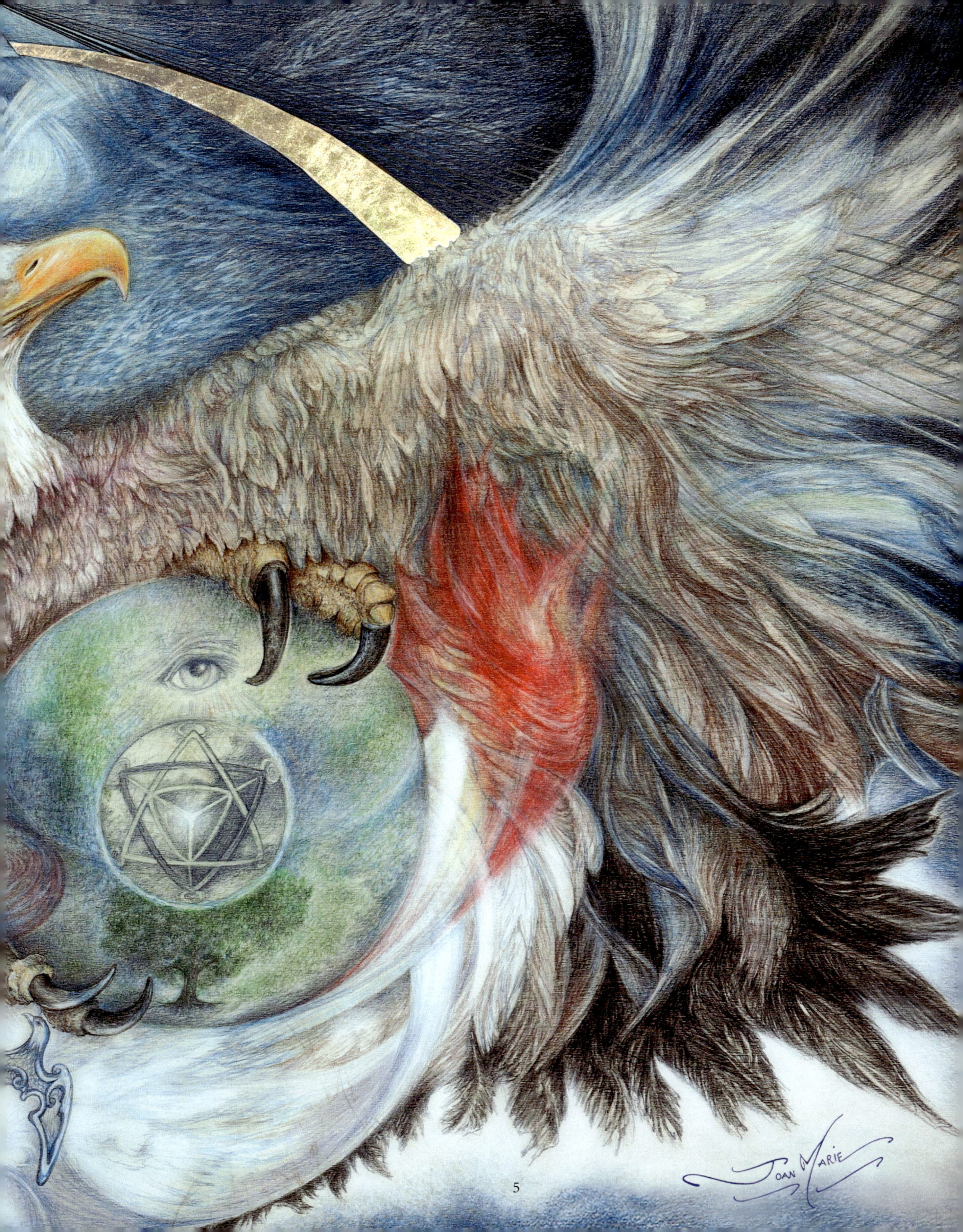
Joan Marie

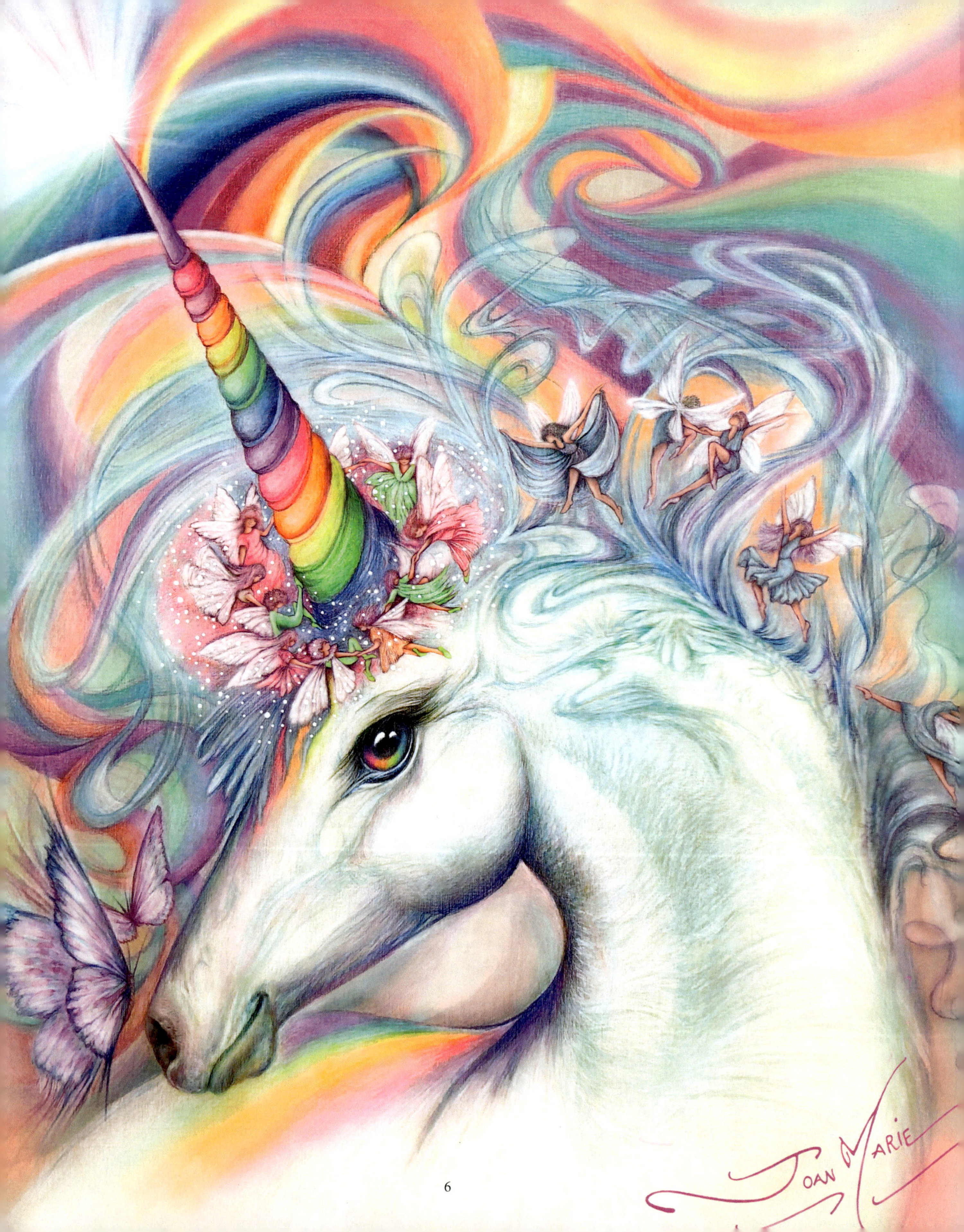
Joan Marie

Life is truly meant to be fun!

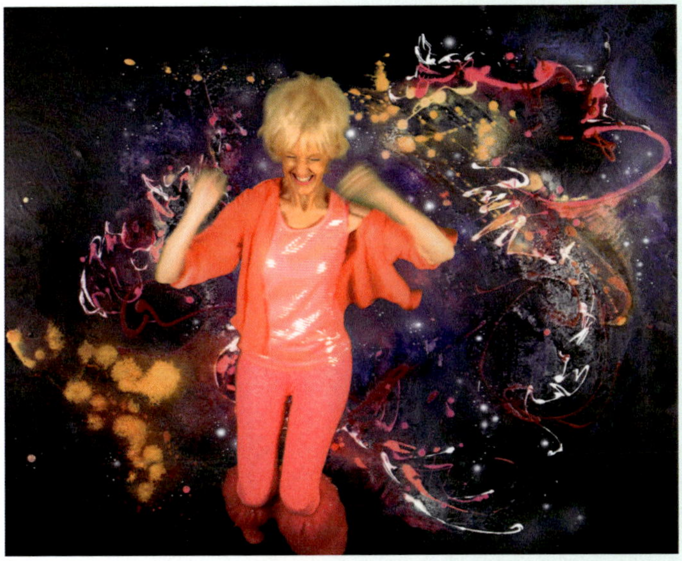

It's true! It's really true! I ran around the house three times celebrating when I learned this wisdom! Now we have permission to be giddy and celebrate EVERY DAY!

Experiment for just a minute. See the world as a little tiny child does. Open your eyes and look at the world without judgment or thoughts of wishing things would be different than they are right now. Enjoy the pure joy of observation and wonder. Through this lens of non-judgement the world glows. Suddenly the world becomes a magical place. Now no matter what is going on, we have permission to stop for a moment to be thankful and get giddy for what is already here. Shift to this place of wonderment any moment you choose.

Do you share these two passions with me?!

Spirituality

The practice of how we can serve others and be all we can be

Creativity

How to free the unique pulsating spirits inside each of us.

Come celebrate!

If you are willing to consider that life is meant to be fun, have fun FEELING GOOD while doing what you love most. Celebrate and stop caring so much about what others think.

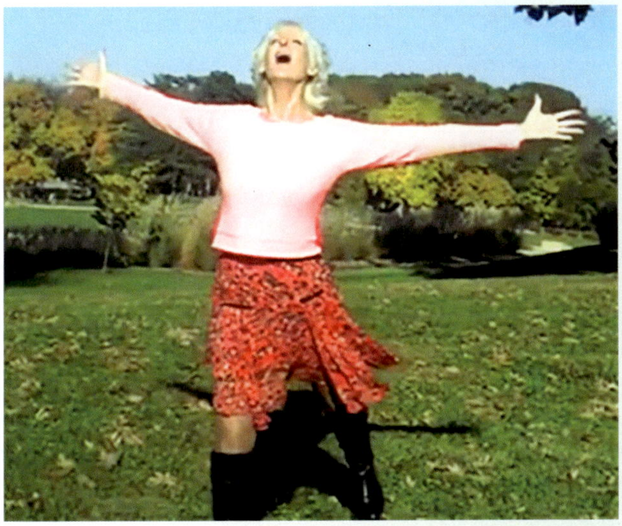

Feel free to follow your heart and listen to your inner desires.

For me, I dreamed about twirling in flouncy-bouncy rainbow glitter skirts on the hills of the golf course singing, "The hills are alive with the sound of music!"

What is that yearning you want to experience? We each have a unique expression to share. Listen to your heart. Stop, take a few breaths and feel what your heart is saying. Then let things go, live with no regrets. Forgive yourself and others. Discover what makes you feel alive. Go out and do it. Do it now!

Truths that Keep You Twirling

1) **Shift negative thoughts to a feel-better place.**
A quick "go-to" remedy for me is to sing a happeee song! Make it fun! Personally, I choose to see myself smiling, singing, and twirling in rainbow fluff for the rest of my life!

2) **Everything is energy.**
Feel energy as it radiates all around you. Check in. Is the energy you are expressing what you want those around you to feel?

3) **What if love is all that matters?**
Try it, when love is your priority, magic happens. It can feel so rewarding to choose love of others and self over possessions.

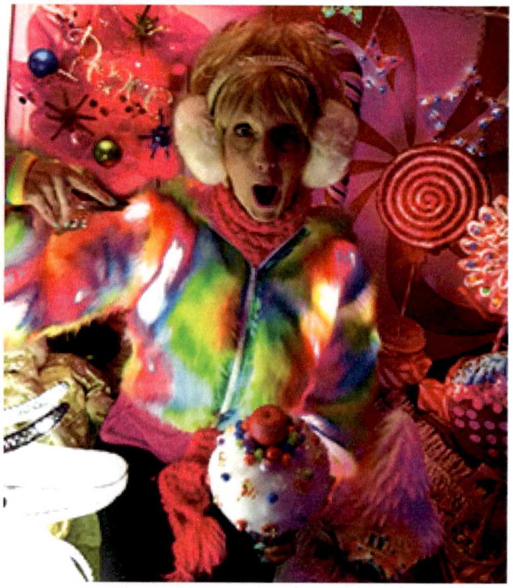

4) **You can *never* be too thankful.**
BE thankful and DO really cool, nice and *fun* things for others! Join me in knowing "Thank you, God" is the greatest prayer and blessing.

5) **Enjoy the *journey*!**
Real happiness is loving the everyday adventure of what you love to do. For some people—life gets so busy that sleeping and eating becomes what they love to do—because those basic needs aren't being met in a relaxed normal balanced way with the push to do-do-do. So, the dreams beyond that—have taken a backseat. But **all we really have is now.** The past is over and behind us. There are no guarantees, the future is unknown.

Be fully present and thankful now.

We don't live in a world of only rainbows...Oh my gosh did I really just say that?! ... So how do we find the rainbow in what appears as muck?

One of the "secrets" to maintaining a peaceful feeling, (which can then lead to smiles!) is creating the habit of being okay with whatever happens. When things do not go as planned,

...Stop to take a breath

...Release your need to control your circumstances

...Go with the Flow

...and be thankful.

Going with the flow means letting things happen as they do and letting go of trying to force change.

...How you feel in this very moment is what really matters.

...Become present to how you feel in this moment.

...Be thankful for what is here right now.

...Accept that you don't have total control of the world around you.

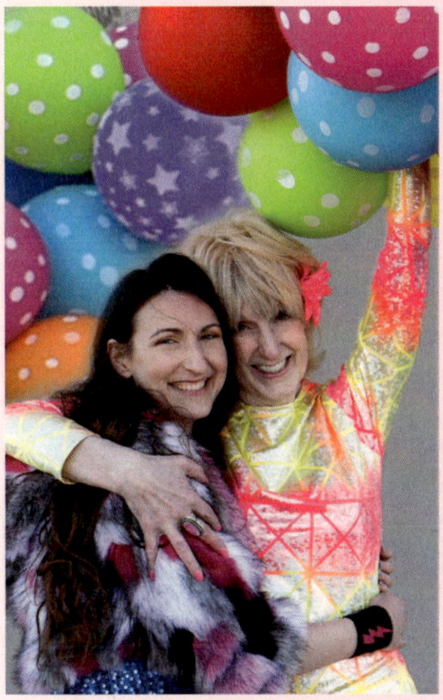

My Daughter, Brittany and me

Develop ways to have fun within the chaos of this world.

Life is how you perceive it.

...Shift your perception of what is happening. Learning to interpret a situation seven different ways is an amazing way to change your perception toward any upsetting situation.

Life flows in miraculous ways when we go with the flow.

We can't always control the outcome, but we can always control our feelings in this moment. When we allow flow, it's possible that solutions could occur that we could not have created with our limited brainpower.

The one thing we know for sure is that we have the power in this moment to choose an inner smile and enjoy the feeling of trust and acceptance right now, no matter what.

... Life is an amazing ride when you add the fun and wonder of a child when seeing things for the first time. Accept the ebb and flow of life, and regularly shift to the best feeling place. This welcomes magic into your life every day!

Start with an inner smile. Do you feel a glow coming from within? Many are not aware of the power of an inner smile. This is one of my "secrets" to happiness that truly works: Lift the corners of your mouth up slightly. Some call it a Mona Lisa smile. It's amazing what a difference this makes.

Richard Branson, an English business magnate, investor, author and philanthropist who also founded the Virgin Group, responsible for more than 400 companies, wrote 'A Letter to a Stranger' which beautifully summarizes true happiness.

"Dear Stranger,

You don't know me but I hear you are going through a tough time, and I would like to help you. I want to be open and honest with you, and let you know that happiness isn't something just afforded to a special few. It can be yours, if you take the time to let it grow.

It's OK to be stressed, scared and sad, I certainly have been throughout my 66 years. I've confronted my biggest fears time and time again. I've cheated death on many adventures, seen loved ones pass away, failed in business, minced my words in front of tough audiences, and had my heart broken.

I know I'm fortunate to live an extraordinary life, and that most people would assume my business success, and the wealth that comes with it, have brought me happiness. But they haven't; in fact, it's the reverse. I am successful, wealthy and connected because I am happy.

So many people get caught up in doing what they think will make them happy but, in my opinion, this is where they fail. Happiness is not about doing, it's about being. In order to be happy, you need to think consciously about it. Don't forget the to-do list but remember to write a to-be list too

Kids are often asked: 'What do you want to be when you grow up?' The world expects grandiose aspirations: 'I want to be a writer, a doctor, the prime minister.' They're told: go to school, go to college, get a job, get married, and then you'll be happy. But that's all about doing, not being – and while doing will bring you moments of joy, it won't necessarily reward you with lasting happiness.

Stop and breathe. Be healthy. Be around your friends and family. Be there for someone and let someone be there for you. Be bold. Just be for a minute.

If you allow yourself to be in the moment, and appreciate the moment, happiness will follow. I speak from experience. We've built a business empire, joined conversations about the future of our planet, attended many memorable parties and met many unforgettable people. And while these things have brought me great joy, it's the moments that I stopped just to be, rather than do, that have given me true happiness. Why? Because allowing yourself just to be, puts things into perspective. Try it. Be still. Be present.

For me, it's watching the flamingos fly across Necker Island at dusk. It's holding my new grandchild's tiny hands. It's looking up at the stars and dreaming of seeing them up close one day. It's listening to my family's dinner-time debates. It's the smile on a stranger's face, the smell of rain, the ripple of a wave, the wind across the sand. It's the first snow fall of winter, and the last storm of summer. It's sunrise and sunset.

Don't waste your human talents by stressing about nominal things, or that which you cannot change. If you take the time simply to be and appreciate the fruits of life, your stresses will begin to dissolve, and you will be happier.

But don't just seek happiness when you're down. Happiness shouldn't be a goal, it should be a habit. Take the focus off doing, and start being every day. Be loving, be grateful, be helpful, and be a spectator to your own thoughts.

Allow yourself to be in the moment and appreciate the moment. Take the focus off everything you think you need to do, and start being—I promise you, happiness will follow."

Happy regards,
Richard Branson

So...
Lighten Up... Love What Is
Live in the Moment

We are in this world together each with incredible potential. Let's be part of the solution. The solution is Love, loving ourselves and having compassion and love for others.

Let's start our compassion at home.

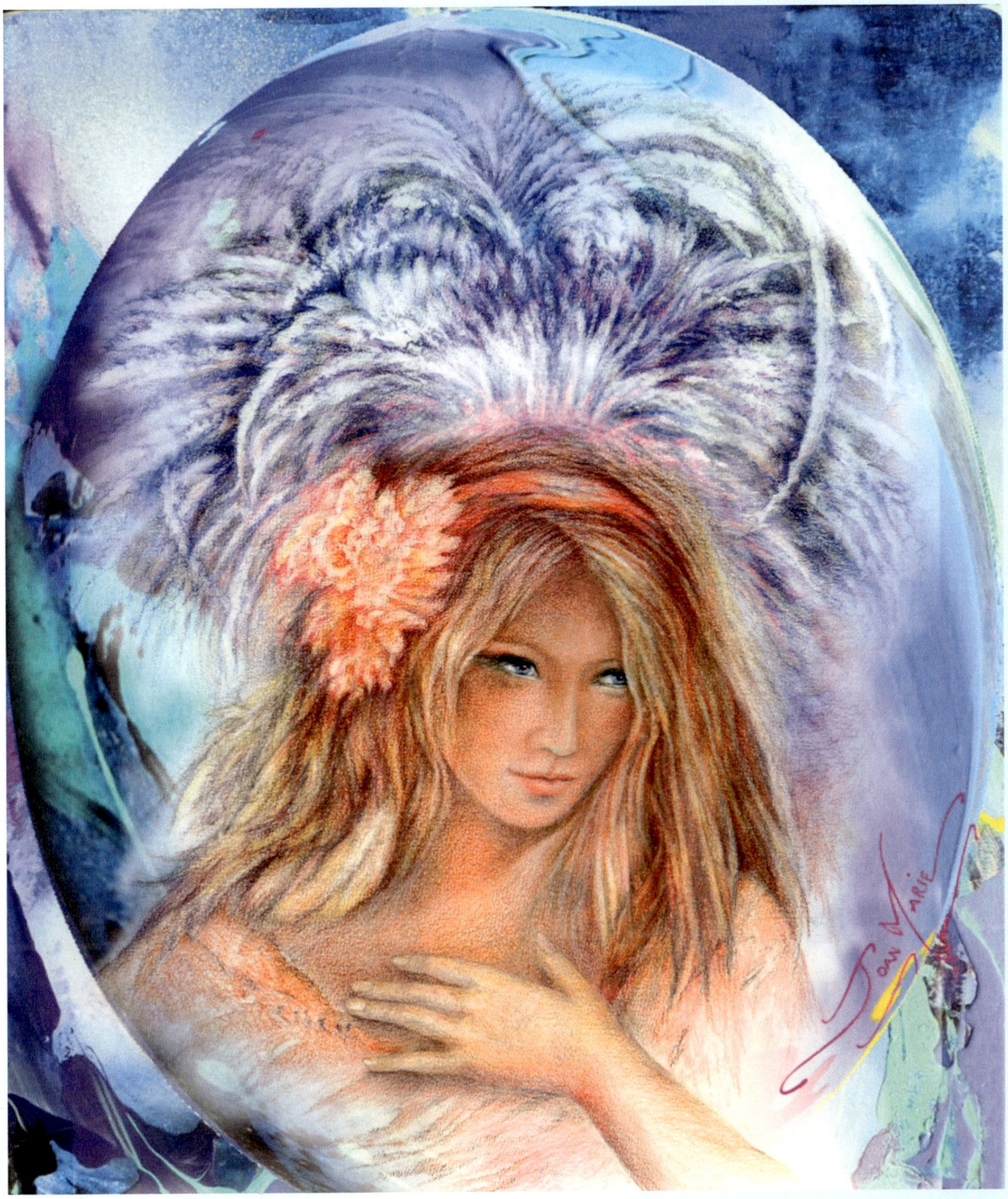

My Story

One of my life's challenges occurred as a college sophomore. As a college sophomore, **a highly respected Art professor told me I should not be an artist.** He advised, "You should become a home economics major, you lack creativity…There are 56,000 starving artists in NYC alone…you don't want to be one of them." **Wow!** What would you have said? Would an insult like that have stopped you from pursuing a dream? After privately wiping away tears, I asked him, "Can creativity be learned, or do you have to be born with it?" The professor responded, "You have to be born with it, and I'm sorry."

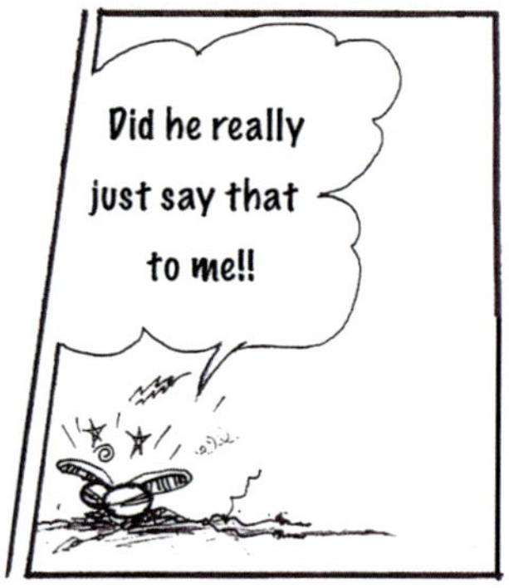

He had no idea how much desire I had in my heart.

My intense determination to become an artist began at age 19, when I was awestruck by Michelangelo's Sistine Ceiling. "If art can be that powerful, I have to be a part of it," I thought. Profoundly inspired, art became my burning passion. I felt my life's purpose was to add positive energy into the world through my art even though I continued to hear that professor's limited beliefs in my head for fifteen years. Unfortunately, I developed negative thinking patterns that reminded me constantly that I did not have what it took to be the expressive artist I dreamed to be.

When my art began to shine,
negative self-talk became a challenging habit to break.

What I have learned:

…Insults only hurt us if we believe them (obviously, I believed them)

…The innate artistic talent I must have been born with was buried under layers of insecurity.

If you have an intense drive to do a particular thing, you might share my experience and discover talents buried under years of low self-esteem.

After years of dedication to develop my skills, I realized **hard work is *not* the key to success or happiness.**

Feeling peace and unbridled achievement requires having respect and love for yourself just as you are, as well as for all living beings.

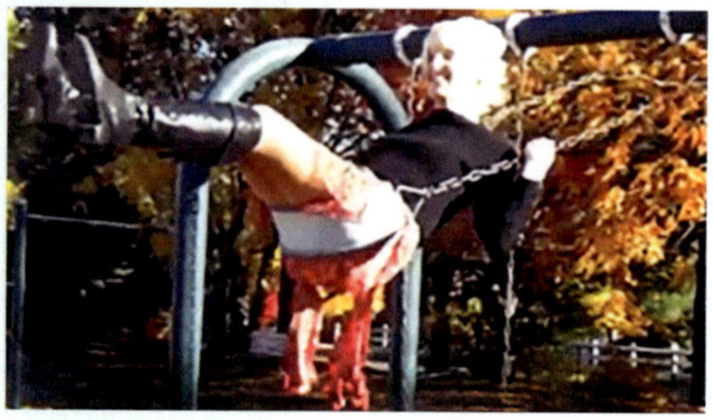

Love what is!

Do you hate your job? I always dreamed of being a full-time artist.

While working on that goal, I taught high school art for 28 years. In the middle of my teaching career, I had extremely negative feelings about being an art teacher. One morning while driving to school and feeling particularly upset about teaching, I began listening to an inspirational tape that proclaimed,

"You are never stuck. You always have a choice. Either quit and get happy with another job or shift your attitude and give your current job your all. If you stay in a job filled with angst, your life will stay stuck."

I chose to shift my thinking and gave teaching my all while I continued to create art during evenings and week-ends.

When I developed positive ways to view every conflict while I taught, I shifted my experience completely.

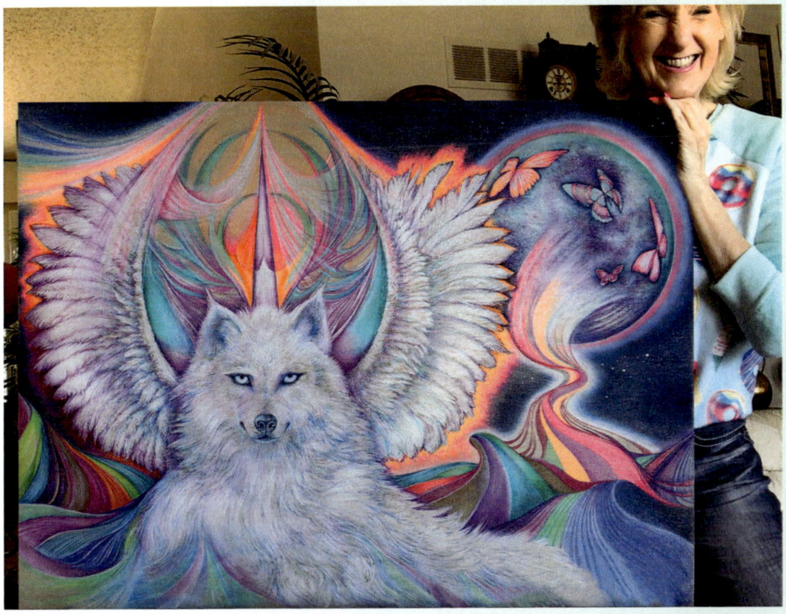

Magical Fairy Parade

Suddenly I felt as though the days were glowing with fun. I experienced exciting challenges and phenomenal rewards while I chose to give my all to teaching art.

I always felt like I had two full-time jobs, as a high school art teacher, and an artist. With so many things to accomplish, it was helpful to understand the difference between being in overwhelm, as opposed to being busy.

"Overwhelm is having lots to do and no priority. Busy is having lots to do and prioritizing"

Jim Fortin, TCP, see Contributors

Creating priorities allowed me to feel comfortable letting some things go for the moment.

My goal as a teacher was to give each student skills to help them increase their love for themselves. When a student said they wanted to be an art teacher because they too want to love their job like I did, I asked if they would be able to **feel compassion for every student that would come through their door.** Effective teachers must be heart-centered. I gained many strengths once I shifted my thinking and decided to give teaching my all. In my last year before retirement, I did not count the days. I lived in the moment and enjoyed every moment until the end.

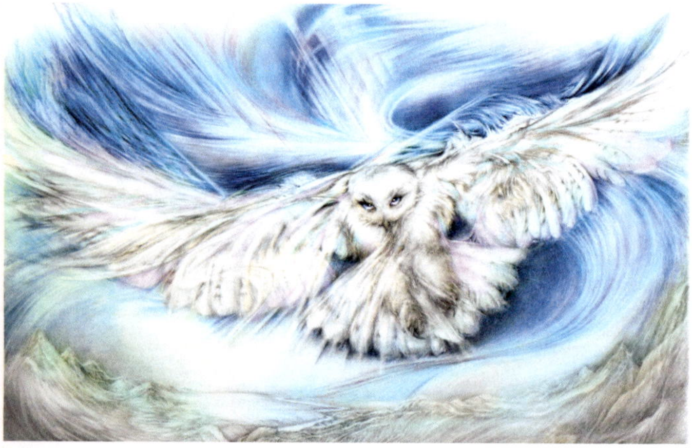

Destiny

At my teacher's desk, the photo displayed shows the **love of toys** I made available for students. It was such fun to watch the giant rainbow slinky 'walk' down the school steps. Even today, I keep glow rings that flash in my car ready for a sad or bored child. **Keep the smiles coming and imagination alive!**

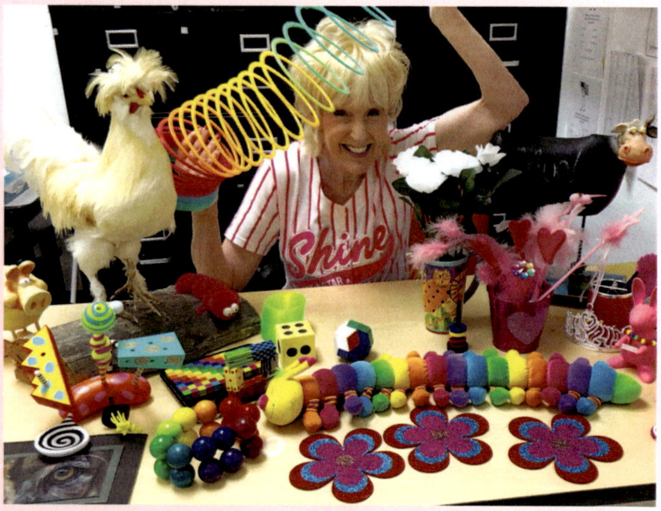

Displaying rainbow toys was one way I began expressing my personal passions. This was one sign that my confidence was building. Today, it's hard for many to believe I was ever insecure.

I have overcome insecurity by accepting what is.

Learning to think and feel I am okay just the way I am in every moment' gives me the peace needed to fully enjoy this very moment, right now. The more I imagined mental images of myself as a successful artist, the more I felt successful. Then I began to believe it.

The most challenging habit for me to break was destructive self-talk.

I believed that being a hyper workaholic would lead to success. Now I understand that committed hard work alone does not guarantee the feeling of well-being.

...First enjoy feeling how you will feel when being who you would love to be.
...Daydream and connect with that feeling.

Up until a few years ago I refused parties and most social life, always feeling too busy focusing on being the best artist and high school art teacher possible. **Maybe that's why I'm now having such fun twirling in huge fluffy skirts, glitter, and flapping butterfly wings with others**!

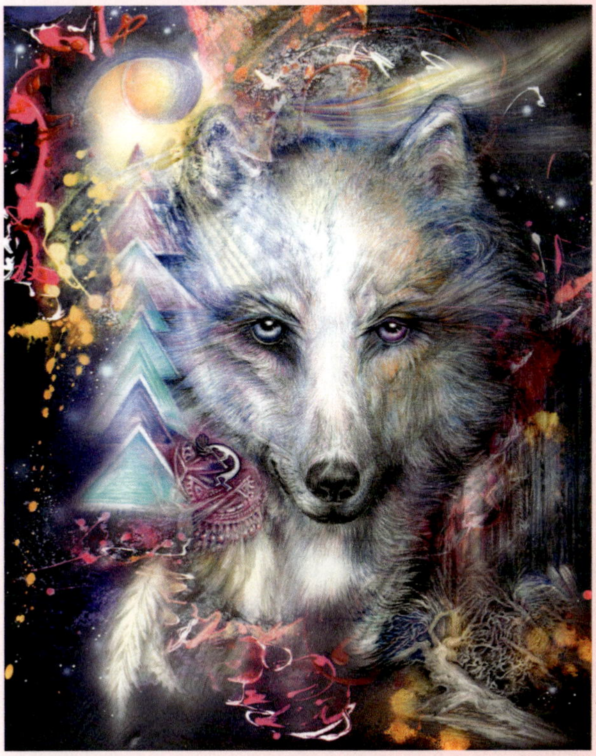

Spirit Protector

The freedom to twirl and move in any way that feels good began a few years ago when I attended a weekly **free-form movement dance class**. We moved in any way we choose as music awoken and inspired communication between bodies, minds and hearts. When I began class with a connection to my heart's desire or a problem to solve, **I felt amazed at the solutions that popped into my head while moving.** This has proven to me how answers come in the silence. Answers come in silent movement as well as while sitting in silence. Separating ourselves from constant busy activity and smartphones

... to be quiet, listen, sit in nature,
...take a walk
...or allow inner voices to be heard,
are the moments that refresh ourselves.

This is when life's magical moments occur.

I pursued multiple directions in the business of art and had huge success in art licensing, selling millions of kitties and unicorns internationally. Yet my heart yearned for freedom from the demand to create successful designs for the commercial world.

Since I supported myself as a teacher, I had the financial freedom to explore the dynamic voices inside me that craved to be expressed.

Since seeing Michelangelo's Sistine Ceiling at age 19, I've had an intense need to express a pulsating energy within me. It took years of dedication, daily creation of art, and above all else the development of inner belief and feeling that **I already am who I crave to be.**

I can only describe this inner energy as an excited child who wants to speak. The continuous nudge from within kept me committed while I experimented with new subject matter and forms of expression.

One of life's greatest celebrations is when you are enjoying doing what you love. We all have our own path.

One thing I finally understand…

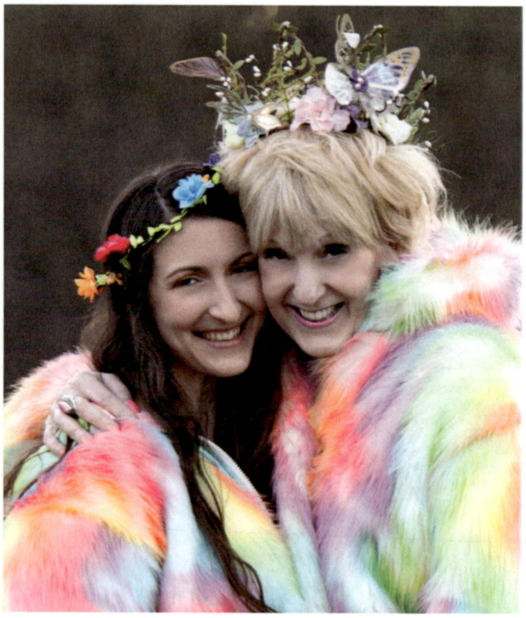

"Fairy Sisters", My Daughter, Brittany and me

Work, work, work is not the answer.

Enjoying doing what you love is the answer.
You may still work a lot, but it sure won't feel like it!

What is your passion?!
What do you really …REALLY want?
What do you love?
What really matters to you?
Go do it…then feel the glow of feeling joy in every moment you choose!
When you're happy, your energy radiates love.
Your energy glow helps heal the world.

Here's to living life to the fullest!

What is Magic?

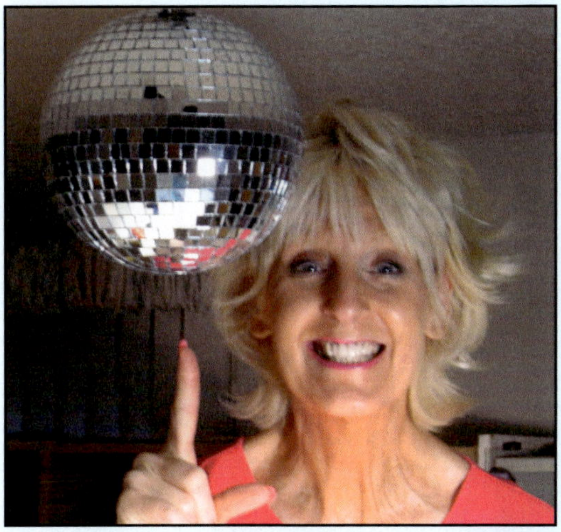

Magic is the glow in your heart when you are smiling,

It is when that stranger sits next to you on the airplane and answers the question you have been asking yourself.

Magic surrounds you when you consciously choose to see the storm as a blessing.

It is the positive feeling you get because you lift the corners of your mouth to create an inner smile.

It is a pulsating enthusiasm that circles the air and is available to you when you are enjoying doing what you love.

It's when taking out the trash becomes a happy dance, either in your mind or physically rockin' it!

Have fun inventing entertaining ways to "wake up" in the morning or to create fun ways to act during everyday activities. Talking like 'liddo' kids or 'tawkin' with a southern drawl can instantly create a shift to a 'let's play' feeling.

Take a breath, stop for two seconds to say "Thank you, Thank you, God!" No matter what, there's always so much to be thankful for.

**Saying "Thank You," instantly shifts energy to a better feeling place.
You can help heal the world with these moments of appreciation.
Your radiant love can circle the globe and touch a sad soul so far away.
WOW! You are powerful beyond measure. It's really true!**

It can be so simple to shift to both love and compassion instead of "oh-poor-me".

It is entertaining to view bills as a blessing. Feel blessed to be who and where you are.

Counting blessings is an action that can create instant happeee-dance feelings!

Ask many people who have recovered from a near-death experience, many of them will tell you about a refreshing new appreciation for the chair in their living room and the sound of the neighbor's dog barking.

Thankfulness leads hearts to a newly found giddiness.

It's all your choice.
Being able to change how we see and experience the world is the magic of transformation.

Choosing to feel optimistic leads to instantaneous vitality.

Walking outside feeling thankful or helping a neighbor can free your mind from negative chatter.

All of a sudden with space, your imagination will soar with creative ideas and solutions to the puzzles in your life.

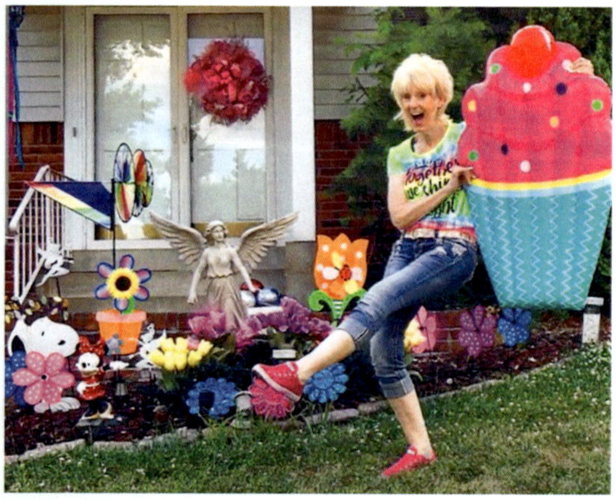

This kind of magic is at your fingertips every day. It all flows from the moment you choose to shift from:

anger to worry
worry to boredom
boredom to hopefulness
hopefulness to belief
belief to enthusiasm
enthusiasm to passion and then to ***Pure Joy!***

It's fun to have reminders around what lifts your spirit.

...Draw a smiley face or a radiating sun on a post-it and put it on your mirror.
...Place a favorite pillow in your special cushy chair.
...Hang a painting that lights you up and reminds you of who you really are.
DREAM! YES DREAM! DREAM BIG!
Then...Create MAGIC!

How about creating magic at a party?

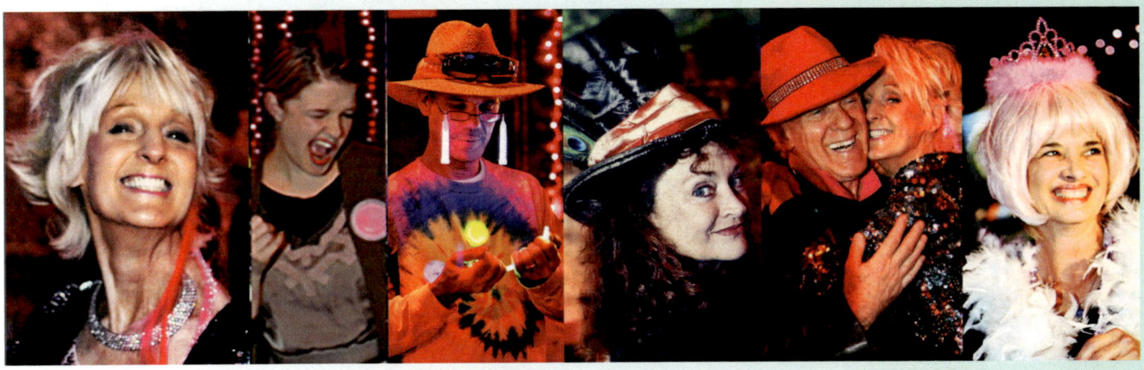

Getting together to party can be the best fun ever! The formula for a great party? Provide ways to help people release their alter egos.

Invite them to come in **costume** if they choose. Provide **wigs, hats, ten glow sticks for each guest** to do with whatever they wish, glow buttons, line the walls with soft lighting, choose a space with an elevated platform, or **bar for a few people to be featured dancing.** Have fun with a **photographer and videographer** encouraging them to animate their feelings, and a **DJ** playing a variety of music that stirs various memories or moods. **Watch alter egos appear.**

My dream for my 60th birthday was to dance on a bar! Ha! We made it happen!! Feeling so blessed to have awesome fun-loving friends showing up to shine! Oh, Thank you for these inspiring memories! It's exhilarating to see **party animals** released! It's Party Time! HURRAY!

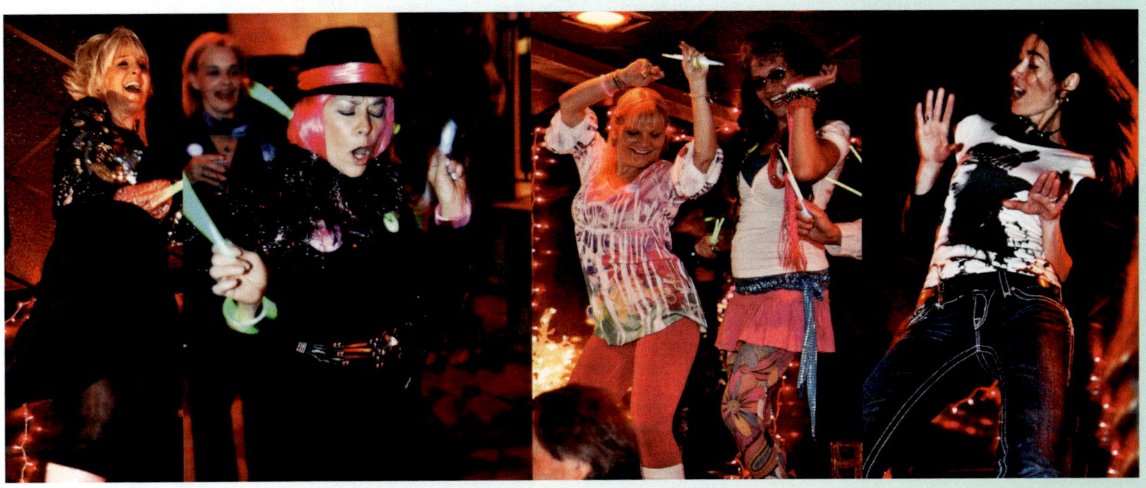

My 60th birthday dream to dance on a bar with awesome friends!

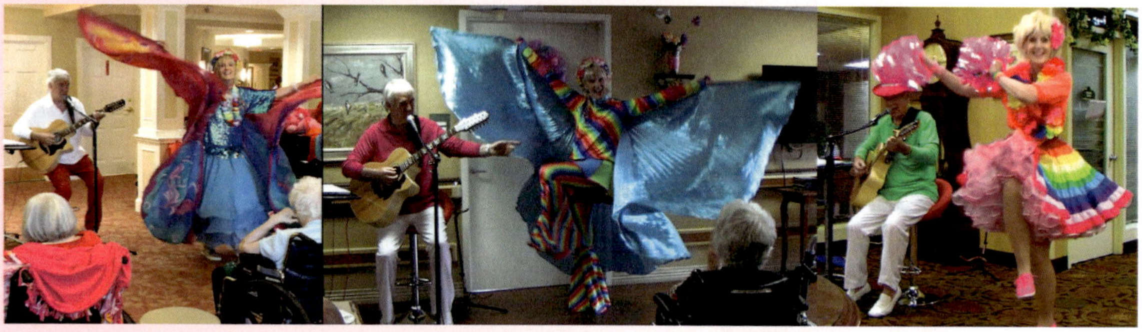

More magic appeared with my new 'I just don't care anymore' confidence. My sweetie, George Hinds, entertains with his beautiful voice and upbeat songs at many assisted living homes.

A few years ago, I joined him and encouraged others to dance. That appearance has evolved into me arriving in full costumes with a different crazy-fun prop for every song. Feeling connected to their hearts and exchanging smiles is truly the most heart-filling moments in our lives

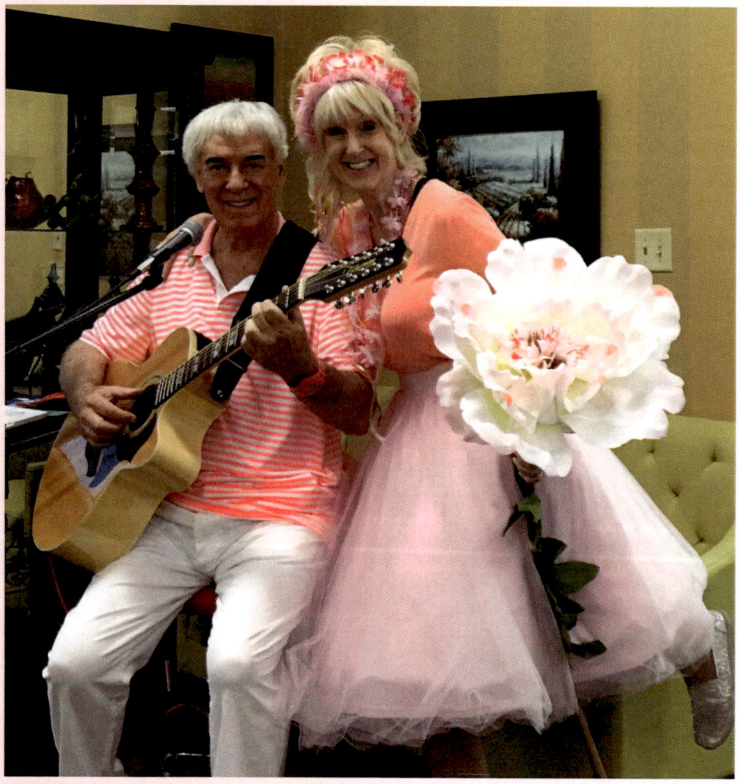

My sweetie, George Hinds and me entertaining in an assisted living home

Speaking of MAGIC, how about a phenomenal day on the BEACH! I had a vision to bring one hundred balloons and eleven pair of Isis wings to the beach on a trip to exhibit my art in California. My daughter Brittany and I asked whoever happened to be on Venice Beach that day to join us, as a drone, photographer and videographer captured the energy of how wild wind controlled our actions. What a magical day.

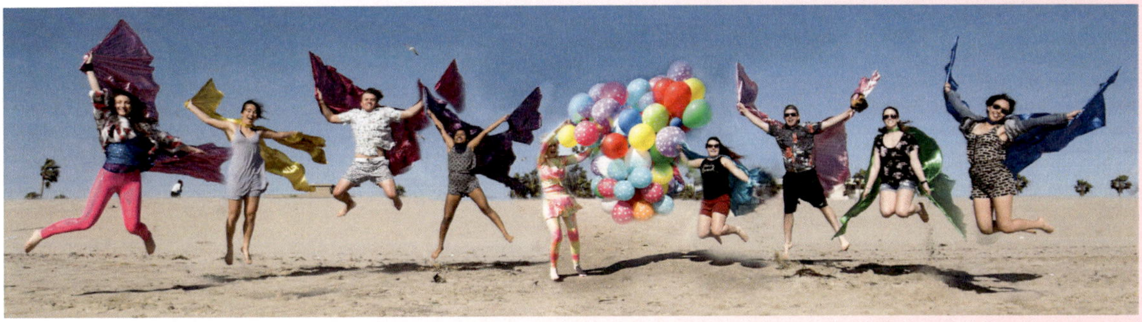

On Venice Beach with Balloons and Wings

Use your imagination. Then make it happen!

So…What is MAGIC?
… Create it!
… Have fun with it daily!

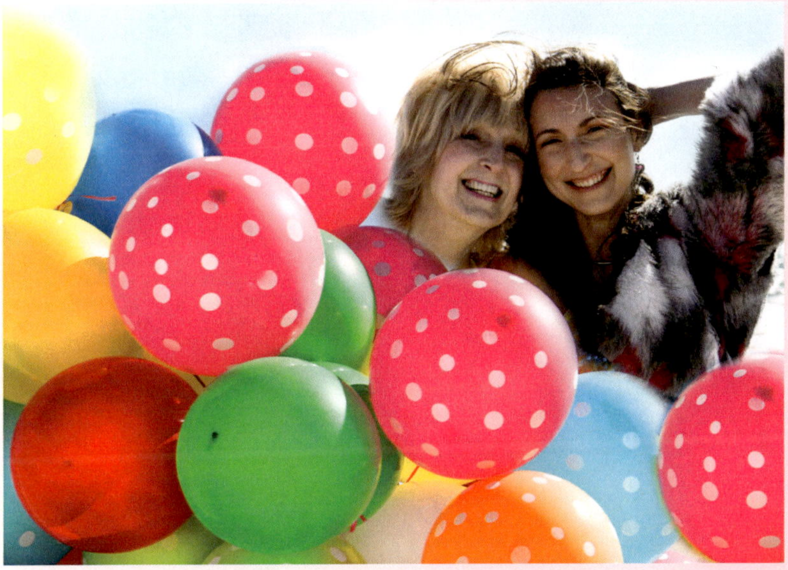

My Fabulous Daughter, Brittany and me (Toki Lee Photography)

Receiving the Wisdom and Truth

Life is meant to be FUN!

First, Love Yourself

If you are reluctant to love yourself because you see your flaws, remember what Eleanor Roosevelt said, "*You wouldn't worry what other people think of you if you knew how seldom they do.*"

The most important thing you can do is develop love and trust in yourself. Follow your heart, your intuition will guide you to what is truly important to you.

At age 35, I lived in Sedona, Arizona. My art began to convey a message and a feeling beyond what it had in the past.

Until then I'd been so very hard on myself and felt inadequate as an artist. Even though my artistic skills blossomed previously, I felt my art lacked a message. Until this drawing, **"Receiving the Light."** I felt I'd gained the ability to draw, however I wouldn't consider myself an artist, nor could I feel fulfilled until my art expressed a passionate spiritual message.

Art created in the spiritual environment of Sedona began to express my passion for life and love for myself.

As you love yourself, and feel passion and joy for living, inspiration begins to be received.

This image captures the profound inspiration of receiving spiritual awareness that shifts lives. In return, we feel the desire to give back and share what has been received.

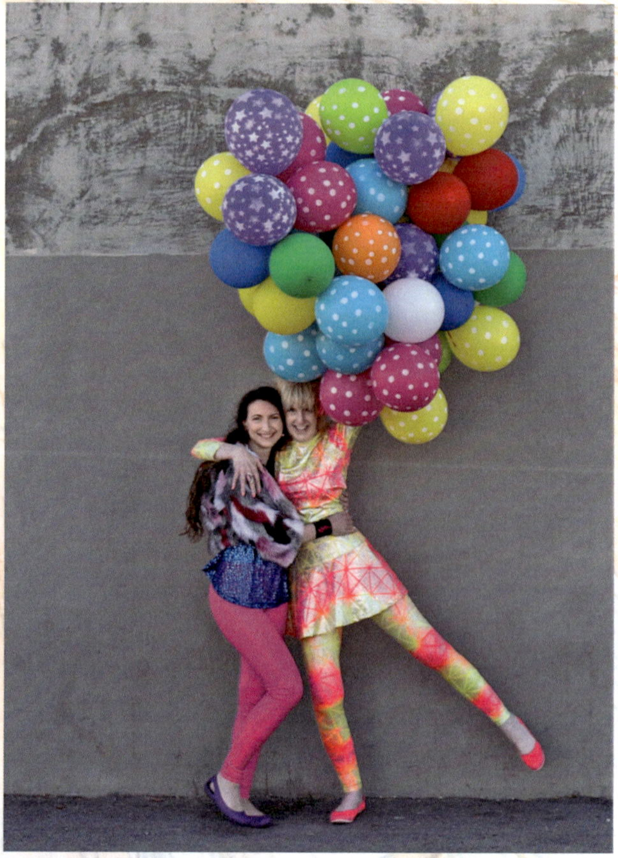

My Daughter, Brittany and me, (Toki Lee Photography)

Opposite page: *Receiving the Light*

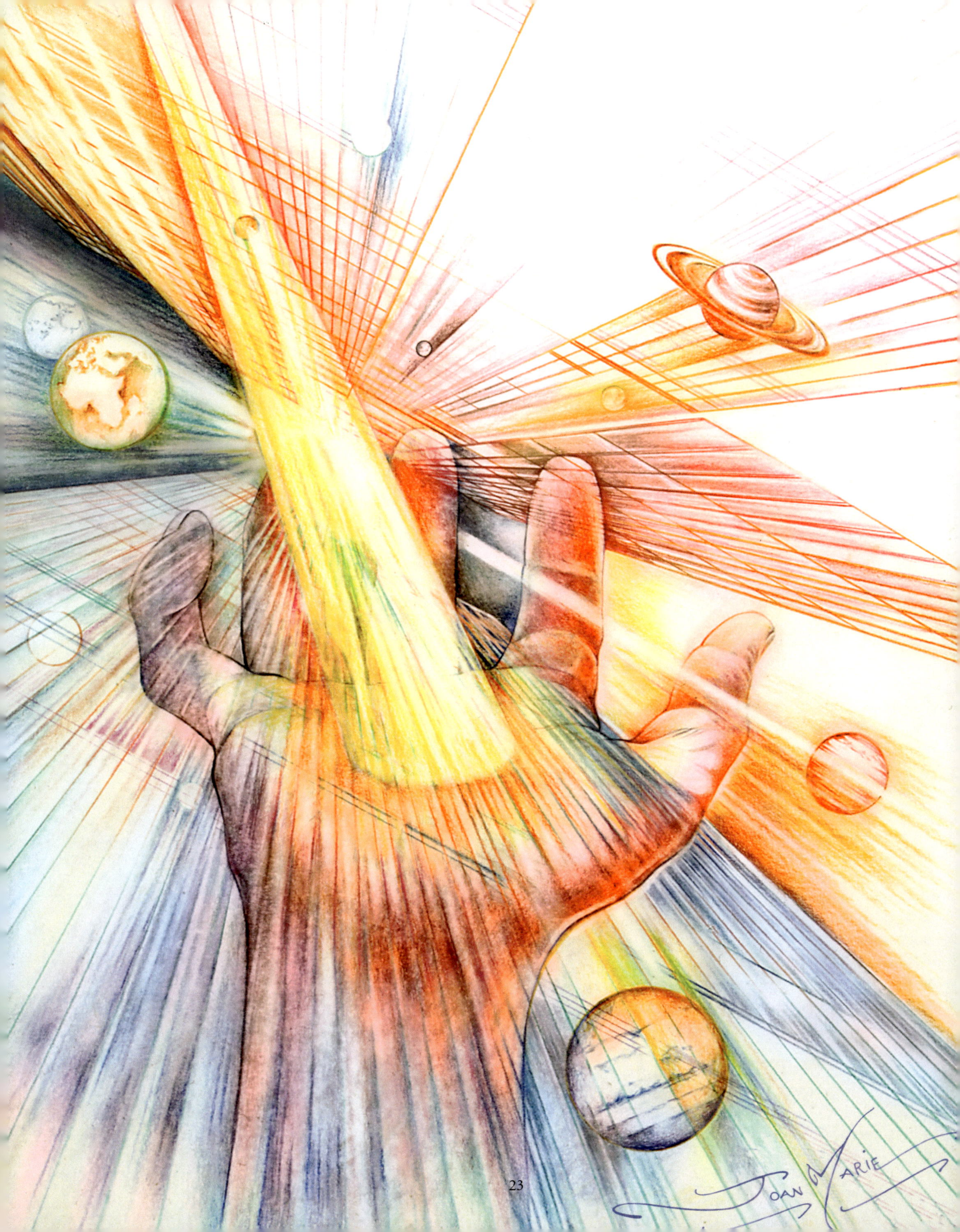
Joan Marie

FOCUS

Celebrate who you are, NOW!

Waiting until something gets better or waiting until you feel lovable prolongs the experience of what you desire.

The trick is loving all of who you are right now.

Fun Activity: Expand your idea of who you really are. You have so much potential. Create a vivid movie in your mind feeling yourself being your ideal self. Stop, relax, and vividly feel. Then see your ideal movie several times a day. These uplifting daydreams or visualizations can feel so good. You will begin to look forward to pausing everything for those few moments to experience yourself in an uplifting mind-movie, feeling as though you're on a refreshing mini vacation.

Make it entertaining for yourself, but the most important thing is to get into the feelings of the experience.

Having a positive self-image is the number-one most important thing to develop. Fully loving and accepting yourself as you are, is where the magic begins.

Make your dreams feel real and entertaining, then count your blessings.

Trust that those unexpected turns in life increase your wisdom and add another voice to the already unique and special you. How you respond to the challenging events in your life is up to you. Wouldn't it feel great when you choose to believe that everything works out? It's all good.

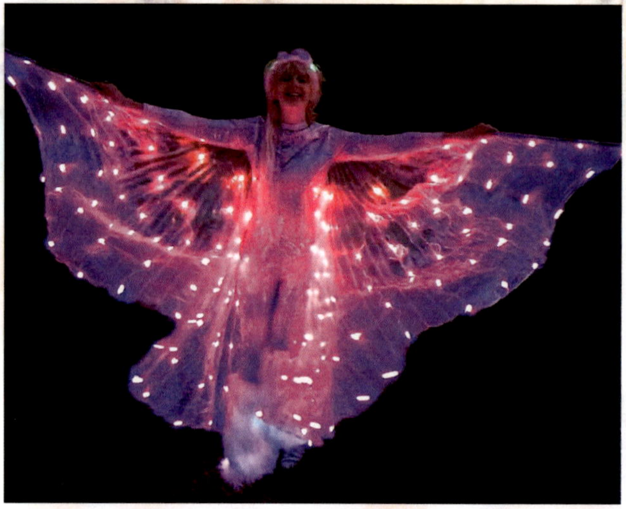

Opposite page: *Chrysalis*

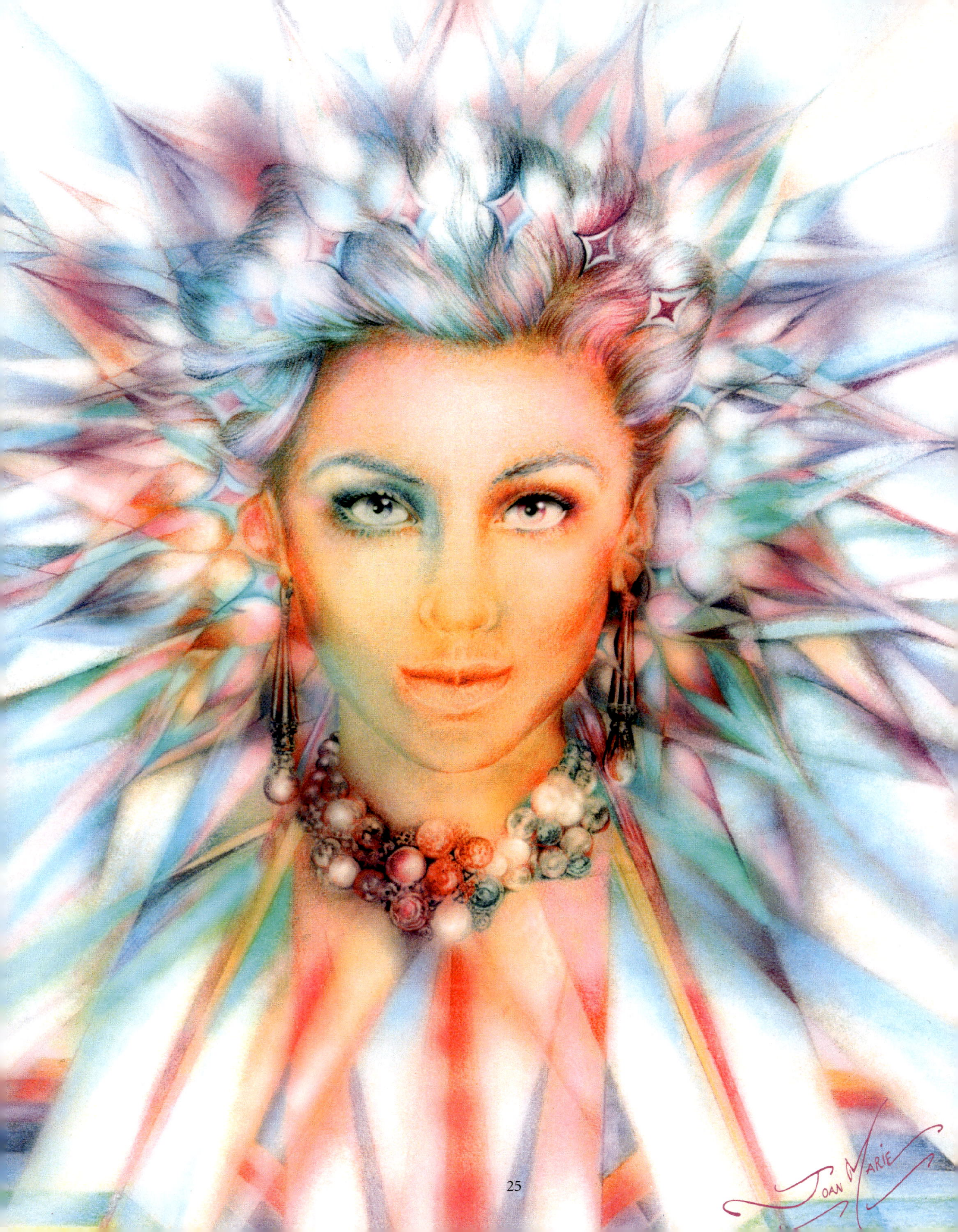
Joan Marie

Life is truly meant to be Fun

PLAY! Make Exercise Fun

Jumping? Dancing?
Roller skating? Fast-walking? Hiking? Yoga?
Free-form movement dance? What exercise feels like fun? What exercise enlivens your spirit?

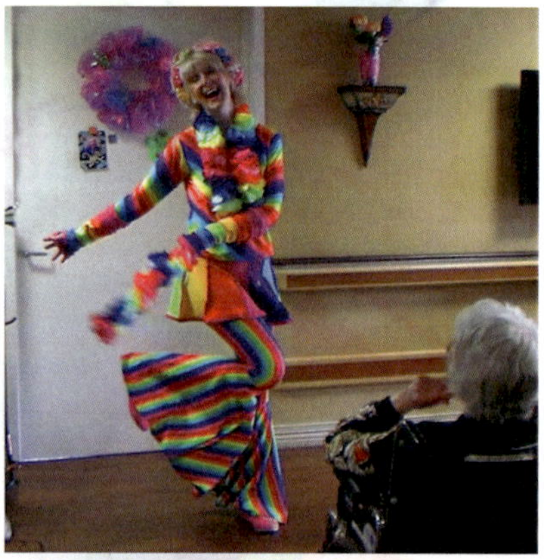

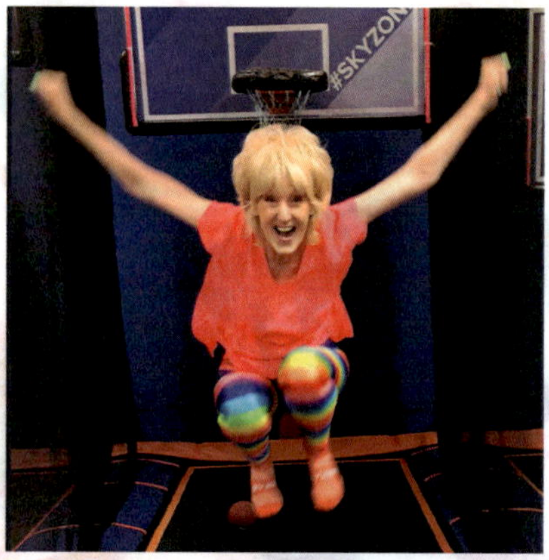

The more vitality you feel the more joy you express through the work you do.

As an artist, I feel enjoying fun movement is a requirement for expressing passion for life on canvas.
If it sounds entertaining,
go ahead
and put on a glowing
fluffy skirt and twirl.
Feel happy joy come pouring
out of you!!

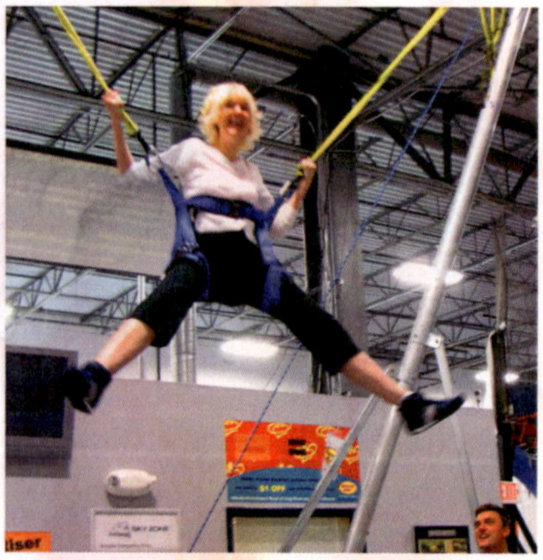

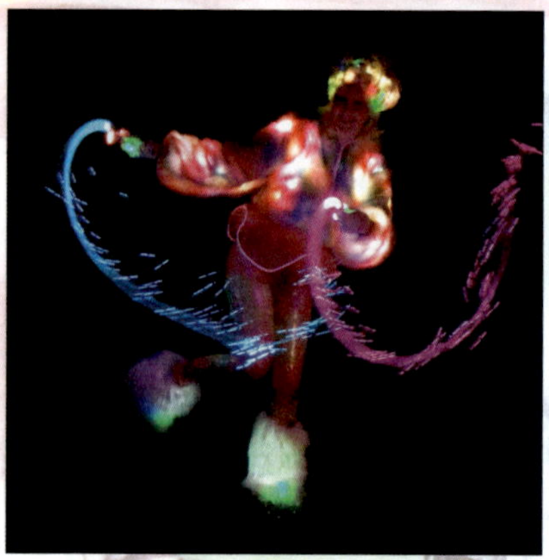

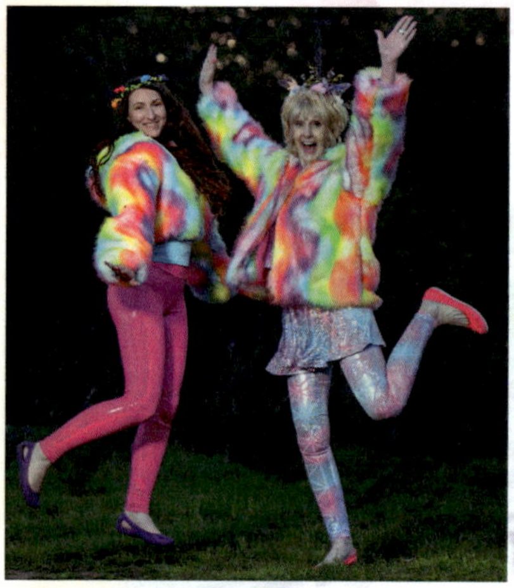

My Daughter, Brittany and me, (Toki Lee Photography)

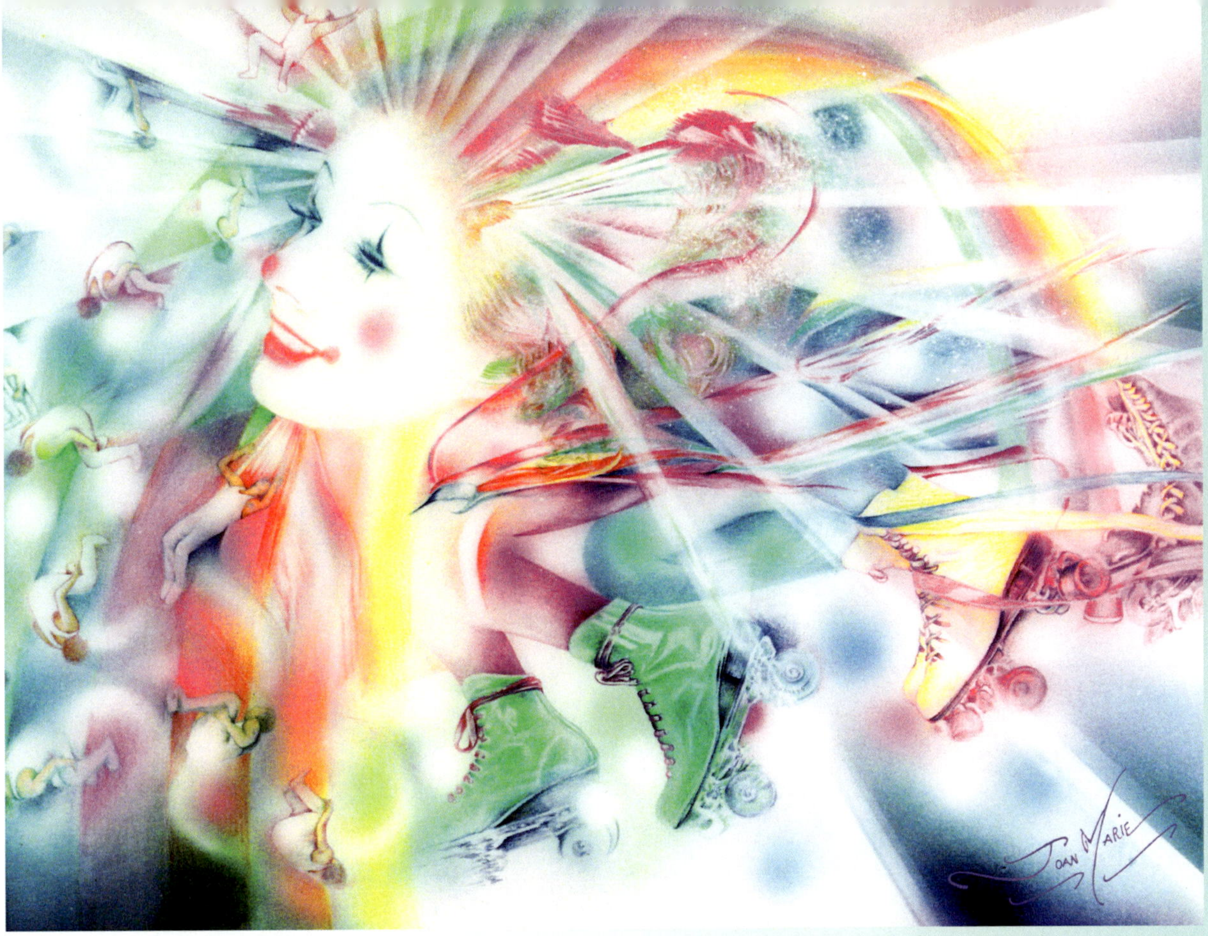

Sedona Radiance

'Trampoline Heaven'

When I lived in Sedona, while I listened to a guided meditation tape, I had a vision of a trampoline in my back yard. Within 2 weeks, I made that happen.

Use your imagination. What will you visualize? What will you create?

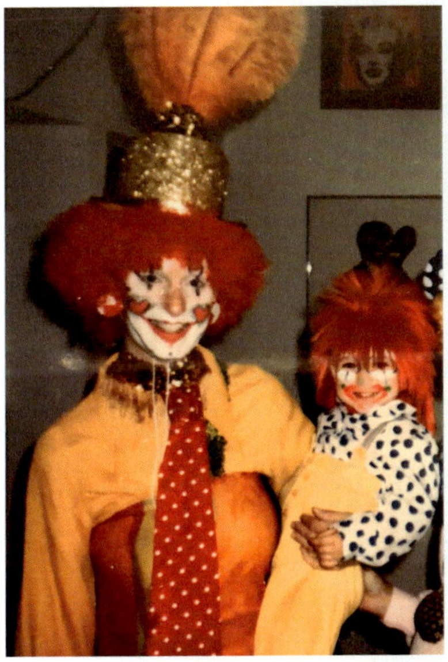

My Daughter, Brittany and me

This painting expresses the fun of roller skating, jumping on a trampoline, and becoming a mime clown with my daughter Brittany. We learned from the famous mime, Robert Shields, who told us never to speak a word when performing. "If you make a sound the magic will be gone." He was right. Have you ever experienced not talking for a period of time? Not speaking while being a mime clown is different than silence during a meditation, yet both allow enchantment into your life. Someday soon, consider not speaking for a period of time or becoming a mime, whichever sounds most compelling to you.

What You Focus on Persists

Are you aware of your thoughts?

**"What you think about is what comes about.
What you give attention to grows.**

If your thoughts are constantly about what is missing in your life,
you will continue to miss these things.
When we focus on what we don't have, such as feeling we don't have enough talent or money, that becomes our reality.
The opposite is then true.
The more we focus or imagine things going well, the more we open the door for things to flow to us in magical ways,
ways we could never have imagined.
If you ask for success, but prepare for failure, you will get what you prepare for.
Act as if you have what you want.
Say thank you before you have it.
Feel it, hear it, picture it, taste it, smell it…Most of all, feel it!"

Jim Fortin, TCP. . .See contributors

Are you aware of what you are thinking right now?
Are you aware of what you are feeling?
Shift to the best feeling place you can in every moment.

You might shift by singing your favorite song.

Shift from:
…anger to worry
…worry to boredom
…boredom to hopefulness
…hopefulness to belief
…belief to enthusiasm
…enthusiasm to passion and
then to ***Pure Joy!***

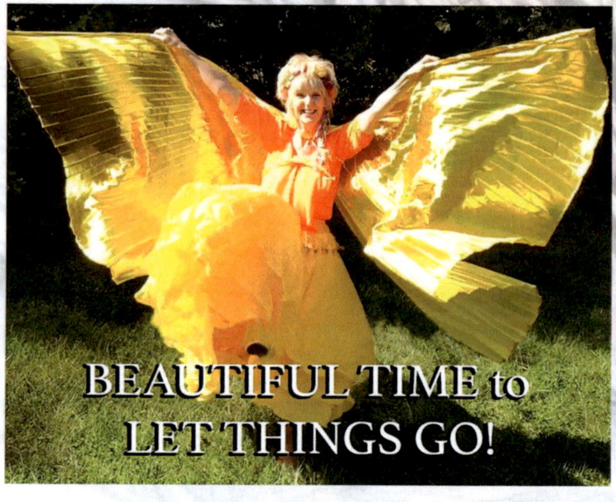

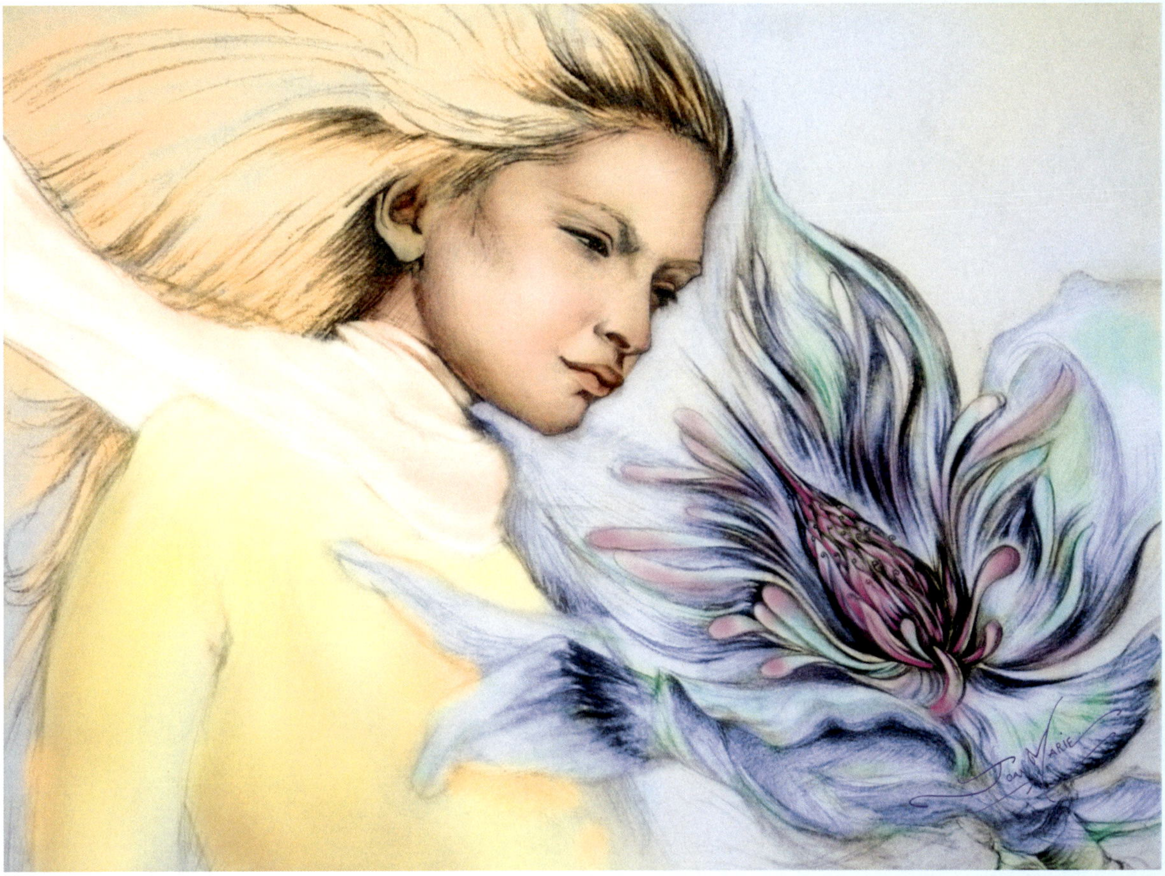

Forbidden Flower

I Believe

When facing challenges, feel grounded and stand in the power of love and experience trust throughout your body by saying,

"Thank you, God."
Then calmly watch fear move away as
you shift your focus to a better feeling place.

Feel a calm sensation of peace fill your heart. Breathe deep, relax and move forward with your dreams!

The Ecstasy of FEELING FREE!

Create new stories in your head about fears.

Two common fears: "Will people reject me" and
"Am I good enough?"

Over and over again you may have found yourself in one or both of these fears. Thoughts could be an enemy if you allowed them to control you.

Worrying creates pictures of unwanted experiences. These mental images put negative energy around the situation and never helps anything.

Worrying about a loved one actually creates negative energy. Yikes! Shift from visualizing fears to picturing positive images of the desired outcomes.

This can actually help, and it feels so much more relaxing, doesn't it?

How do you shift your thoughts to ones that feel good? A favorite trick to replacing negative chatter is to **sing your favorite happeee song**.

Upbeat songs can bring on an instant smile and light-hearted energy.

Do you really want your energy stuck in a spiral of negativity?

STOP THINKING about things so much! Remember when you try hard to think of a name and it only pops in your head when you STOP THINKING?

Stop it!
Worrying doesn't help.
Shift it!
Sing a happy song
or
If tense, shift what you are
thinking and feeling,
**or go dance with rainbow
umbrellas in the yard!**

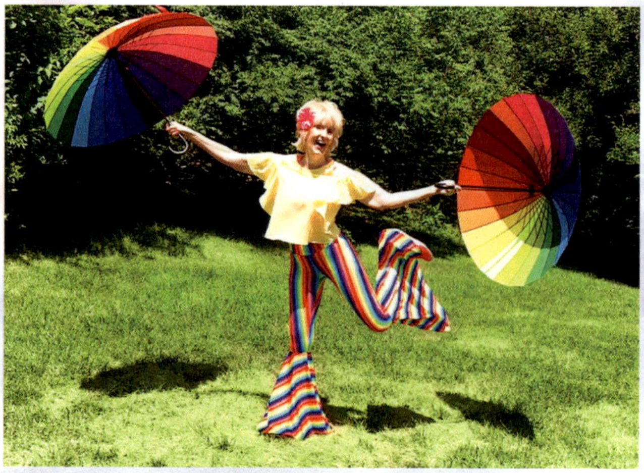

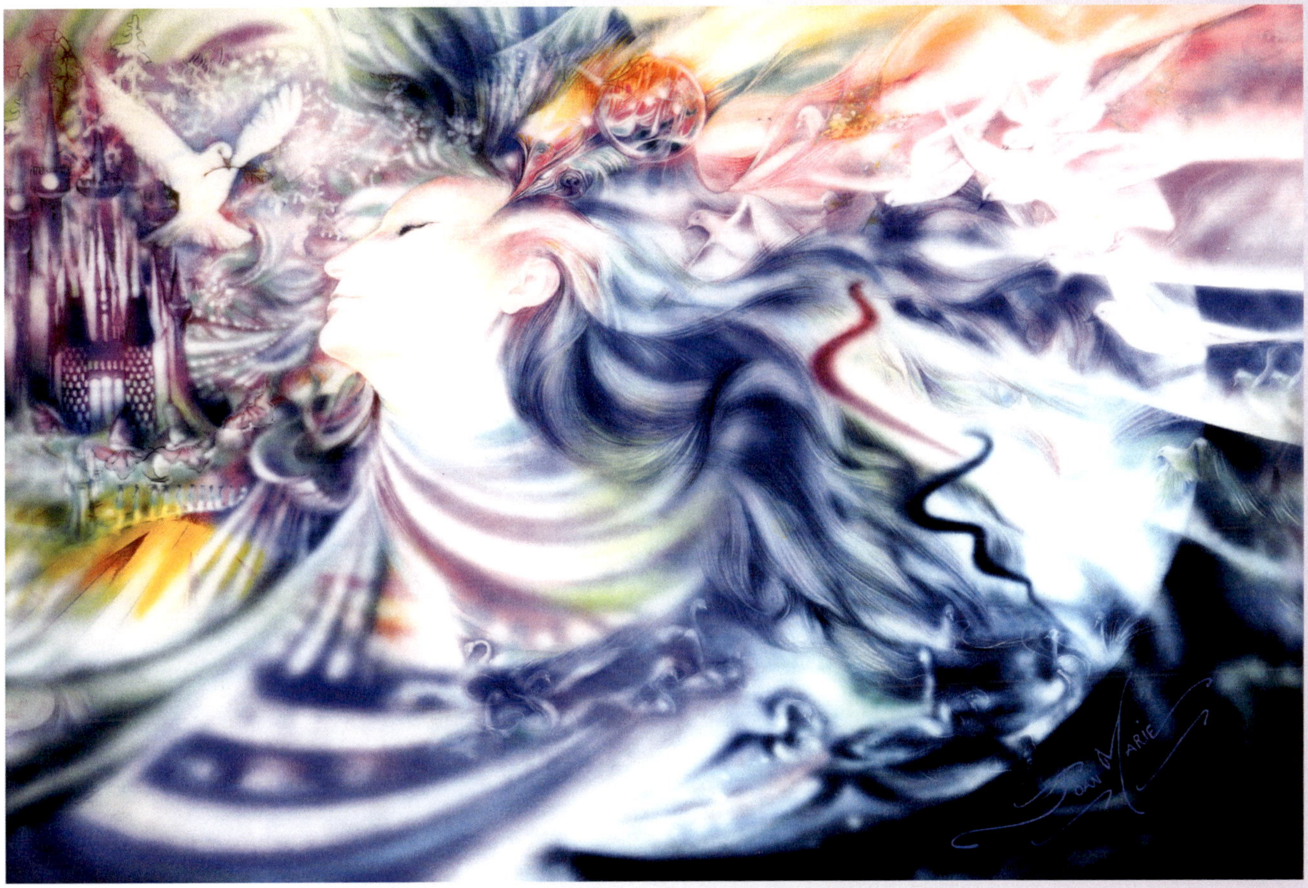

The Ecstasy of Feeling Free

The Ecstasy of Feeling Free!

This 5-foot wide painting came to fruition after a walk across fire. I was one of thirty people who signed up for a 30-day workshop in Sedona to discuss fears.

It was a powerful experience.

We learned to shift our feelings about fears.

On the thirtieth day, we gathered wood and watched it burn to flickering coals.

After several trust exercises, we walked a distance of twenty feet over those red flickering coals.

I was at peace, quiet and in a state of trust while walking across the burning coals.

In the morning, I woke up excited, inspired, and **felt as if I could do ANYTHING!!** After jumping wildly on my trampoline, I began the painting above, which expressed my newfound feeling of confidence and freedom!

Paradise Found

Visualize and Feel it!

Paradise is always available in your imagination.

Daydreaming is an instant go-to mini vacation and it's free.

...What do you want?
...What is your dream?

...Choosing to stop for five minutes, three times a day to visualize a perfect day can be a refreshing and rewarding experience that paves the way for positive future experiences.
...Choose to take a few deep breaths and feel the inspiration of that mini retreat. This could be the most important thing you do.

A short mental retreat could be more important than the next thing on your to-do list. This 3-minute mental paradise might fuel you to move forward on that to-do list with a brighter feeling in your heart.

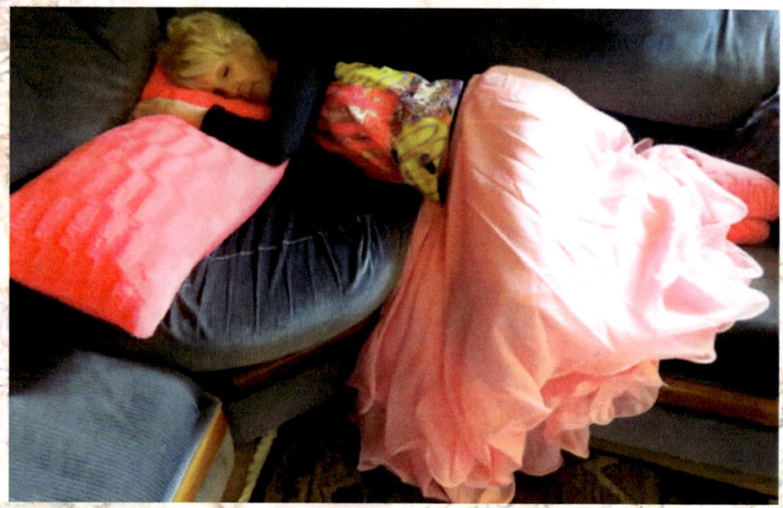

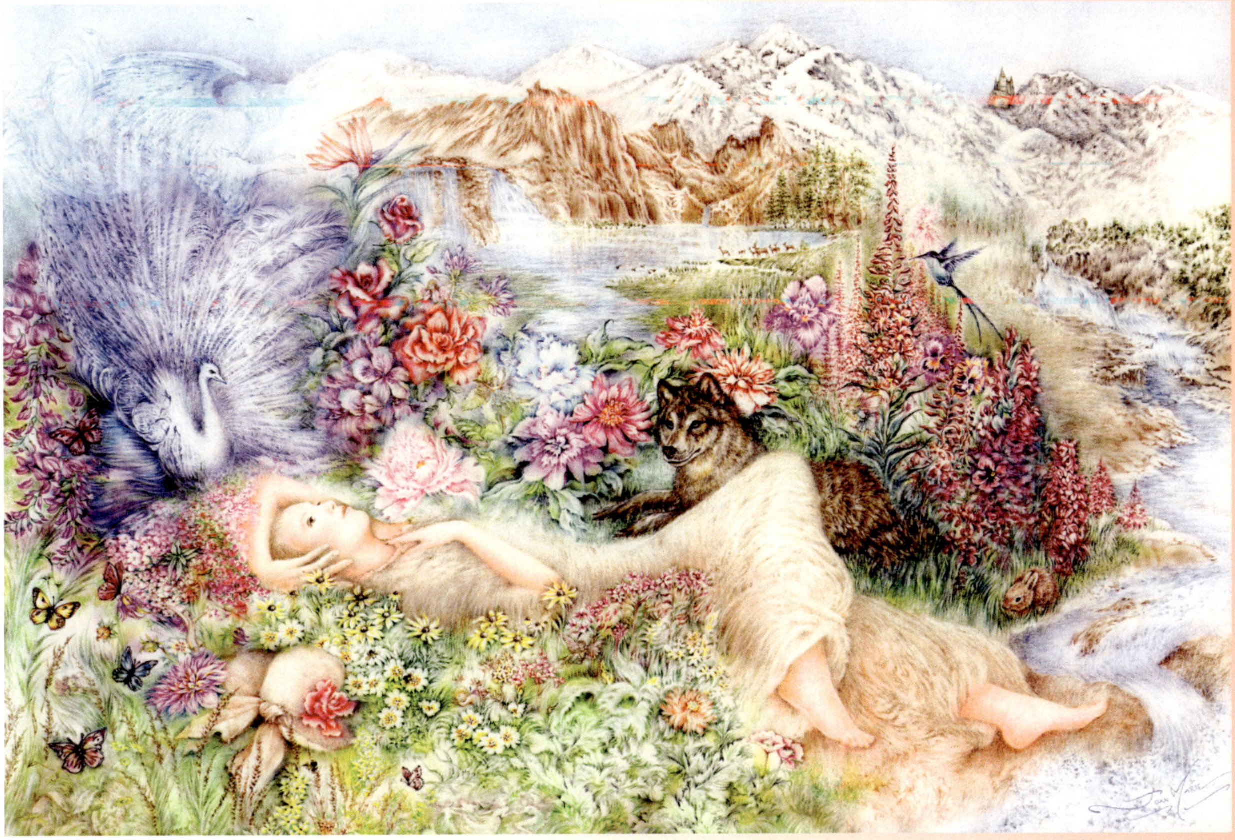

Paradise Found

Paradise Found

As a participant in a spiritual workshop in Sedona, we were guided through a beautiful meditation. Participants were asked to create our ideal environment. Immediately when I arrived home, I recreated the fantasy environment from that visualization on canvas, which included the creation of nature's perfect balance.

Enjoy visualizing this:
Soar to the highest mountaintops. Feel tension in your body float away. Imagine soothing sounds of a river calming you. Let your heart fill with peace and feel free. A connection to nature lures untamed creatures to come and sit by you. The wolf is your masculine protector and the angel surrounds you in peace.

(Note: you will find 11 'hidden' fairies dancing in the flowers.)

Tranquility

Feel Peace: the most powerful place from which to work!

Success is learning to be at peace with every minute of the journey, not living in anxious anticipation of a "better" tomorrow. Mastering self-love creates true magic in your life.

Magic is feeling the beauty in every moment.

When I developed my artistic skills and devoted myself to the creation of art every day, I created a hyper driven persona to achieve faster results, excited to become a better artist. Then **I was told by a spiritual teacher that being hyper was a sign of being anxious to be somewhere or to become someone else** other than who I was, in that moment.

We must love ourselves as we are right now, otherwise we stay stuck in negative energy, discontent and judgment. The drawing on your right, Tranquility, was created to shift from that place of anxiousness about becoming a better artist to a beautiful place of self-love, peace, and trust.

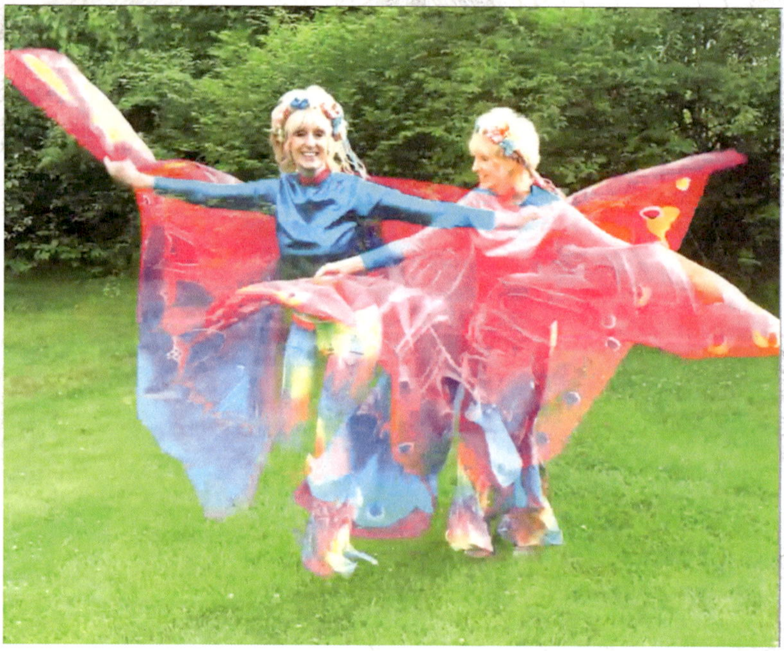

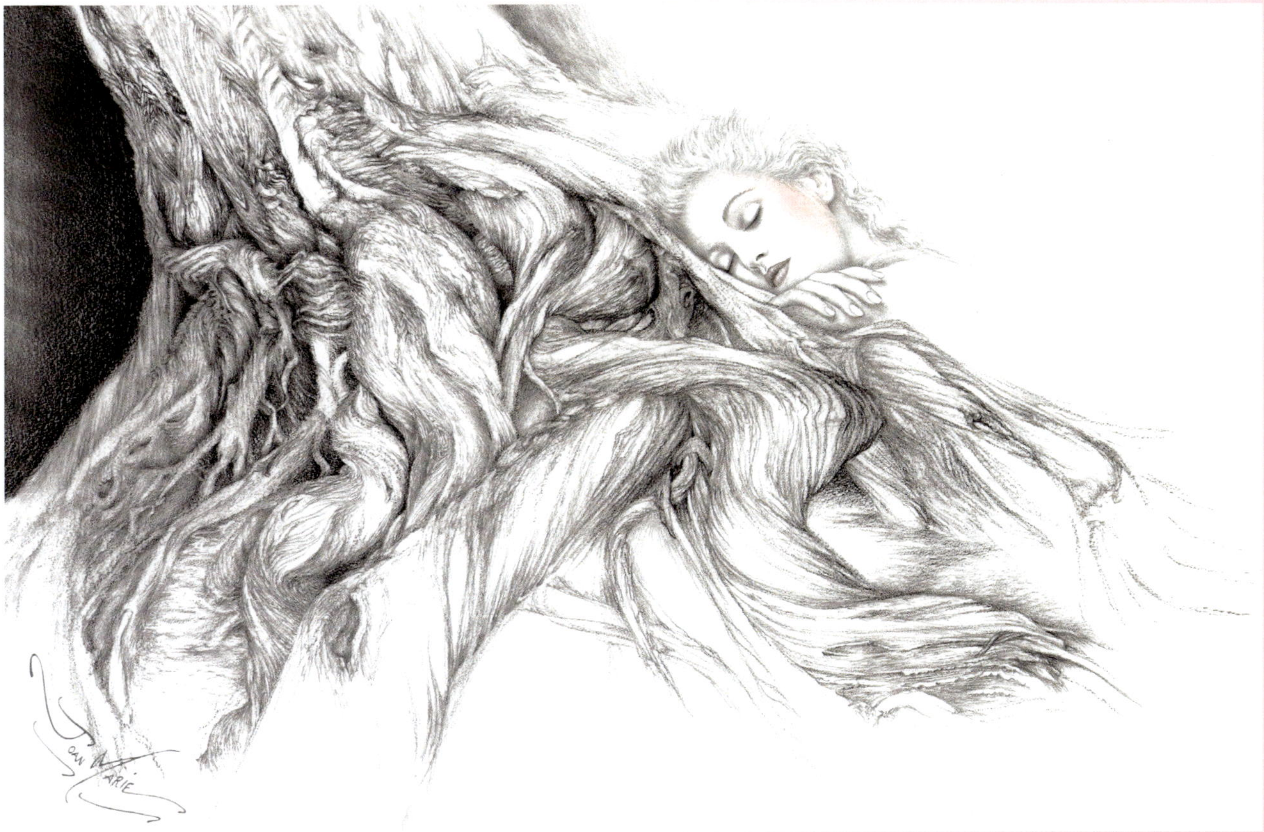

Tranquility

Tranquility

Feel the peace of acceptance.

Close your eyes, visualize and enjoy:

Feel the peace of being spiritually connected, feeling pure love in your heart.

Allow your body to feel as though it is floating in the ethers.

The knots in the tree expressed in this drawing represent

the ebb and flow of life's challenges.

Feel yourself in a state of pure tranquility while flowing with all of life.

Feel the peace of acceptance.

Feel the beautiful balance between Heaven and Earth.

Trust your INTUITION

Quiet…so you can hear…

**Listen to your intuition,
that little voice speaking from your heart.**

Get quiet. Listen.

Wisdom is talking… Love is talking… God is talking…

Following your intuition will lead you unerringly along your spiritual path. Intuition has been called a hunch, gut feelings, following your heart, God's guidance, sixth sense, that "aha" moment, or an inspiration or vision. Which rings true for you?

The girl in the artwork followed her intuition, she didn't know why she felt drawn to this particular tree, but a little voice inside told her to go to the tree. Others have seen this tree as the tree of wisdom or the tree of life. Even though the tree felt like a strange place to approach she followed her feelings. Woven in the tree trunk she discovered a braid similar to the one in her hair, a beautiful connection.

She looked past the magical tree, and saw in the distance a path that lead to the enchanted city where dreams come true.

Trust and Follow your intuition.

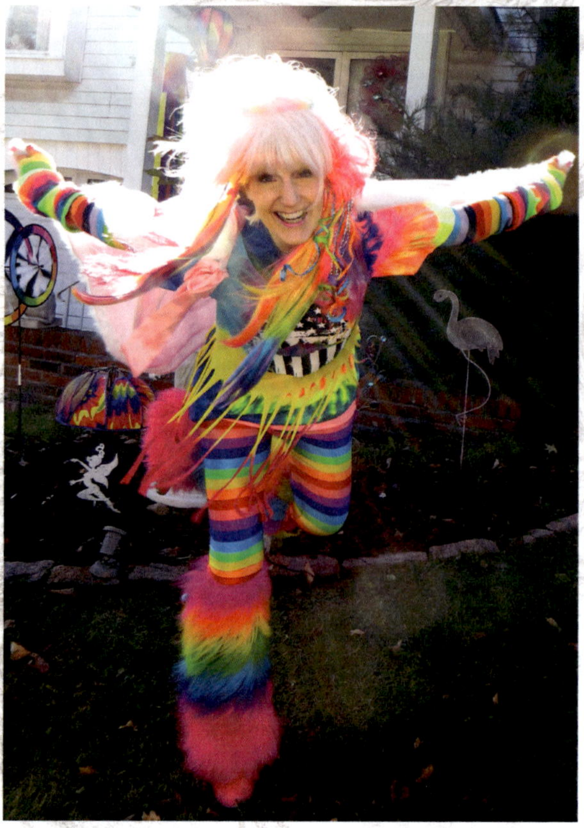

Opposite page: *Intuition*

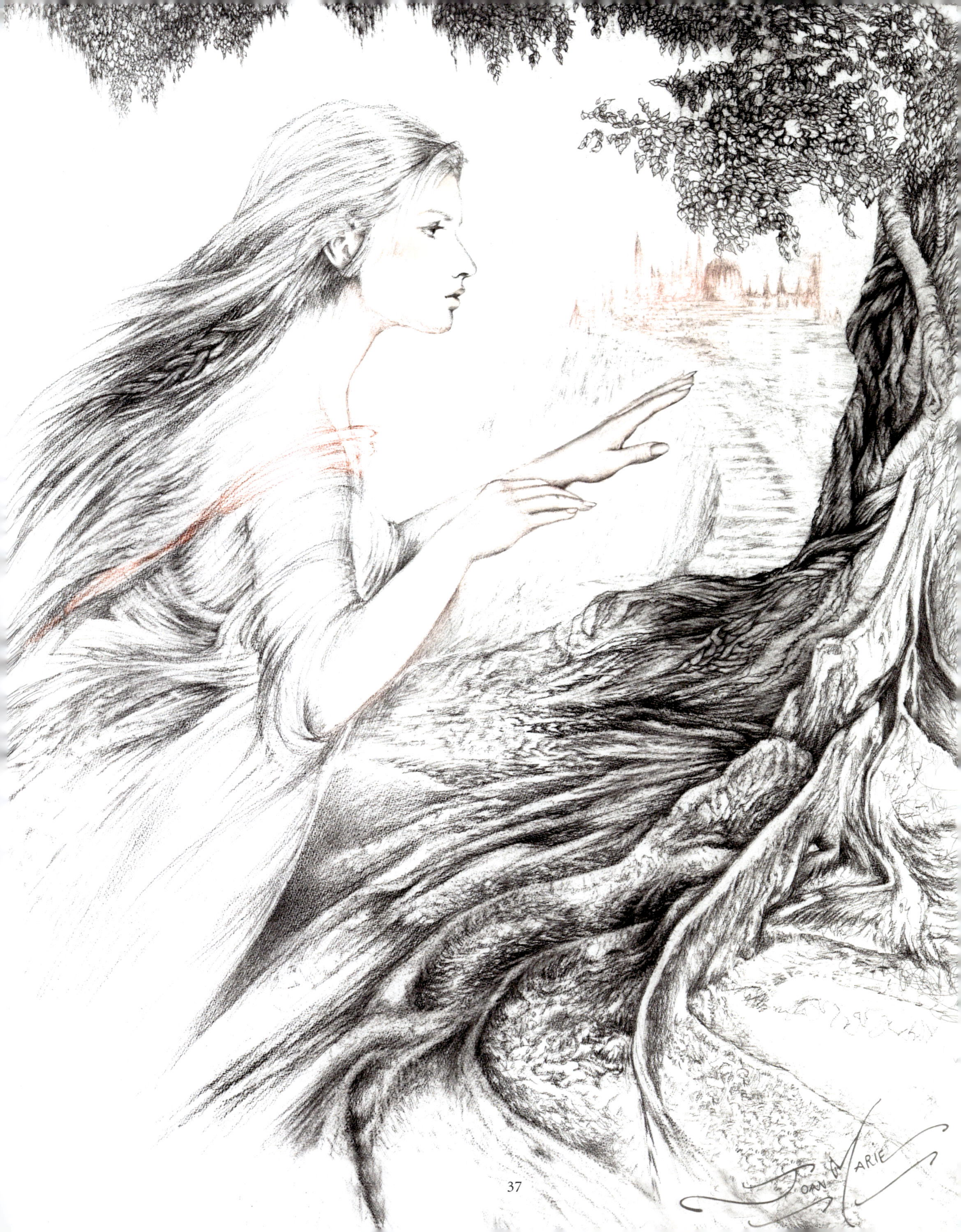
JOAN MARIE

Ingénue

It's time to feel free to express yourself!

Butterflies are a symbol of freedom and transformation. There is a butterfly placed over the mouth of the woman in the drawing to symbolize the transformation from verbal silence and insecurity to an ability to speak freely with confidence. This woman finally voices her thoughts.

Do you relate to this **transformation from insecurity to "I'm free!?"**

Regrets of the Dying may stir more reasons to express yourself verbally:

…I wish I had lived for myself more
…I wish I didn't work so hard
…I wish I didn't hold back my feelings
…I wish I had stayed in touch
…I wish I was happier
…I wish I cared less of what others thought
…I wish I didn't worry so much
…I wish I took better care of myself
…I wish I didn't take life for granted
…I wish I lived in the NOW, instead of always thinking or worrying about the past or future.

From the "Power of Positivity" newsletter

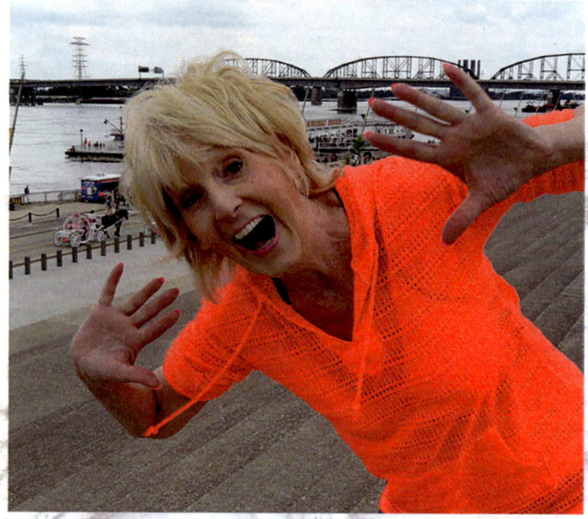

Which wish above feels true for you?

NOW is the time to live with no regrets. Forget the past. **No regrets about anything!** Be at peace, knowing everything had a purpose, even if you don't understand it. **It's the past. It's over.** Move on to live life to the fullest.

It's time to feel free! If you are a people pleaser, it may be time to fully accept that **no matter what you say or do to please others, someone may always be there to share a less than favorable opinion.** Their negative opinions don't have to sway your own positive opinions of yourself. Stay close to those who support and encourage you and be true to yourself.

It's always a good time to smile.

The older I get, the more I just don't care what people think! It's so much more fun to feel this way!

Opposite page: *Ingénue*

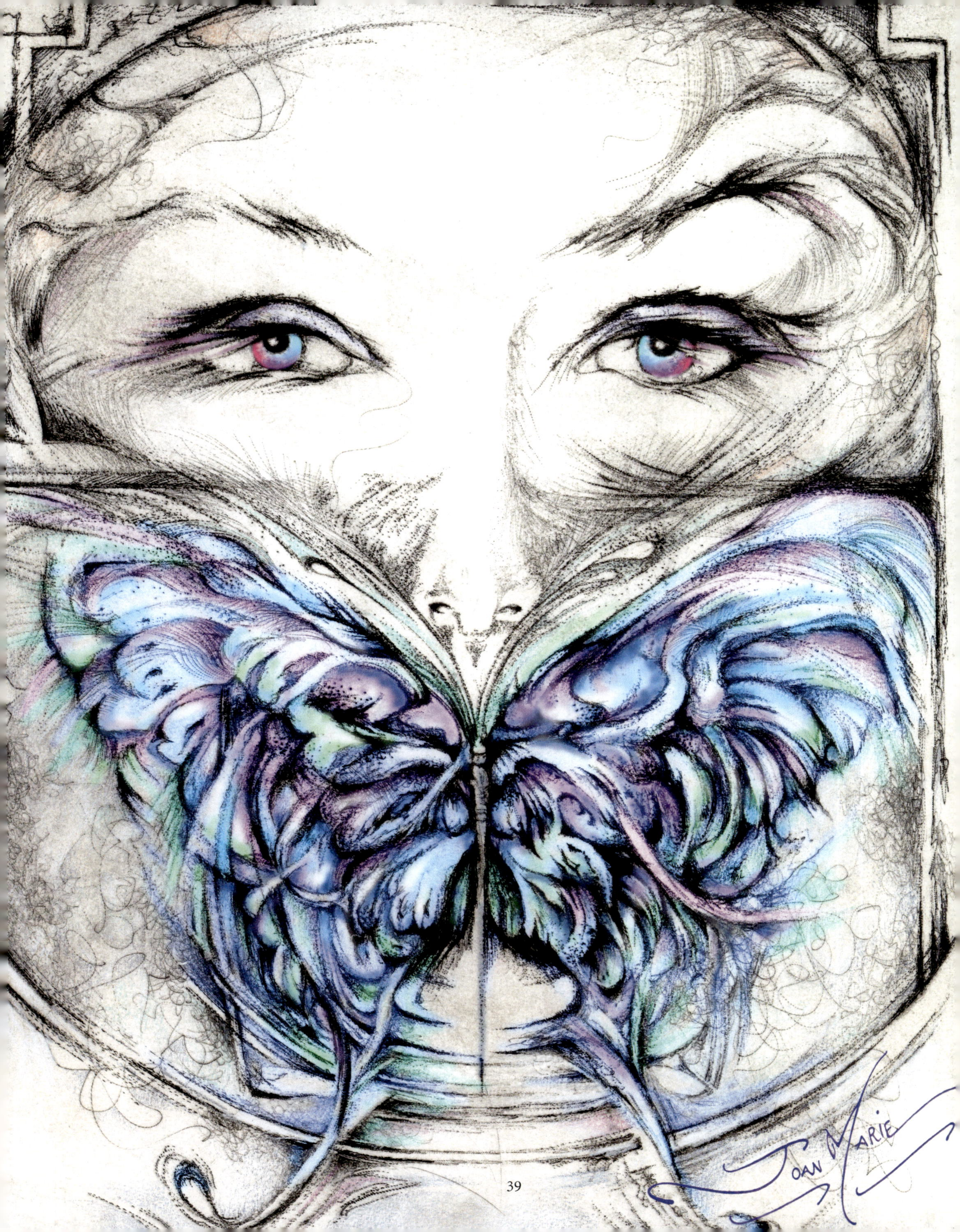
JOAN MARIE

Breaking the Bonds

Visualize the goal - Enjoy the pathway

Einstein's famous quote: "The definition of insanity is doing the same thing over and over again and expecting different results."

Visualization creates images that help generate good feelings.

Good *feelings* direct your life.

List 1-3 things you want or want to make more fun.

Stop, relax, and visualize how you desire to feel three times a day with vivid **feeling**; (notice, ***feeling*** is the most important part of this practice.)

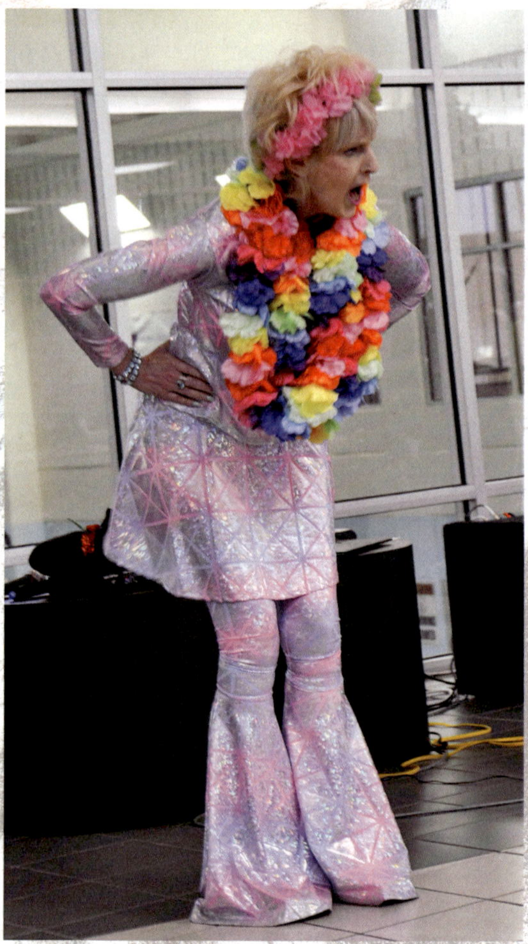

Morning, noon and night, think of what and how you want to feel as often as possible.

This really works! Read the pamphlet *It Works*, by RHJ

How do you view the girl in this drawing? Some see her rooted in wisdom and lessons learned from all the twists and turns of life. Her hair flies with vibrant energy and she keeps her eyes on her dreams.

I originally created this work in response to a personal epiphany. I'd realized that **the repetition of bad habits can prevent the achievement of goals**. The creation of this artwork helped me shift to the choice to visualize my dreams.

Stay on the path you desire, no matter what challenges you encounter. Hair flying in the wind represents the action you take. Do you have a habit that has kept you stuck? Following your feelings, shift your visualization to what you really want. How do these thoughts make you feel? Your feelings direct your life. Shift to the best feeling place.

Opposite page: *Breaking the Bonds*

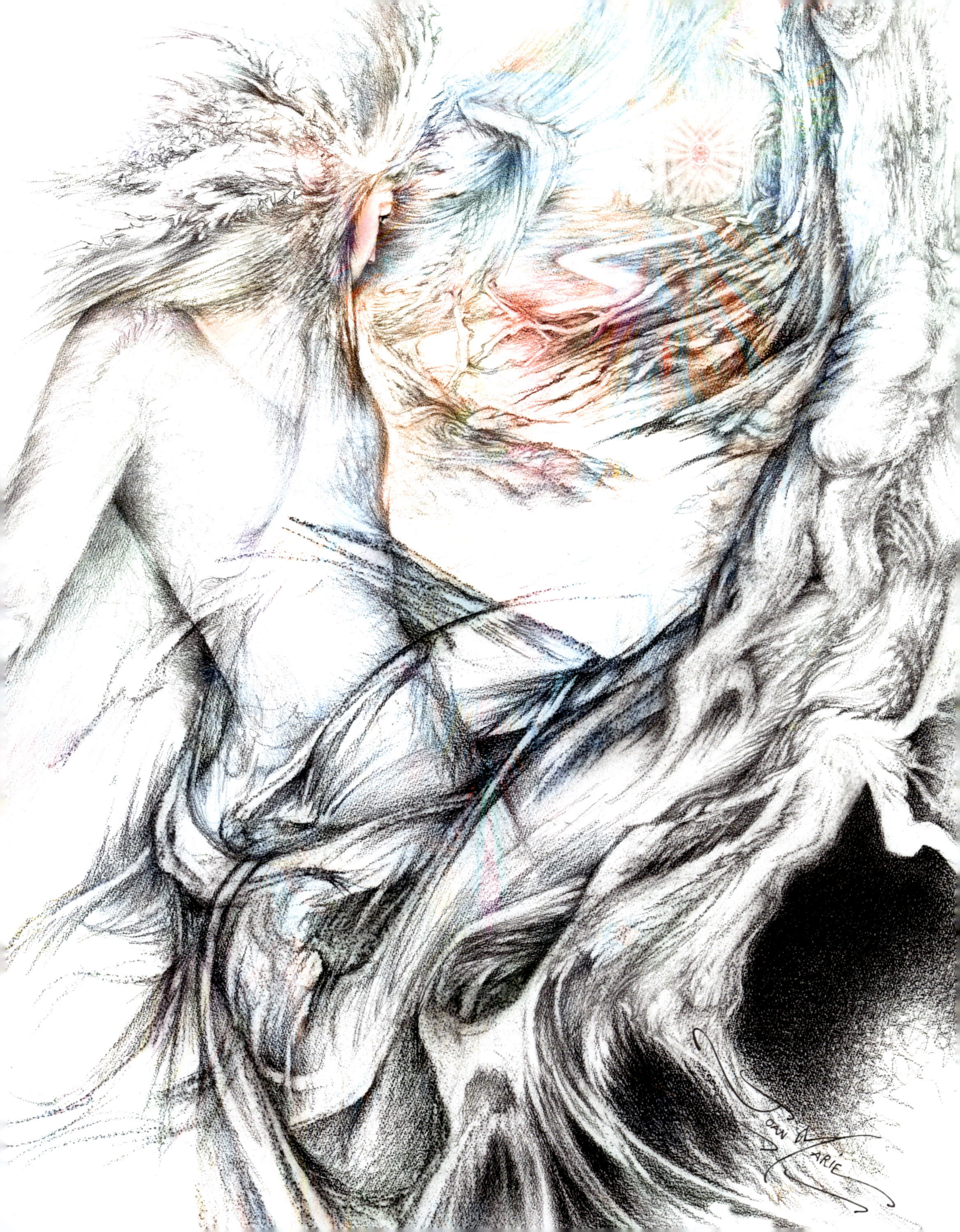

Protection or Challenge?

Life is how you interpret

You have a choice to see life negatively or positively. For example, you could believe getting a speeding ticket is bad luck, or you could view it as a gentle wake-up call that will save lives and reduce tension when you learn to slow down.

Is the cougar in this painting being protective or lurking?

In the photo, are the balloons a huge challenge in the powerful wind, or a dream come true?

Your response is your choice.

Life is how each of us interpret it and the meaning we each give it.

Are you choosing meanings that ***feel*** good?

All emotions are part of life

You can't have day without night. Life is a rollercoaster ride.

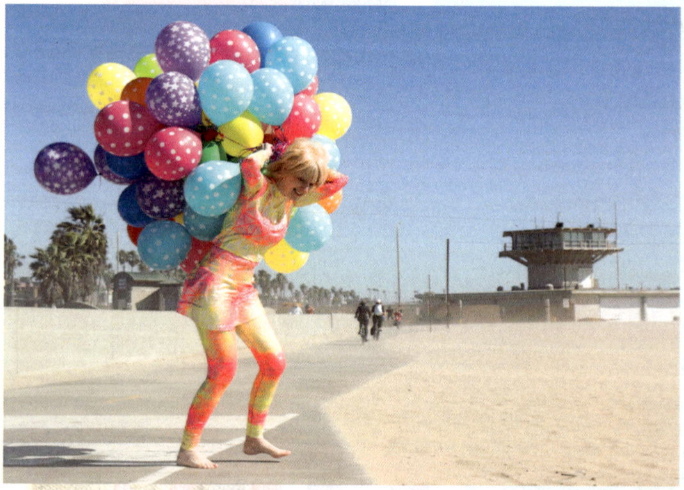

Acceptance of the ebb and flow of life is the key to feeling peace. Stress comes when we believe life should always be one way. Go with the flow and experience the full spectrum of being human.

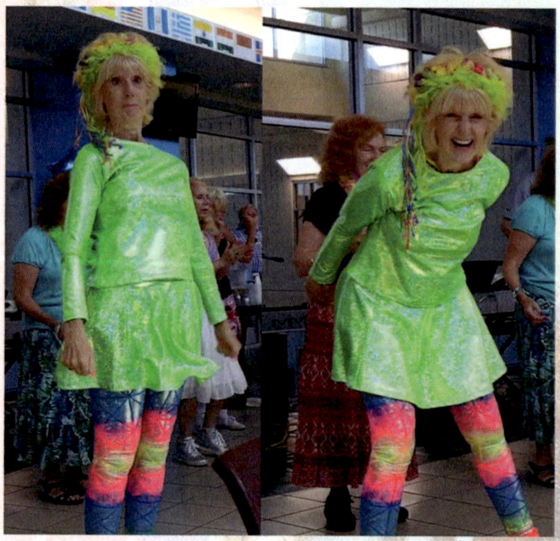

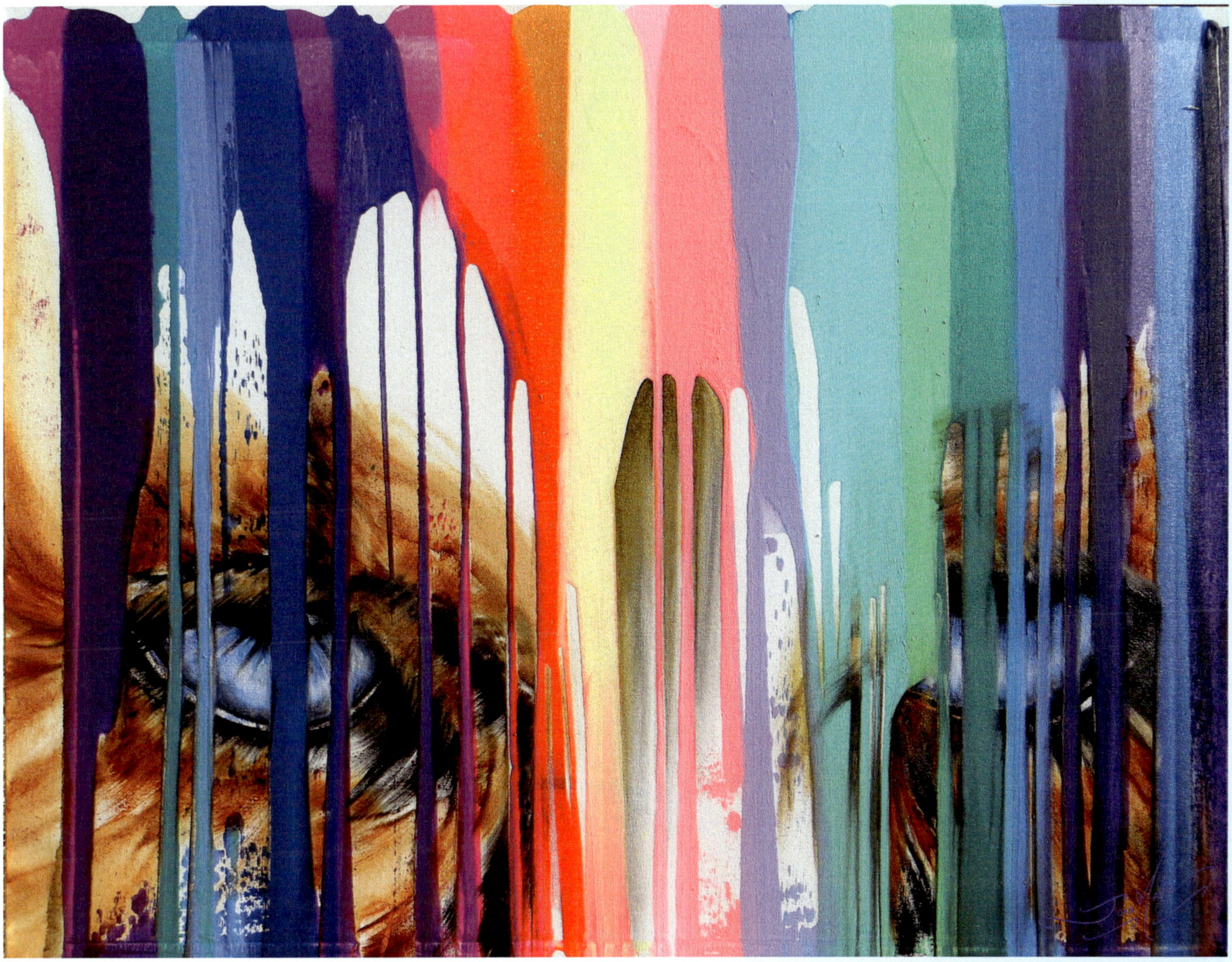

The Guard

The Guard

The mystery of The Guard within. So thankful for his powerful presence. He is at peace while patiently waiting, watching for the moment he is needed.

His great love forever protects you.

Total Trust and Connection to Love

You can always shift your attention.

Holocaust survivor and inspiration, Viktor Frankl suffered horrendously in Nazi concentration camps.

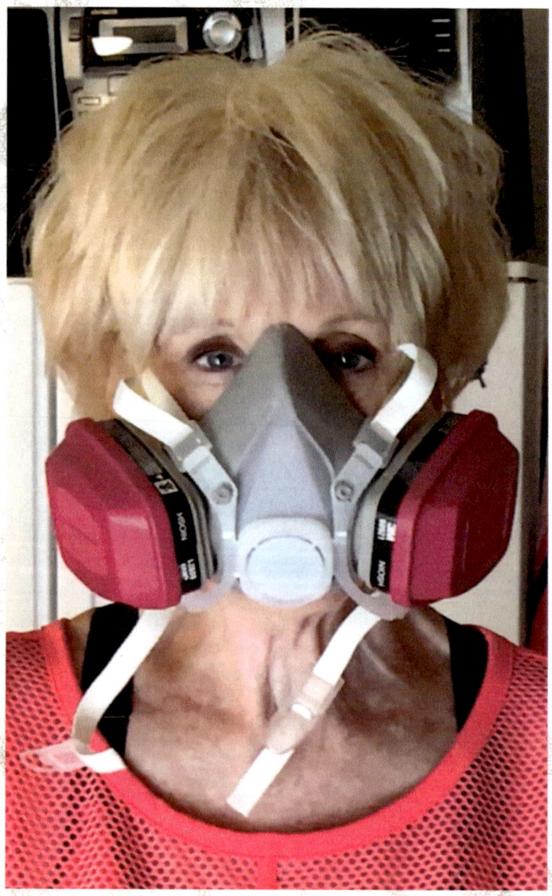

Frankl shifted his thoughts to imagine his wife's radiant smile.

"But my mind clung to my wife's image, imagining it with an uncanny acuteness. I heard her answering me, saw her smile, her frank and encouraging look. Real or not, her look was then more luminous than the sun which was beginning to rise", he stated in his book *Man's Search for Meaning*

"Everything can be taken from a man but one thing… to choose one's attitude in any given set of circumstances…" -Viktor Frankl

In the drawing, *Rising Above* she is

unafraid, finally free and in a state of spiritual tranquility connected to the Divine.

"I feel that this drawing is symbolic of that quiet sacred place we all create in our life to connect to all that is. In that silence, we not only hear and feel from the source of the Universe, but we also remember who we are beyond the day to day busyness and we are energized by it." Yoshi Arima, artist

Opposite page: *Rising Above*

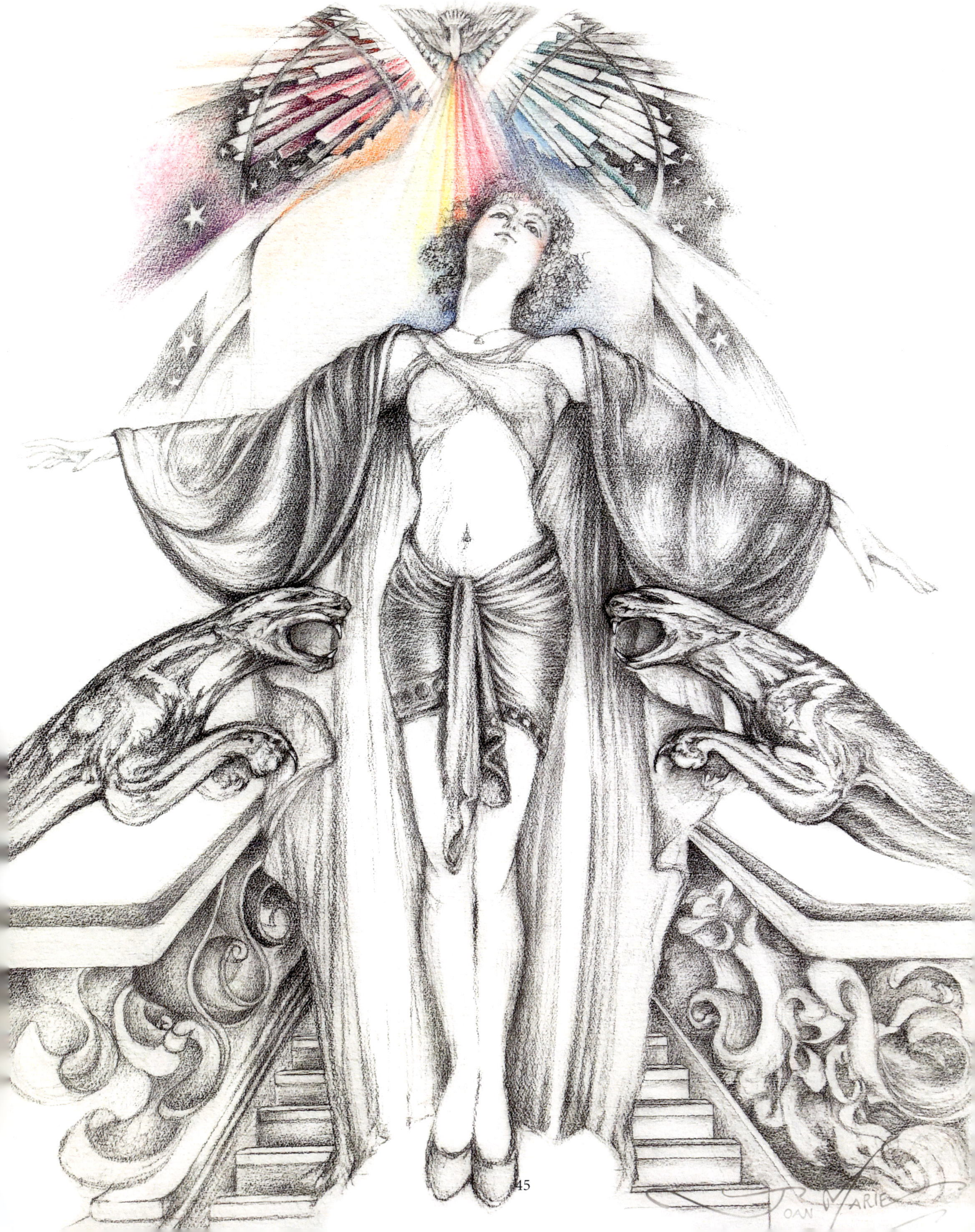
Joan Marie

Return to LOVE

Follow Your Heart

Just as the GPS system corrects the plane's course, you have an inner GPS.

Notice thoughts that create negative experiences. You can correct them to a better ***feeling*** thought.

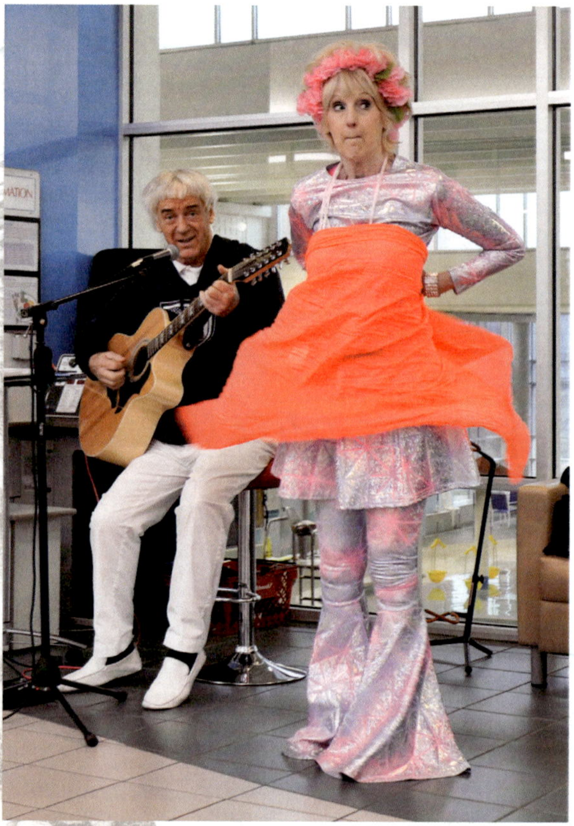

Like the GPS, you can do this repeatedly to stay on a better feeling course.

Notice negative thoughts and correct them to better ***feeling*** thoughts.
Repeat…

Notice negative thoughts and correct them to better *feeling thoughts.*

…Be okay with this

…Be okay with yourself

…Be okay with others

…Notice it. Correct it.

About the Artwork: An ever-present spiritual protection surrounds us with peace. When feeling overwhelmed by life's challenges, we feel comfort as the angels remind us, **there are solutions for everything.**

Breathe…relax…ask for help.
Thank you, God. Feel the peace.

Everything is vibration…What are you vibrating? Where is your energy? Is it in a good feeling place? Yes? Inner smiles *feel* so great!

Opposite page: *Return to Love*

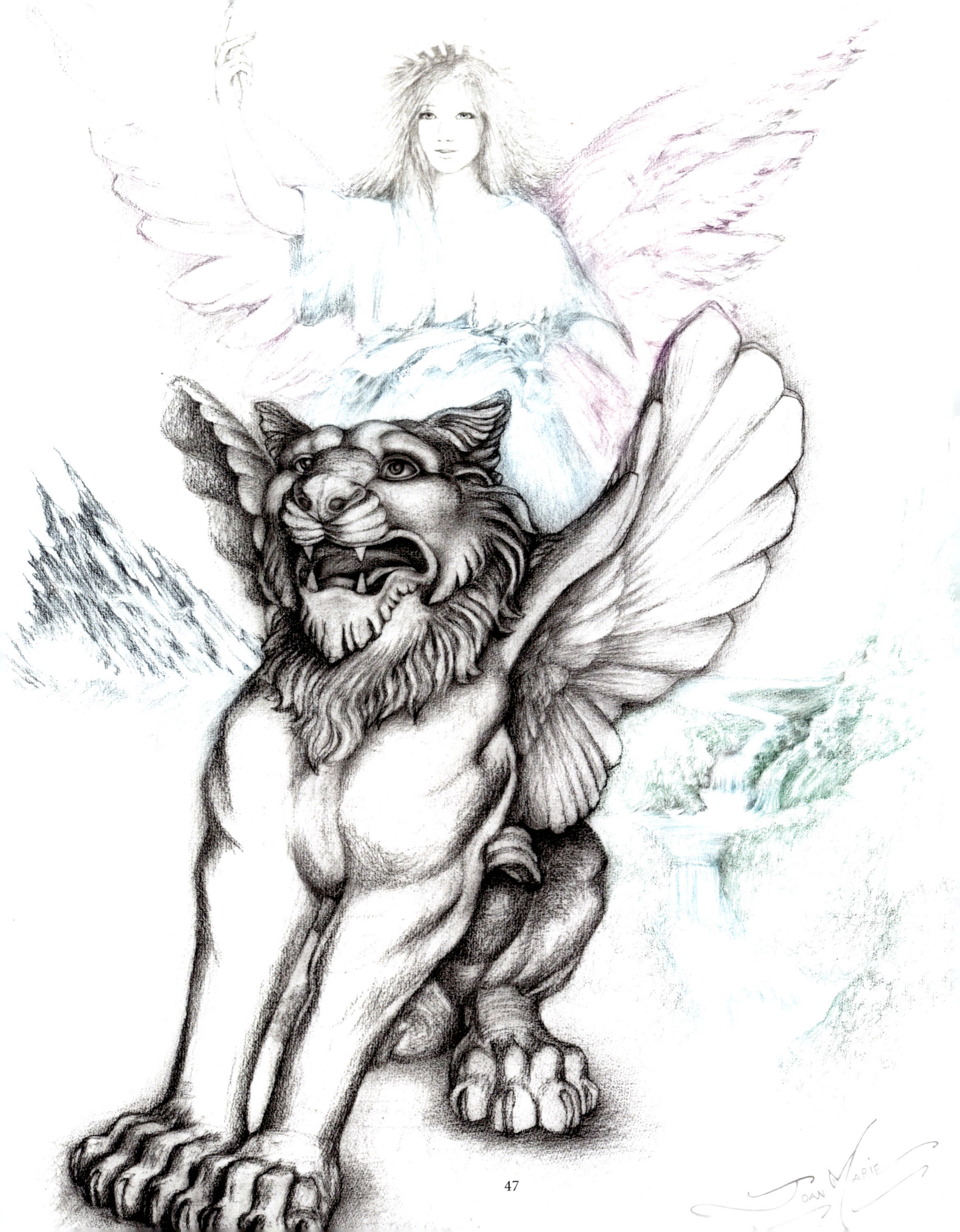
Joan Marie

The Circle of LOVE

Restoring Life

Happiness can come from helping others

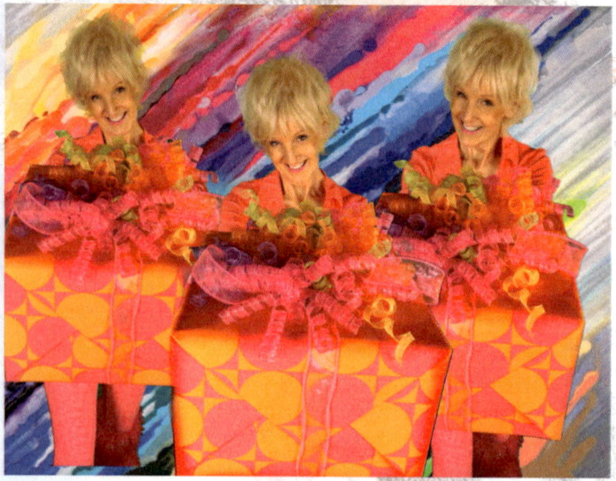

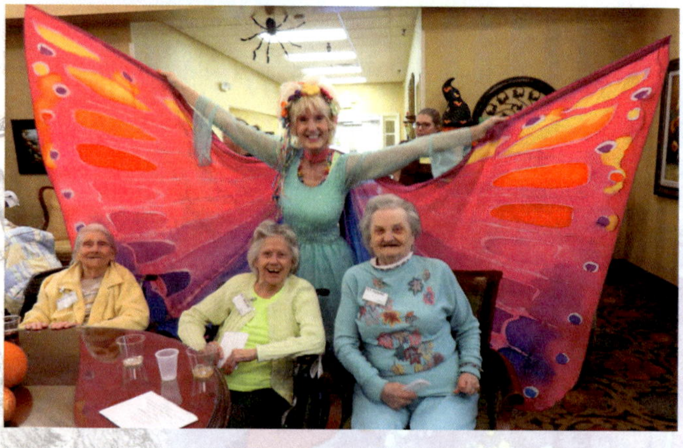

When seeking a way to lift your spirits, doing something for others- even as simple as opening a door or giving a small compliment- will help shift heavy energy to a feel-good place. **The trick is to give without expectations.** Giving unconditionally is the circle of love and life:

Be aware of your power. Love yourself. Then give of your love to others. This is a true FEEL-GOOD place to BE.

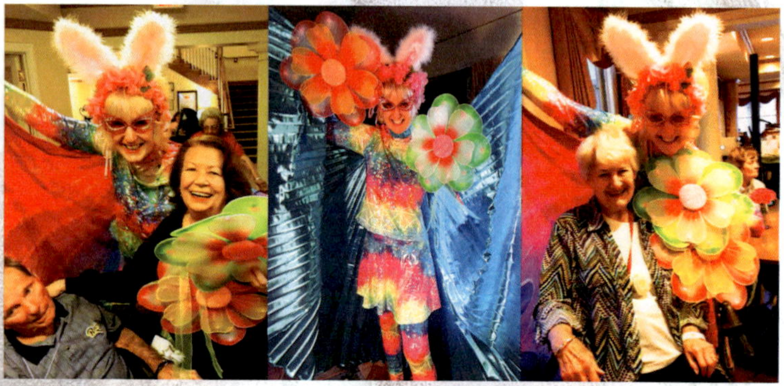

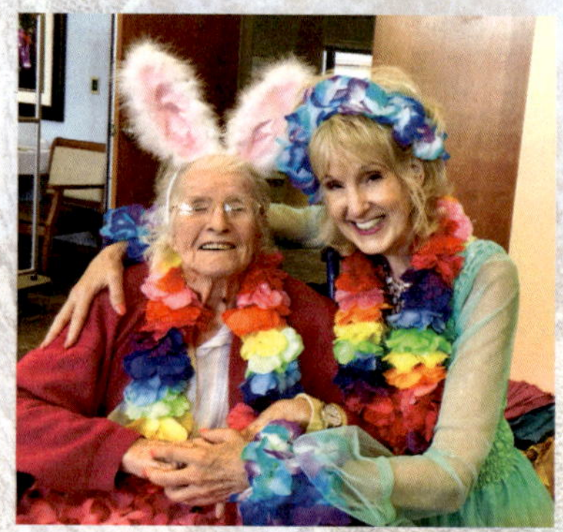

The Greatest JOY of our lives. entertaining in assisted living homes

Imagine being the lady in the painting. You are in your power. You perform the heroic act of restoring a tree to life. Deeply connected to your potential, you have the spiritual power, **the inner trust and wisdom**, to remove the sword from the Cypress and allow the tree to regain its full living beauty. Do you feel the deep joy and satisfaction from helping and sharing your wisdom?

Giving of one's self can be one of the greatest gifts.

Opposite page: *Sword in the Cypress*

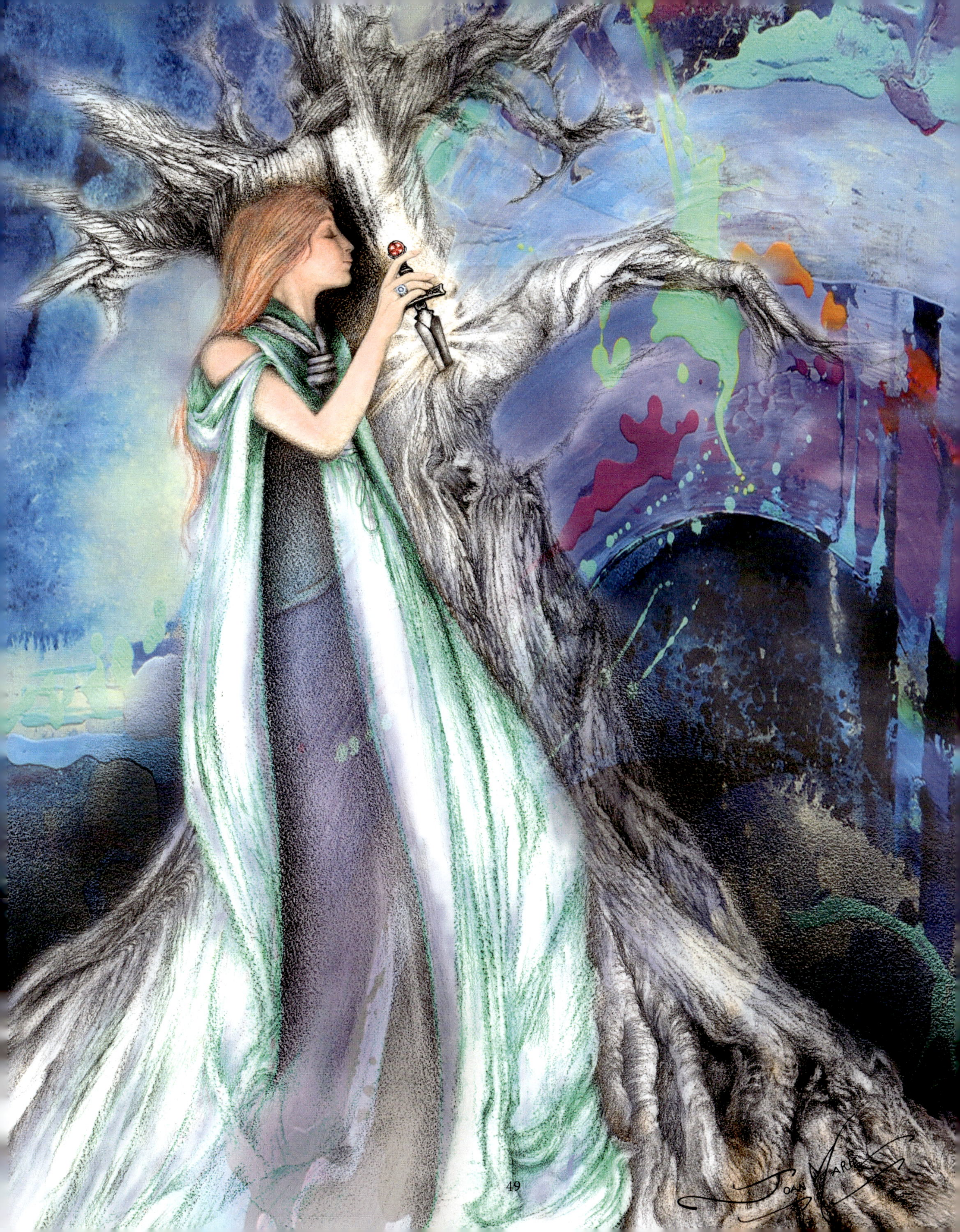

Feeling Free to Be You!

Are you living every day with the passion to be alive?
CELEBRATE LIFE!
Emancipation!

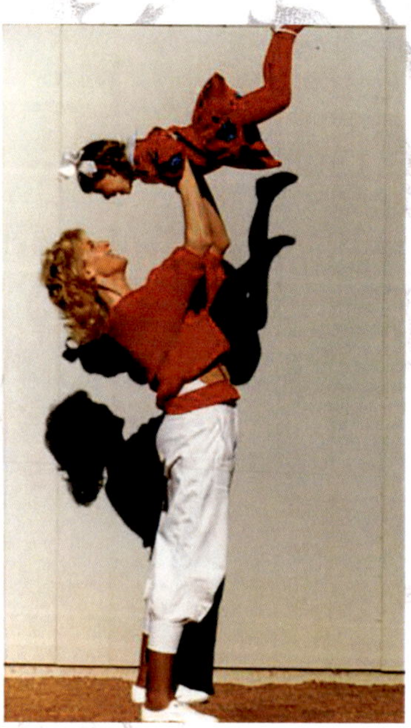

My Daughter, Brittany and me

Yes, you will conquer
old limitations!
Soaring to heights unimaginable!
Finally set free…free to be you!

People ask me how I stay so happy.

Learn to have fun within chaos in a world we can't totally control.

Constantly learning to shift to trust
and acceptance has helped me so often.

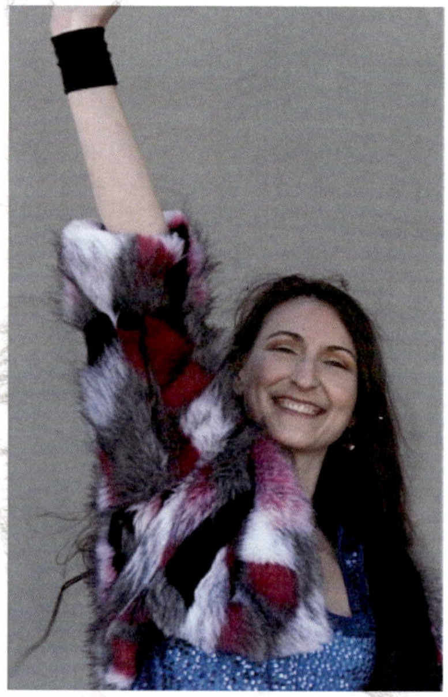

My Fabulous Daughter, Brittany Bishop

When things do not go as planned,
take a breath, feel
and know everything will work out.

Create new ways to view a situation that might have flipped you into worry in the past. With feelings of trust and accepting 'what is' rather than trying to control situations, view what happens with pure observation detached from drama. Developing this skill allows a beautiful state of well-being. This is emancipation!

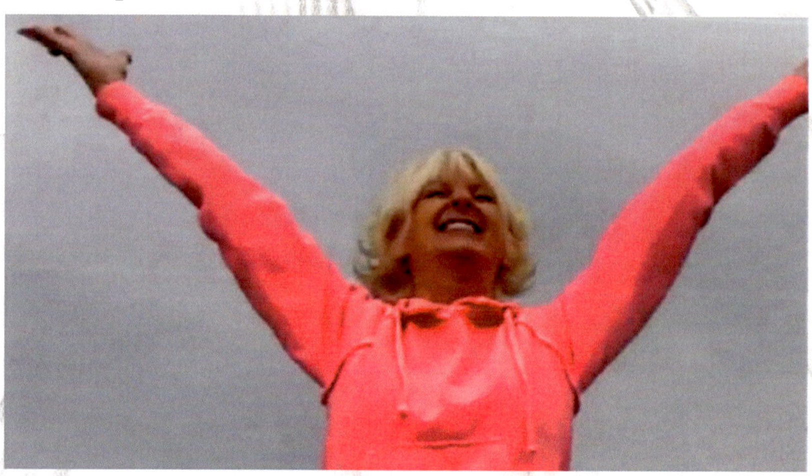

Opposite page: *Emancipation*

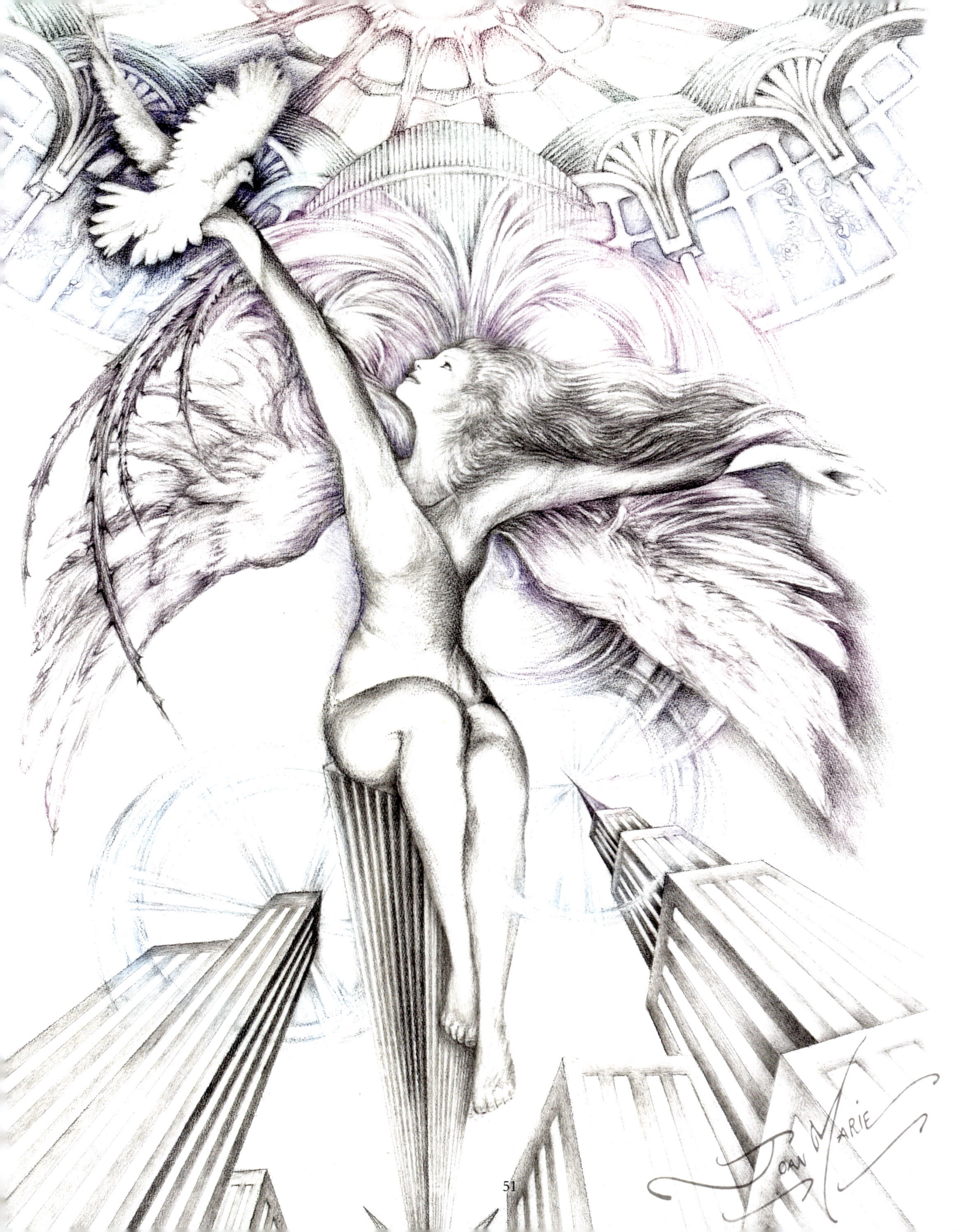

Night Vision

You Are the Warrior for Your Life's Dream

Imagine being a warrior. A warrior has the courage and discipline to face fears and uncertainties while standing strong with clarity and strength. Stand ready for life's challenges.

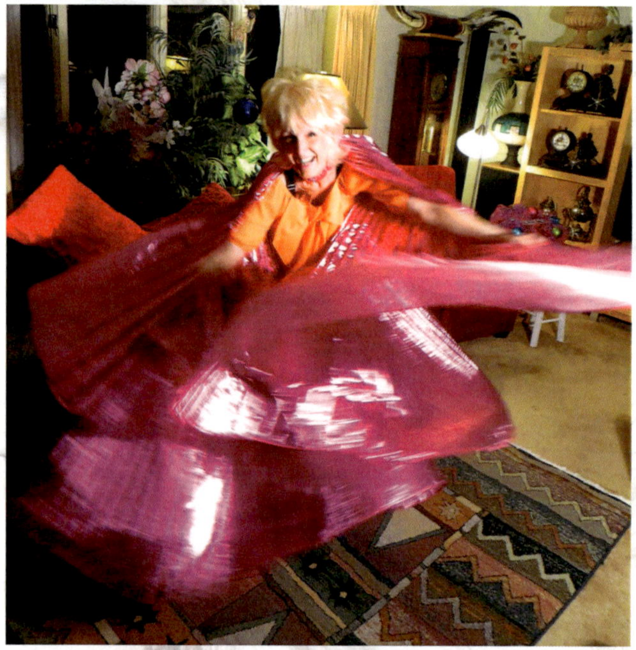

Armed with patience and love, face life with courage.

The warrior in *Night Vision* stands in her power, not allowing opinions or desires of others to deter her from expanding her unique strengths.

The dynamic talisman around the neck represents strength and direction and gives protection and peace. Violet and aqua eyes balance the soul's direction. Aqua allows healing through childlike play and even craziness, as violet stimulates imagination and high ideals. With flowing hair like a powerful lion, free spirited and wild, **stand firm as confidence radiates from your soul.** Yes, you can be the warrior for your dreams

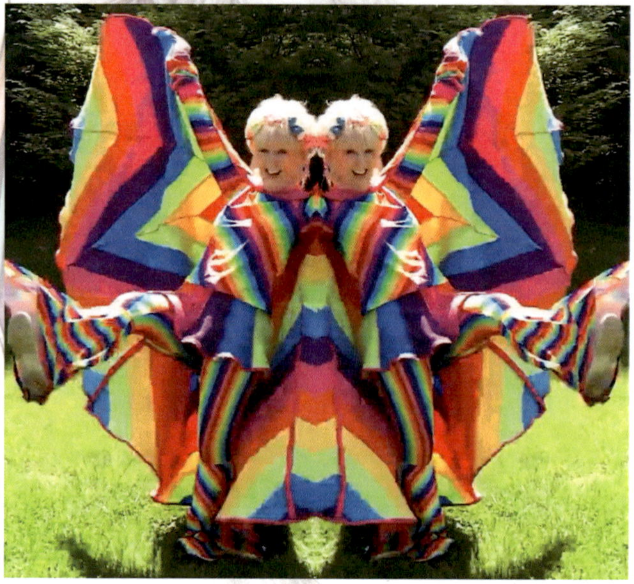

Opposite page: *Night Vision*

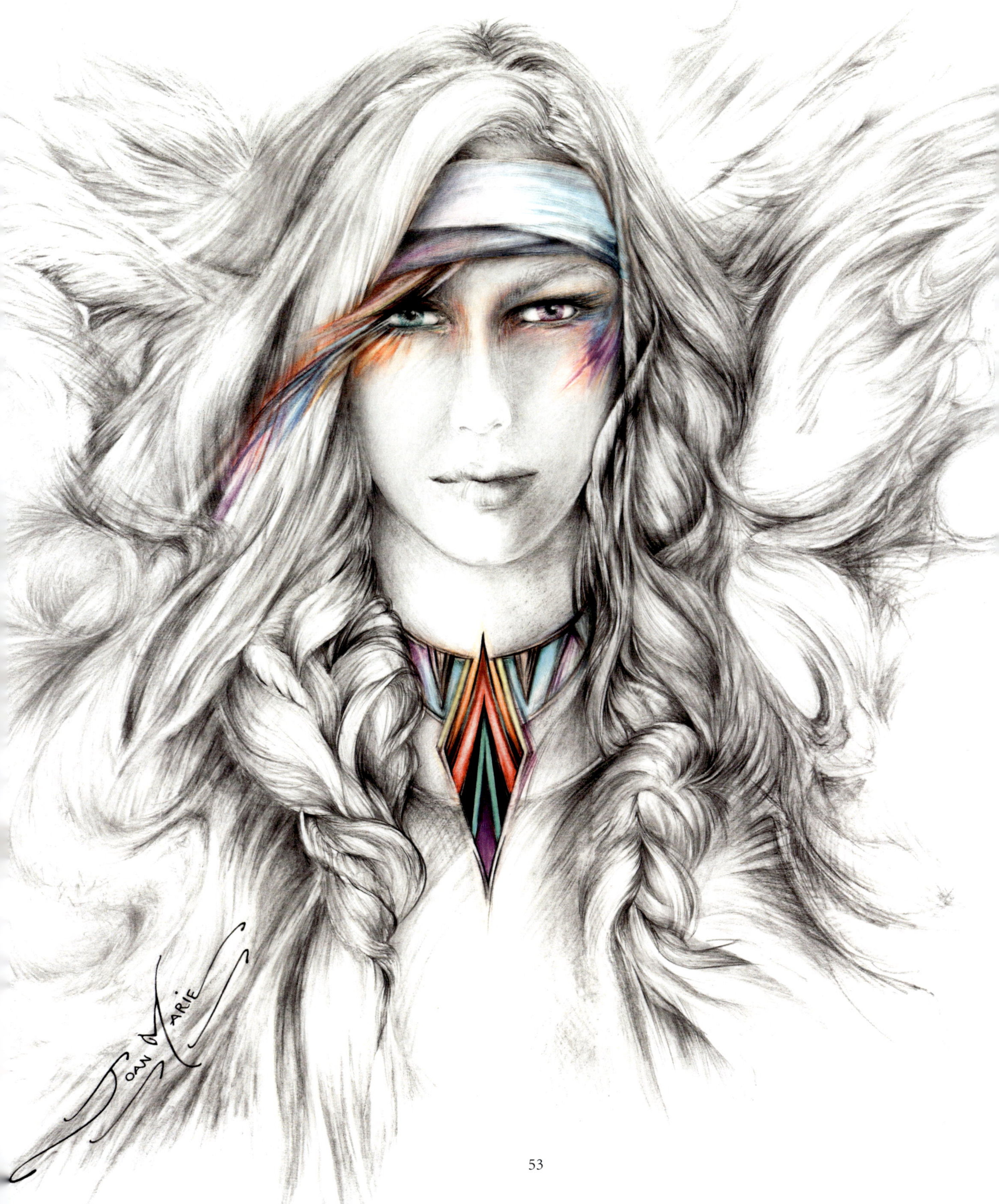
JOAN MARIE

Exhilaration

Take time to Celebrate Anything!

For example: "HURRAY, it's Wednesday!"

...Hurray, "I love the way my rollerball pen flows!"

...Dance down the hall after you hear from a friend!

...Throw out the trash, then break into a boogie woogie. "It's time for a Happeee Dance!"

...Celebrate the snow as a child seeing it for the first time!

OR you could ....

...Decorate a hula hoop, feed the crazy fun llamas, swirl rainbow fans, or buy some Isis wings to share with your friends! Have FUN!

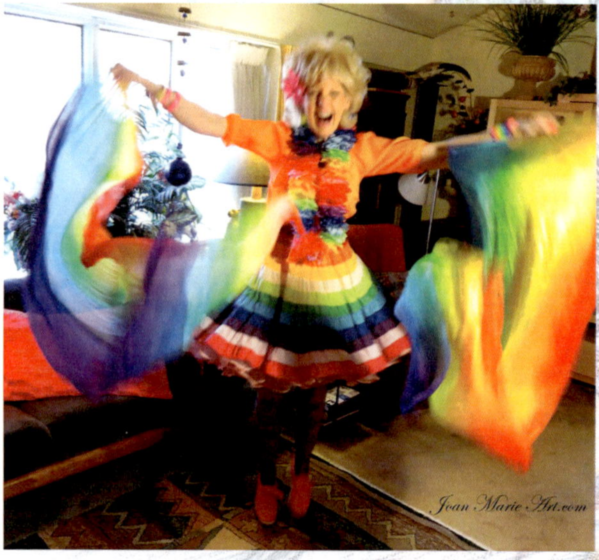

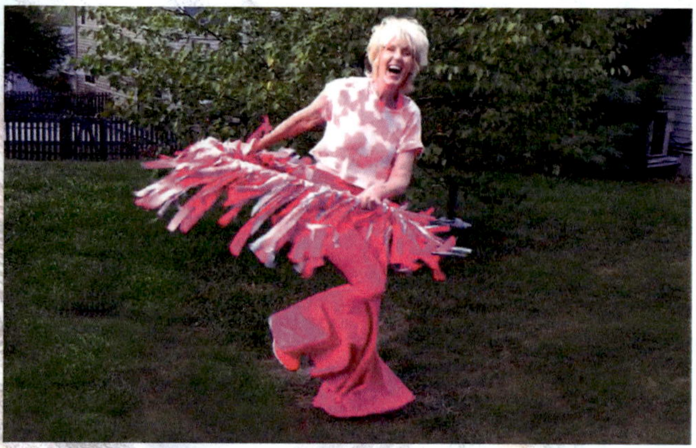

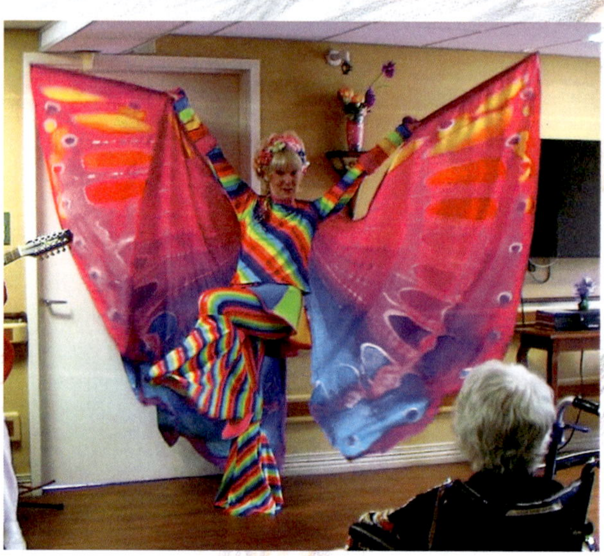

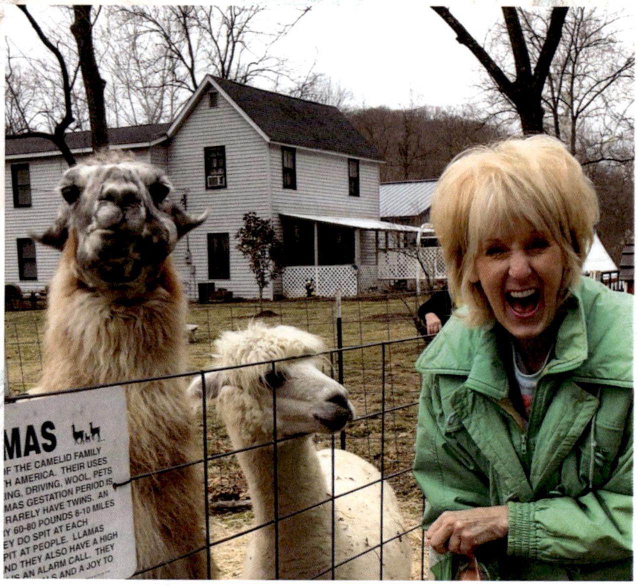

Opposite page: *Exhilaration*

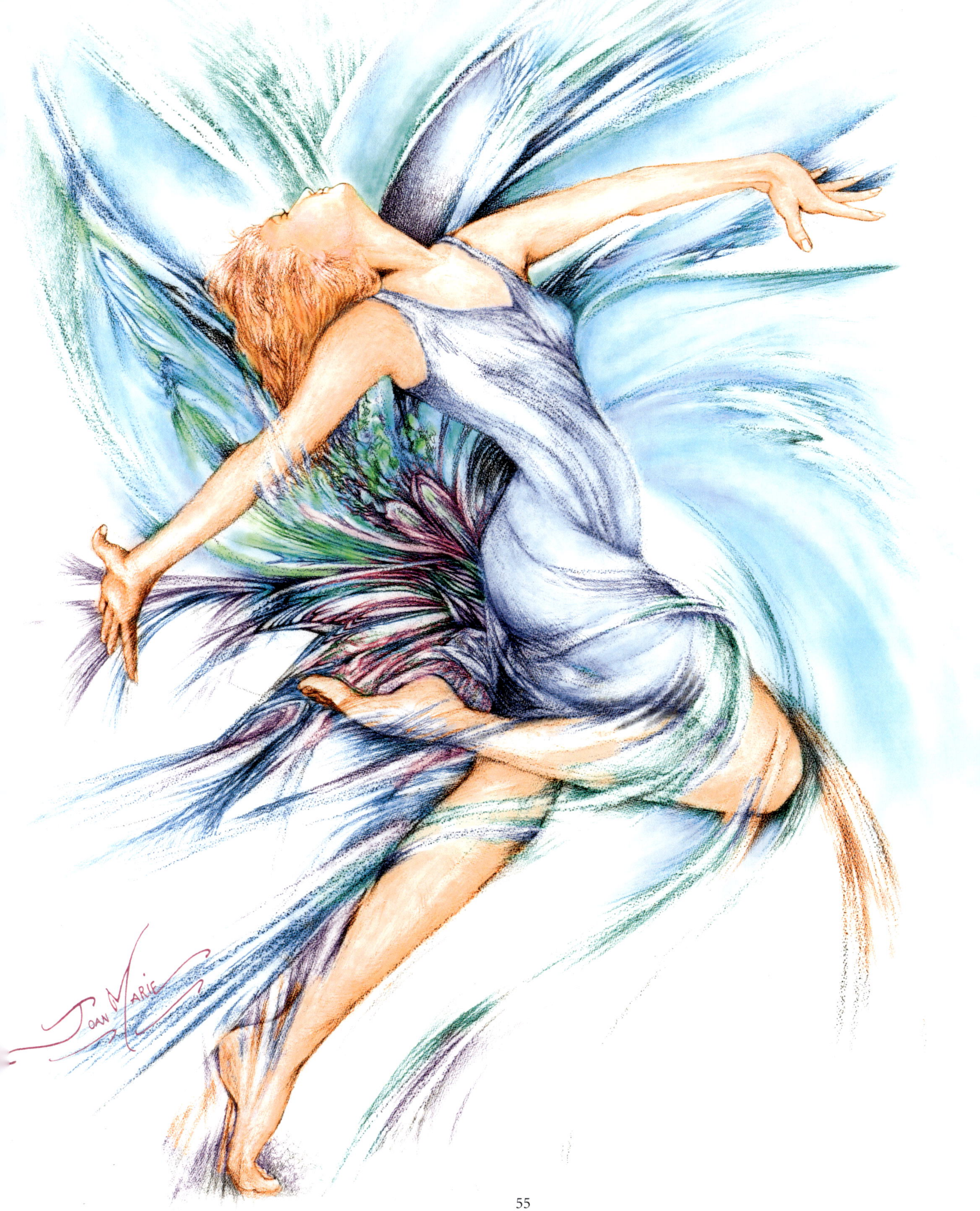
Joan Marie

Sing like the birds sing! Birdies don't worry about who hears them or what others are thinking. Feeling unconditional love from the precious ones.

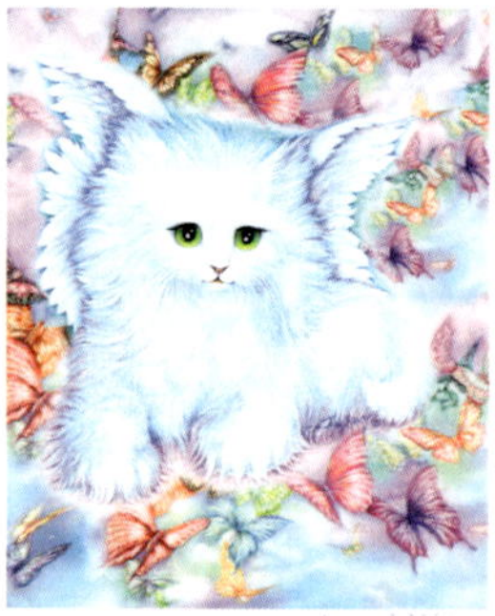
Angel Kitty

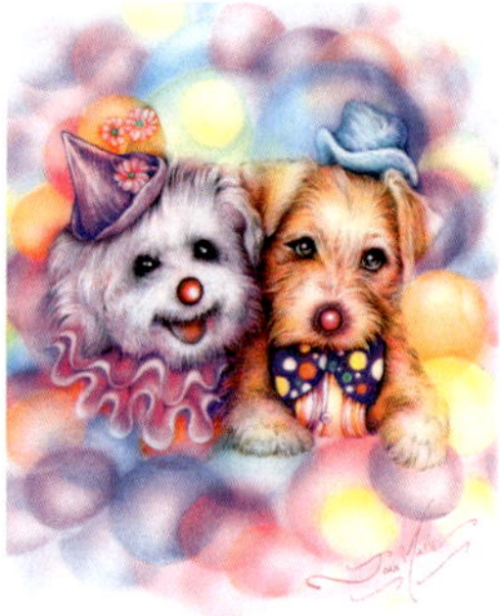
Party Time!

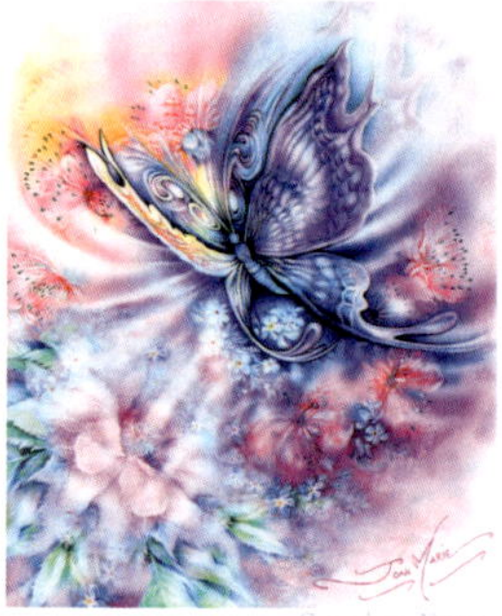
Soaring Free

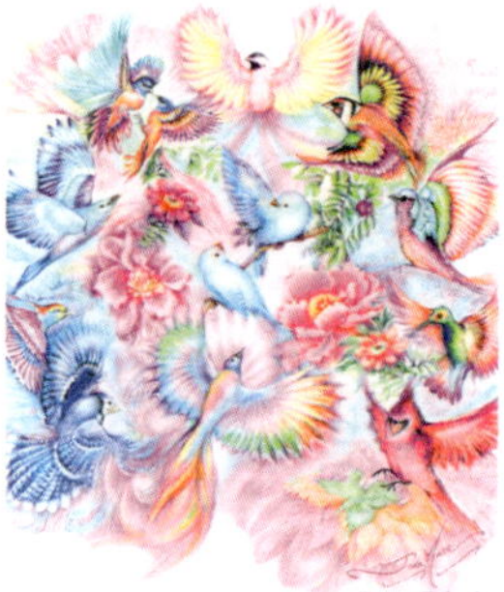
FreeBird

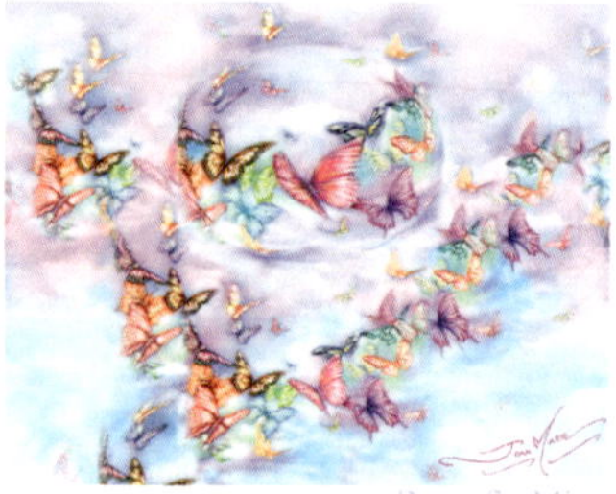
Butterfly Mist

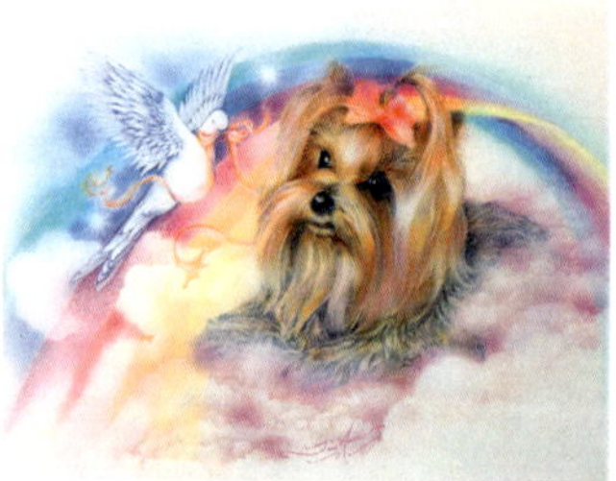
Yorky Dream

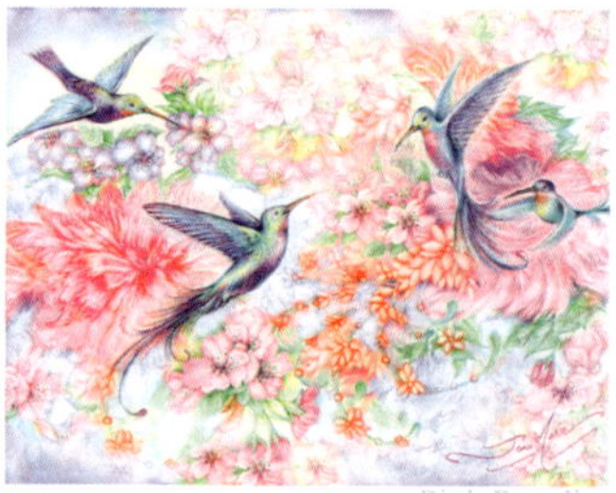
Pink Paradise

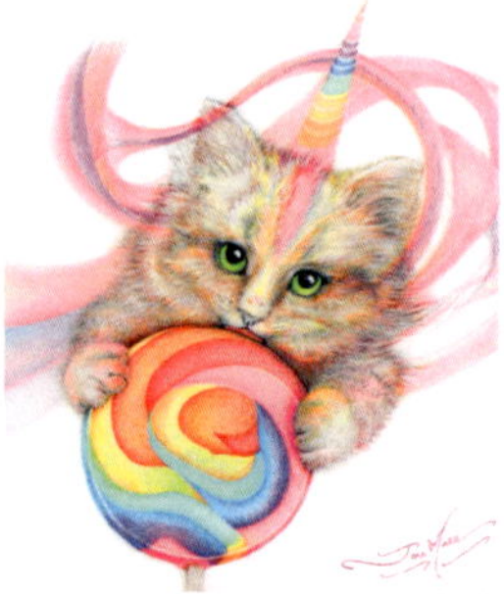
Lolly

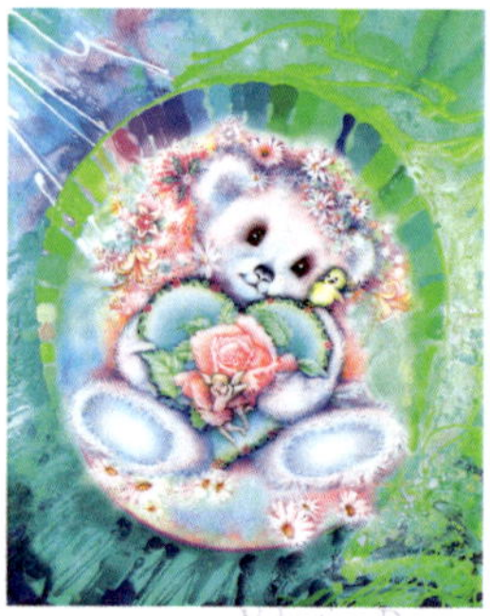
Valentine Dream

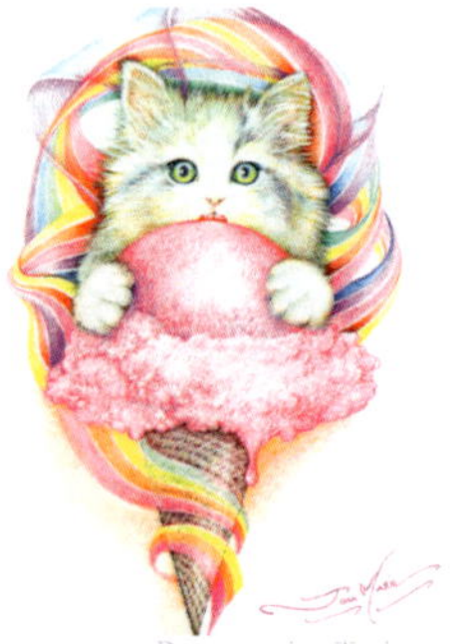
Peppermint Twist

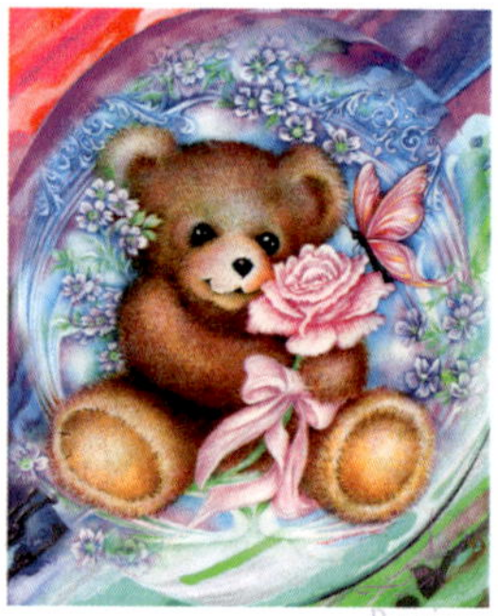
Precious

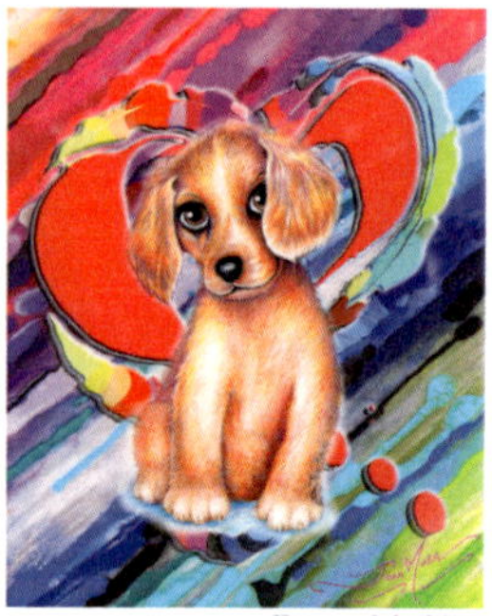
Forget Me Not

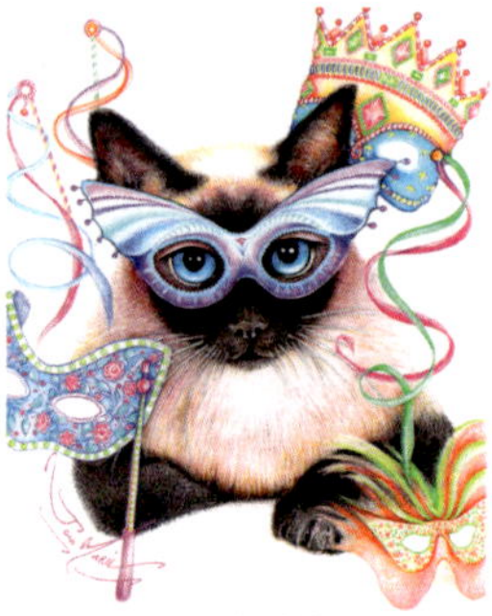
Mardi Gras Queen

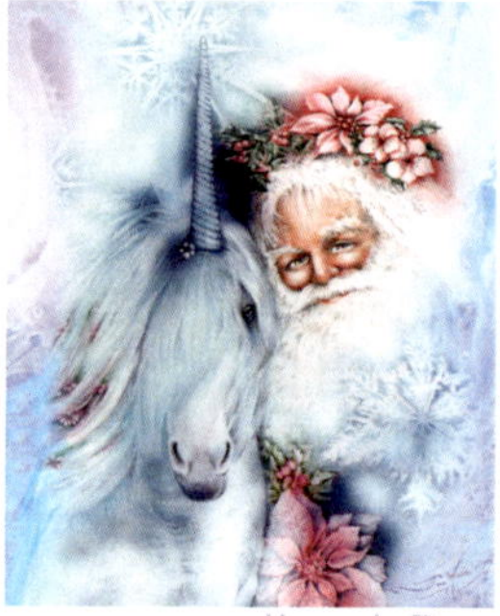
Heavenly Dream

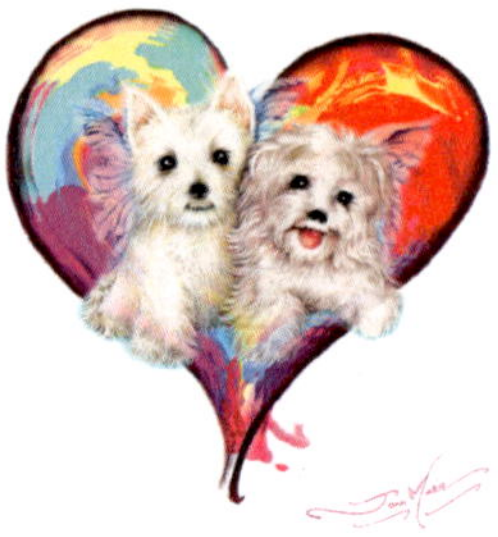
BFF

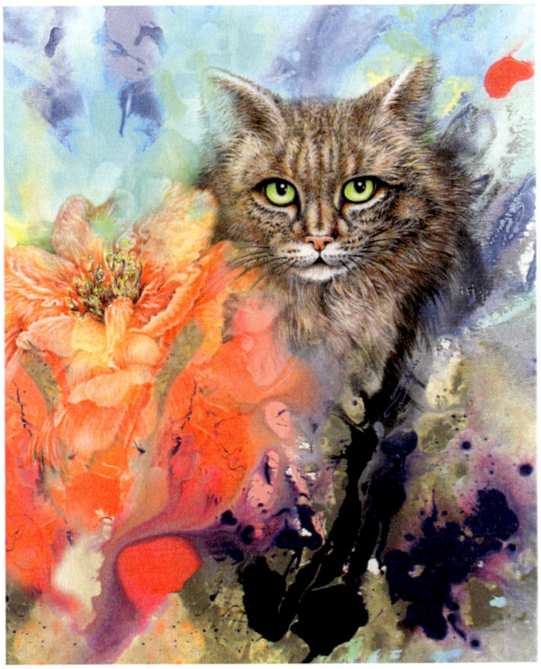

Talullah

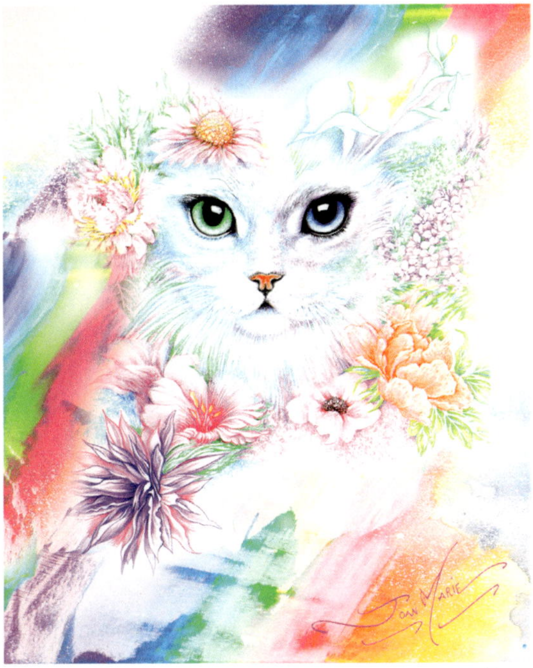

Angelina

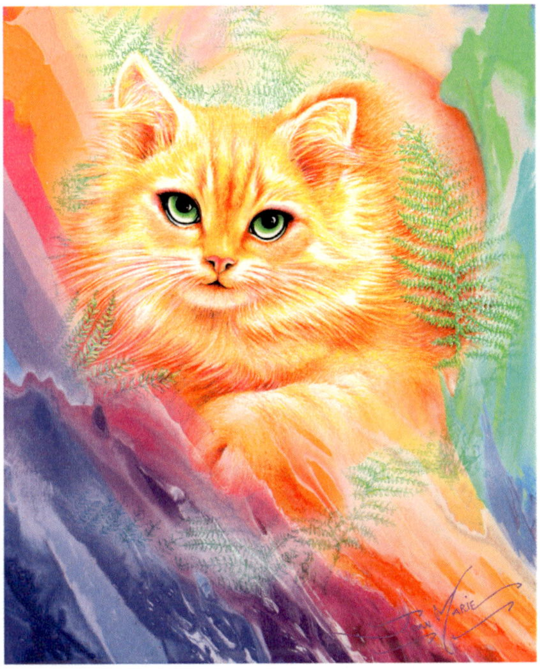

Miranda

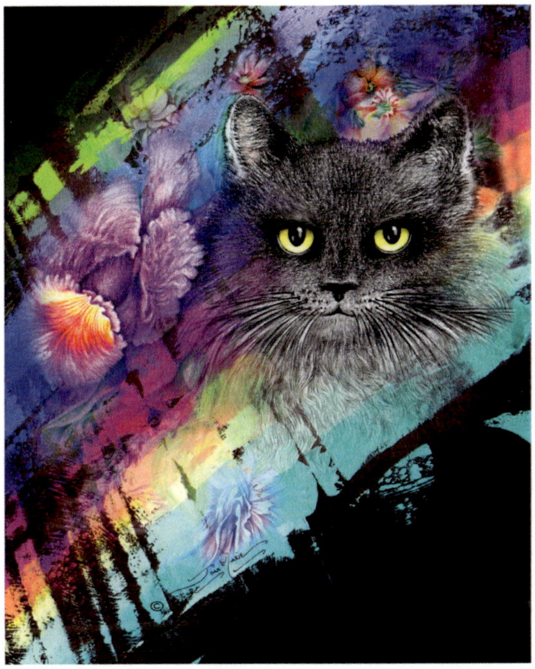

Vixen

Visions of Insight and Strong Gentle Wisdom

Come join our world, where love surrounds us.

Basking in Love

Unconditional Love

Give without expectation from the recipient. Give for the pure joy of giving.
Have no demands of others to perform a certain way when you give.
This is pure love.

"What the world needs is your love and service.

How can you turn your skills into a way to help the world?
What does the world need that you can give?

Don't worry about how good you are; think more about what you can do to help others with love in your heart."

Jim Fortin, "TCP" . . . See Contributors

Are you creating an idea for a business?
Focus on service from your heart.
With love as your focus, you are already a success.

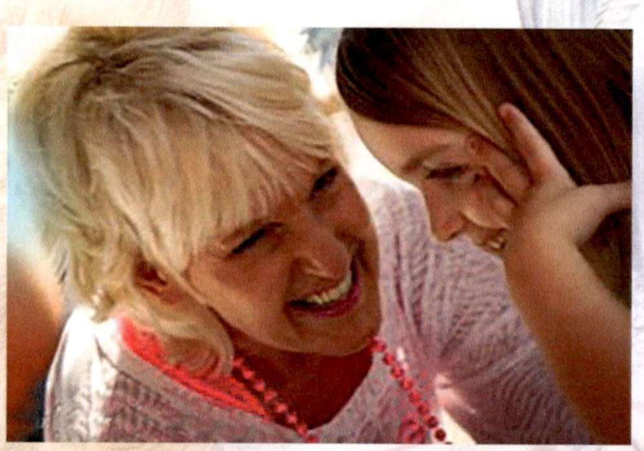

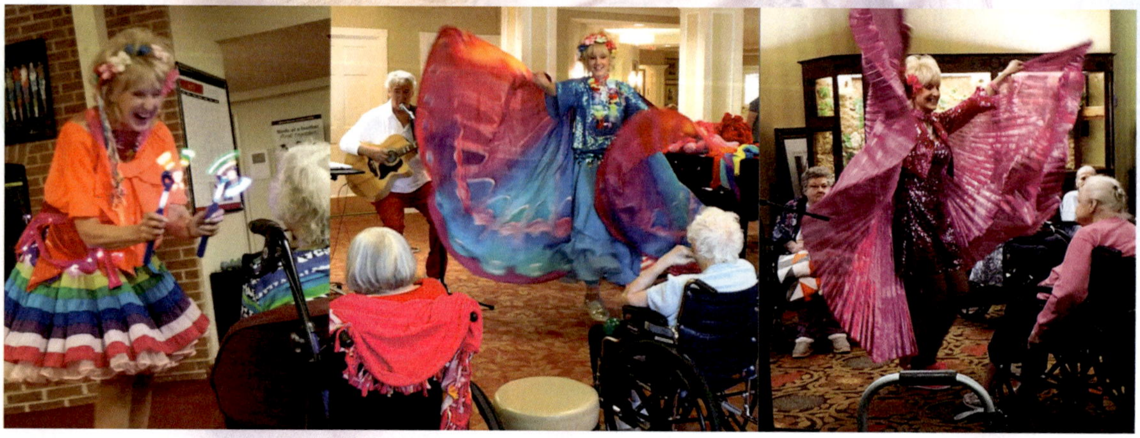

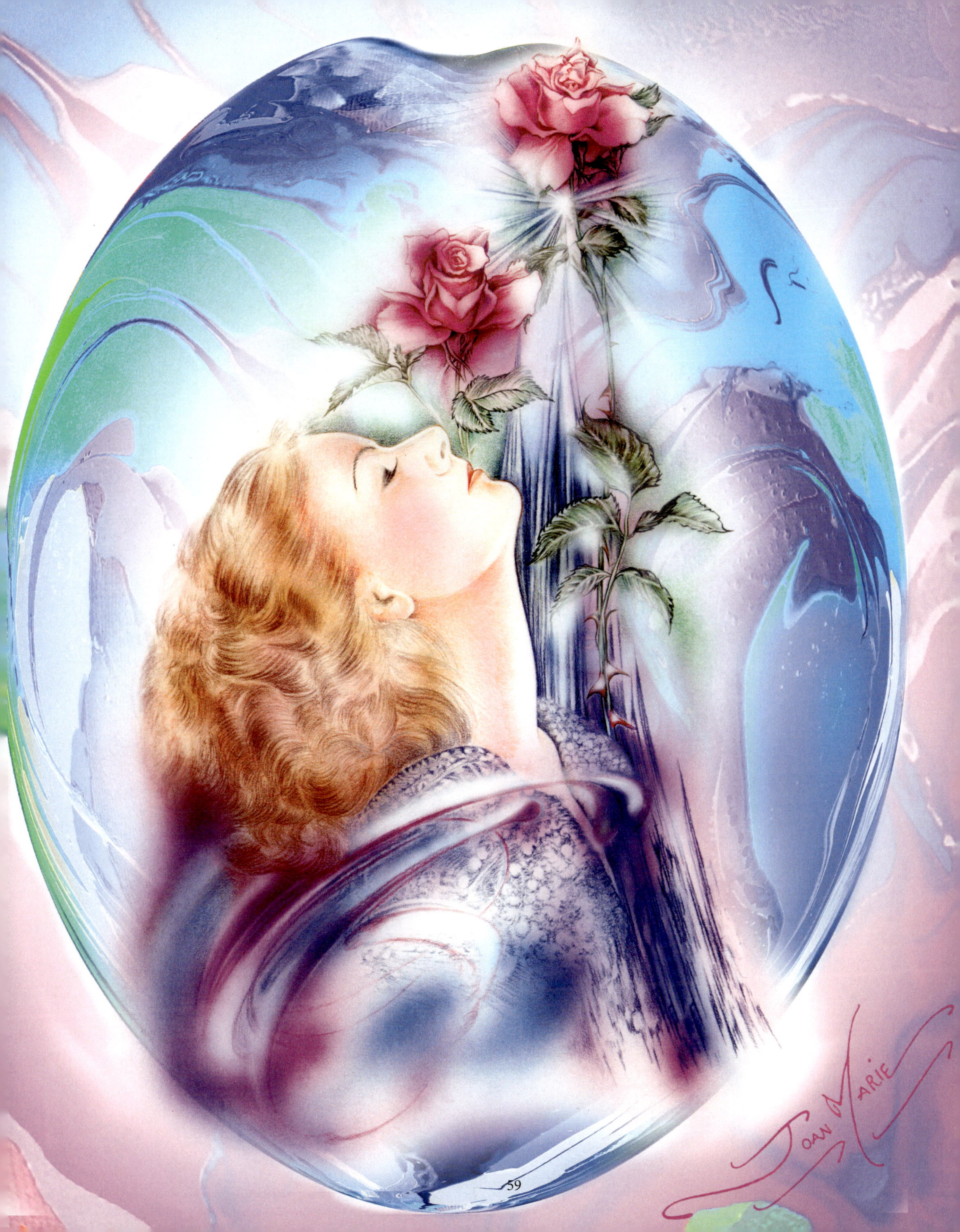
JOAN MARIE

Day Dreaming

Peace of Mind

Peace of mind is the most powerful place from which to work.
There is nothing more powerful than feeling at peace with yourself and with all that's going on around you.

Try it just for a moment. Forgive, forgive yourself and forgive others. Feel tolerance and compassion for all.

Trust the world is healing itself. Be a part of the solution by loving yourself, then sharing your heart and empathy.
Time spent day dreaming can create beautiful moments.
Visualize the way you want to feel in your life.
How do you want to feel in your life?

What does a perfect day look like for you?
Visualizing 3 times a day for a few minutes can feel so refreshing. Imagine your ideal day.

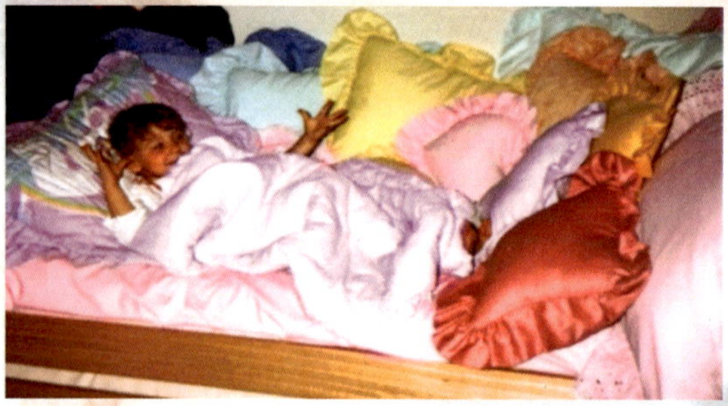

Have you been a workaholic? As I mentioned earlier, I was very hyper for years and loved being that way. Being in a state of hyperactivity felt like productivity. I believed the faster I worked, the sooner my artistic skills would increase, and then I could love and respect myself and be happy.

You have to love yourself first, as you are now, to experience the progress you desire.

The harder you push the further away your goals get. As long as I rushed and pushed to be someone else, I couldn't feel love for myself. The creation of this painting served as a daily reminder to be at peace, now.

Ya' gotta do it!
Ya' just gotta love yourself, just the way you are!

Opposite page: *Dreaming*

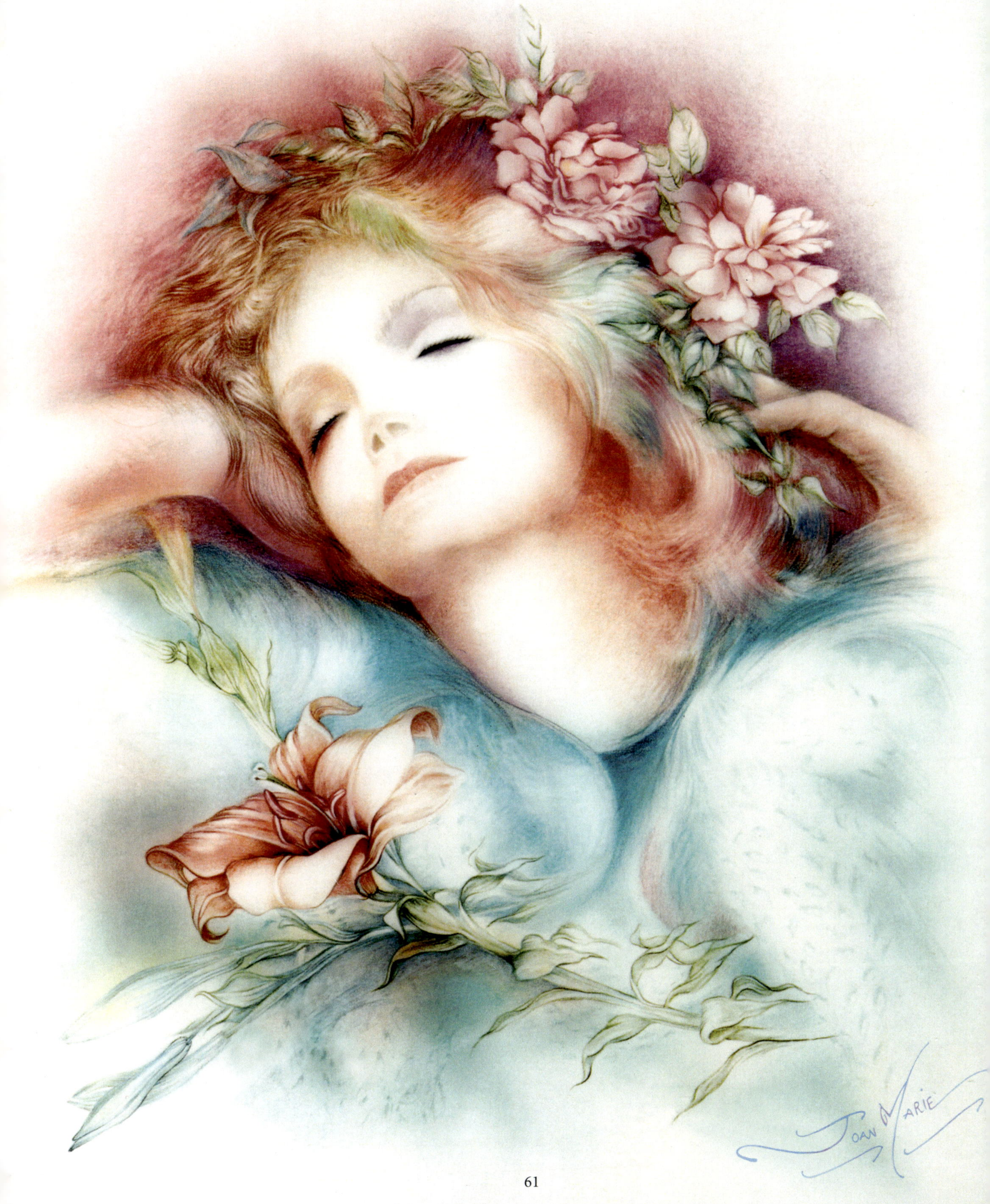
JOAN MARIE

This is what it looks like inside of our hearts

"Oh, Thank You!"

Being thankful and giving of yourself from a healthy place will yield fulfillment.

Feel the Love in your heart beam to others.

Have you made a difference to someone by reaching out to communicate and caring about them?

Have you told the people you care about that they matter and you love them?

Are you spending time with those you love and doing things that you love together?

Butterflies soar in the beauty of your love

All that matters is love!

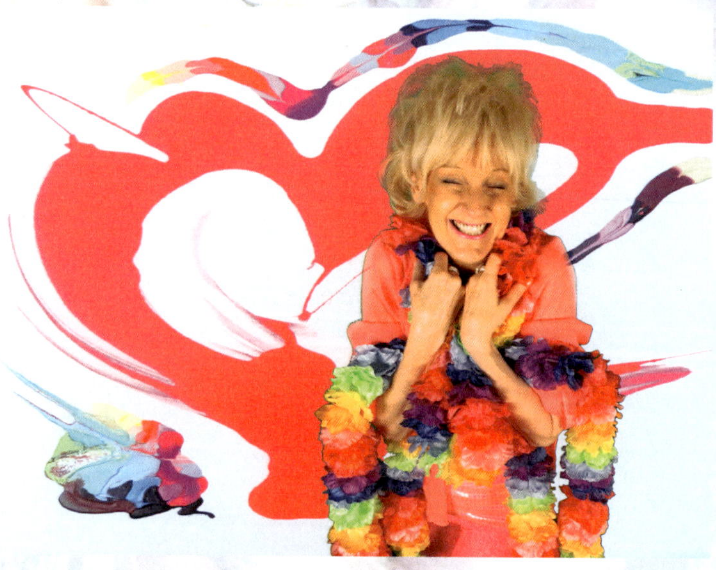

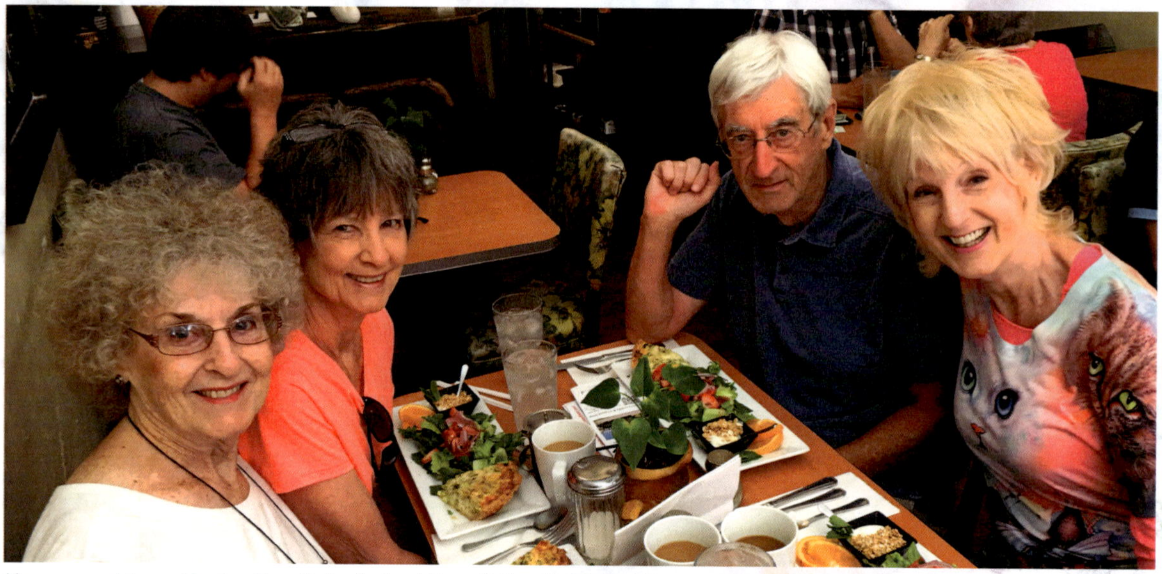

My awesome sisters and brother, Diane Becker, (Lt Front) Donna DeVoto, Paul Gast, and me.

Opposite page: *Blissful Heart*

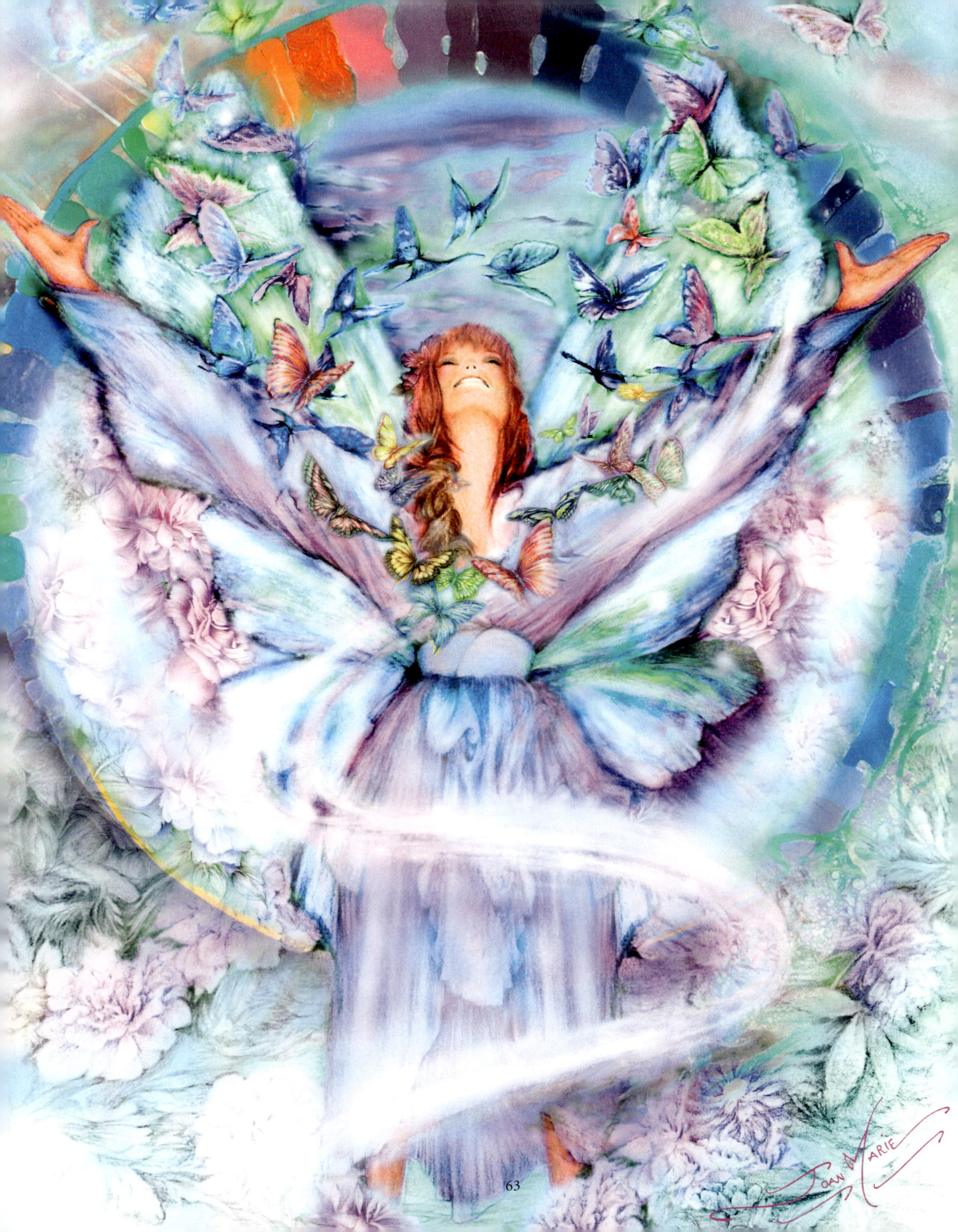
Joan Marie

The Angel of FREEDOM

You feel free!
Time to Boogie-Woogie all the way downtown!

CELEBRATE!!

Join the angel of peace.

...Develop a daily spiritual practice of taking a few deep breaths.

...Then sit quietly for at least a few minutes a day.

...These can become treasured and refreshing moments.

When you quiet your thoughts, ideas may pop into your head. During these special moments create an image in your mind of your ideal self and feel what that feels like.

These quiet moments can be very uplifting. Can you feel it?

Let's celebrate. Come to my house, we can wear wings together and fly around the house. The neighbors are used to it.

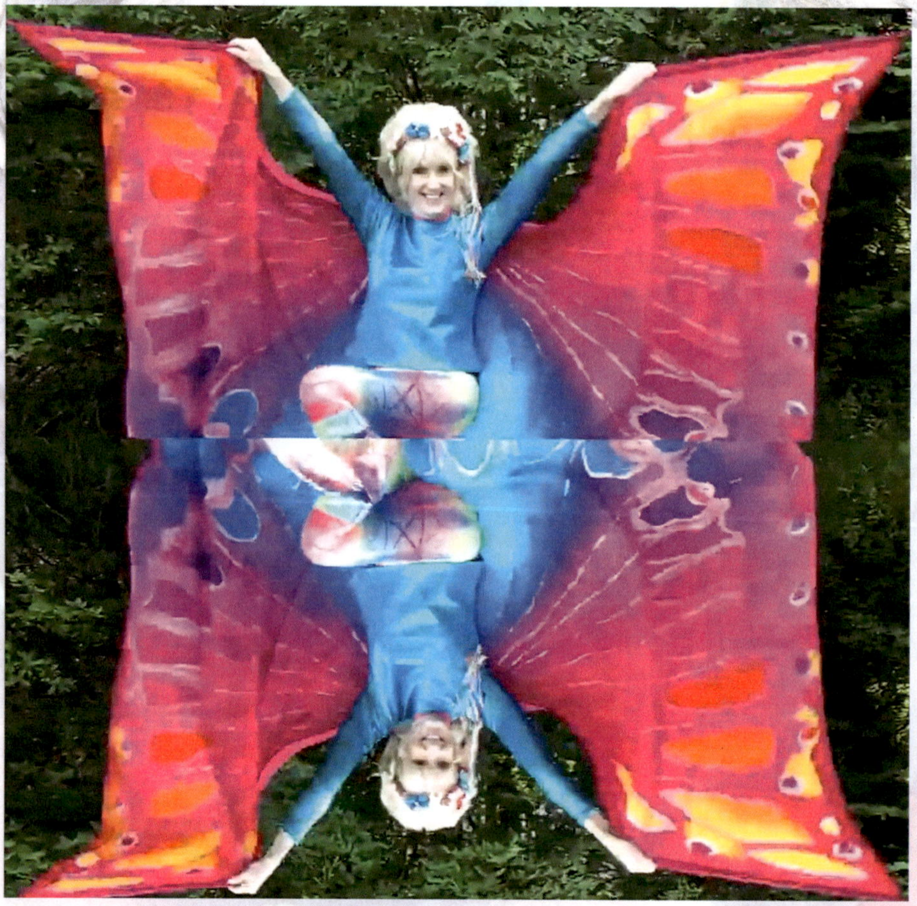

Opposite page: *Angel of Freedom*

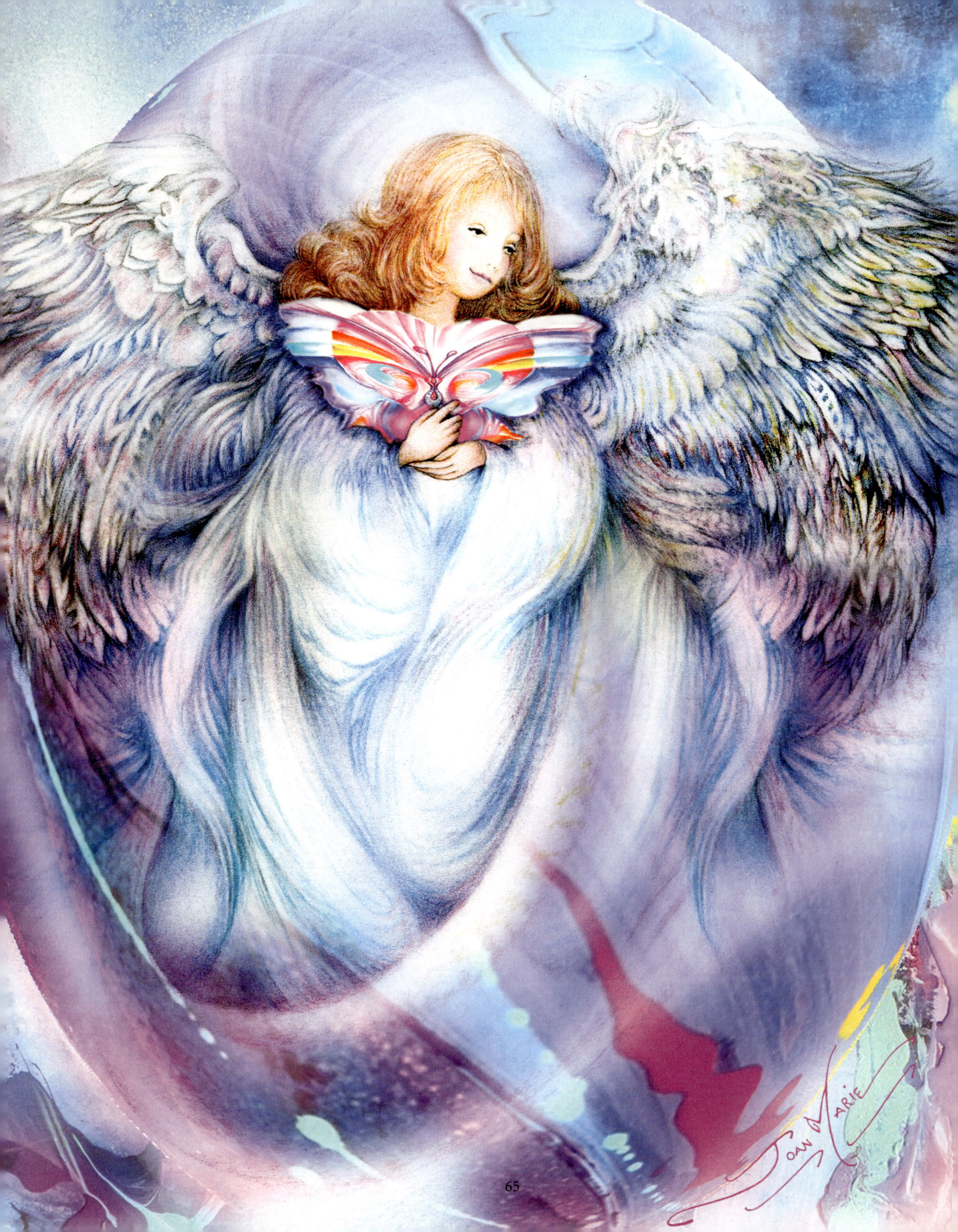
Joan Marie

Fairy BLISS!

People do not remember what you say, they only remember how you made them feel.

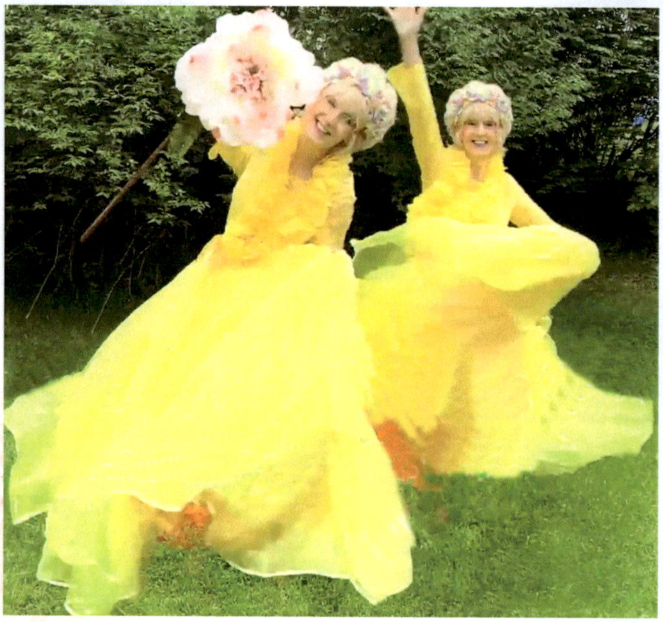

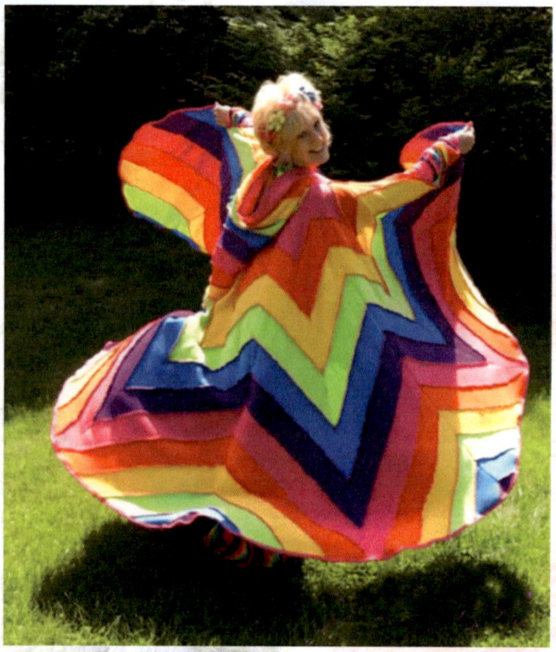

SOOOO leave a trail of smiles behind you!
Do you Love rainbows?
Every color represents a personality trait.

When you are living life to the fullest the entire spectrum illuminates.

I no longer have neutral colors in my closet. Every color from the rainbow is represented in my wardrobe and radiates at its highest luminosity. Vibrant pink, which represents unconditional love and nurturing, is indeed my favorite color. What do your favorite colors represent to you?

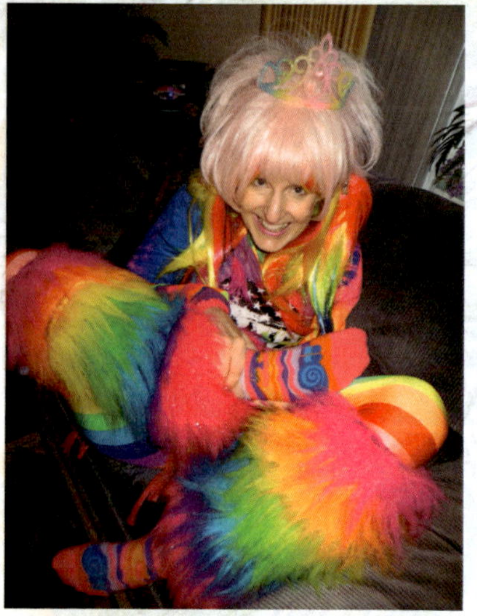

Place the colors you love around you, on pillows, towels, in paintings, in clothing…

Red: energy, power, strength, passion, heat
Orange: courage, confidence, friendliness, success
Yellow: bright, energy, sun, creativity, intellect, happy
Green: money, growth, fertility, freshness, healing
Blue: tranquility, love, loyalty, security, trust, intelligence
Purple: royalty, nobility, spirituality, luxury, ambition
Pink: healthy, happy, feminine, compassion, sweet, playful
Turquoise: spiritual, healing, protection, sophisticated
Silver: glamorous, high tech, graceful, sleek
Gold: wealth, prosperity, valuable, traditional

Opposite page: *Angel of Freedom*

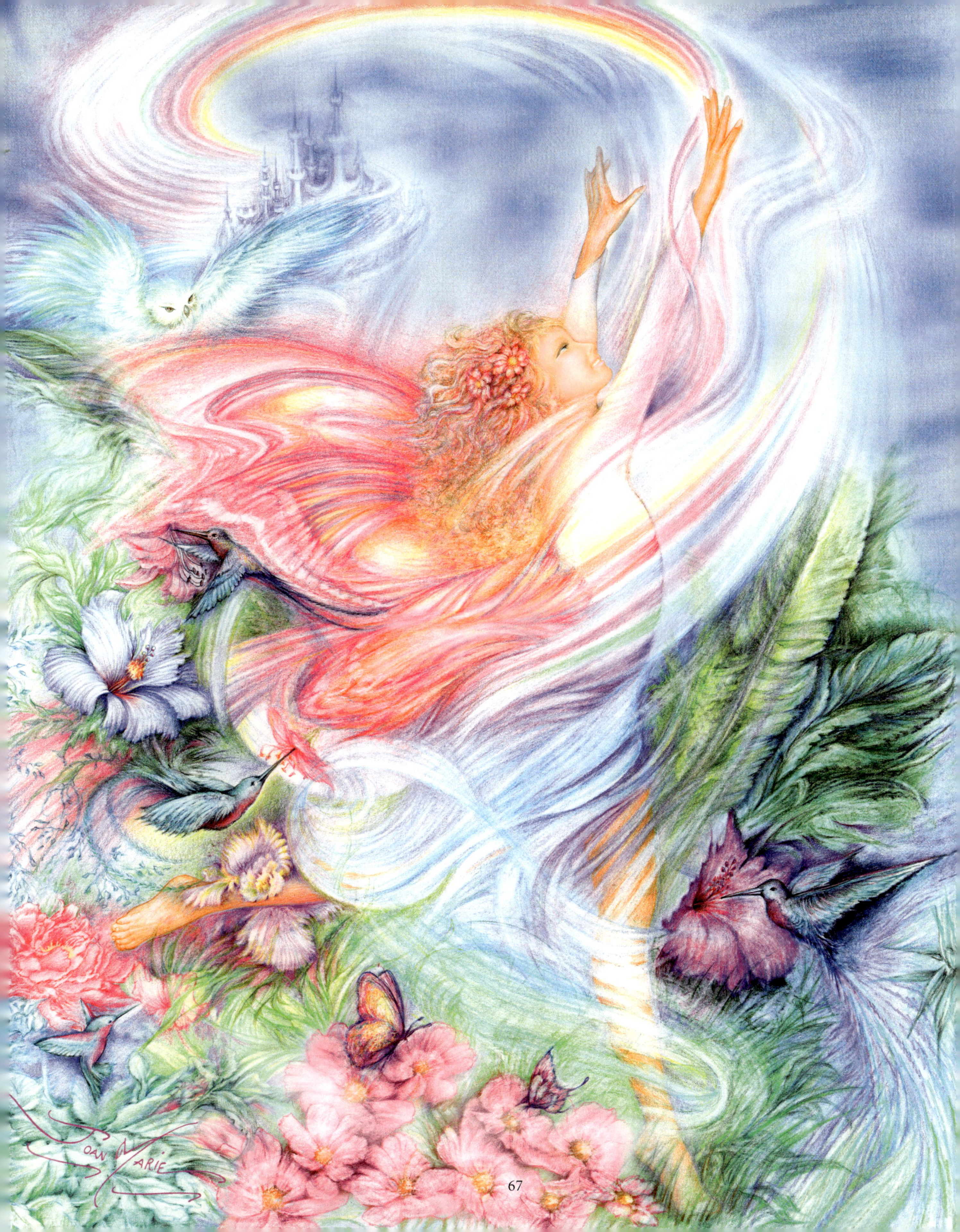
Joan Marie

Moments of BLISS!

We can always change our thoughts and attitude.

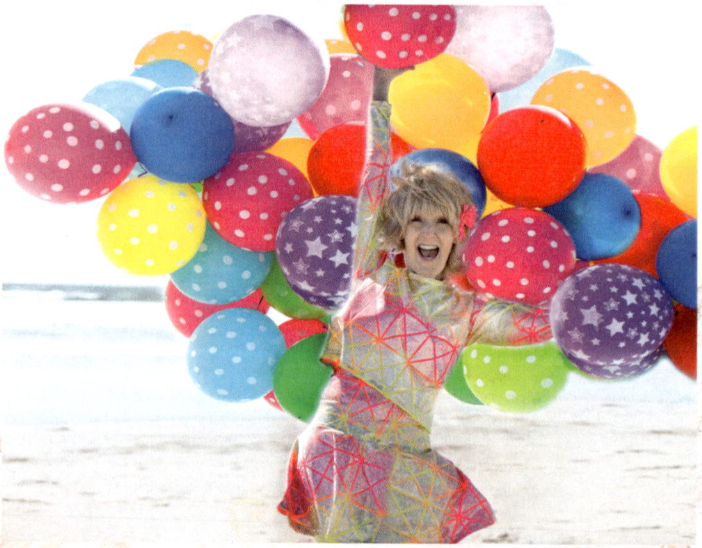

A Miracle Within the Painting

You might not be able to change your financial situation or where you live at this very second, but **you can shift your thoughts immediately**. Changing your perception of a situation can happen right now. During a sad time, I chose to shift to a better feeling place. I chose to create a work of art that expresses all the things that I love:

…a woman with a scarf turning into wings while on top of mountains in Sedona
…an angel of love sending the dove of peace
…the majestic mountains of power escalating to the castle of magic and trust
…a sunrise that says, "It's the dawn of a new day!"
…a lighthouse beaming a path to belief and trust
…free-spirited butterflies floating with ease and joy
…dolphins playfully flipping with grace
…three fairies frolicking and playing in the flowers

When I asked my friends, "How do you like my new painting?" they said, "We love it, but we really love how you drew Christ in the sky!" "What? I did not draw Christ in the sky!" I replied. They pointed a bit to the left of the castle's peak, and there it was, Christ's head. Long hair, and some said they saw a bit of pink symbolizing thorns around his head. What? I got goose bumps! Chills! If I had intended for Christ to be in that sky, I certainly would have drawn him better than that! **Yes indeed, it felt like a miracle!** God's presence assures us that shifting our thoughts from negativity and fear to all that uplifts us is certainly a feel-good solution to feeling peace again. Soon after that, I received unexpected requests for more designs, which activated more business.

Turning to what feels good is the answer, once again.

Oppostite page: *Moments of Bliss*

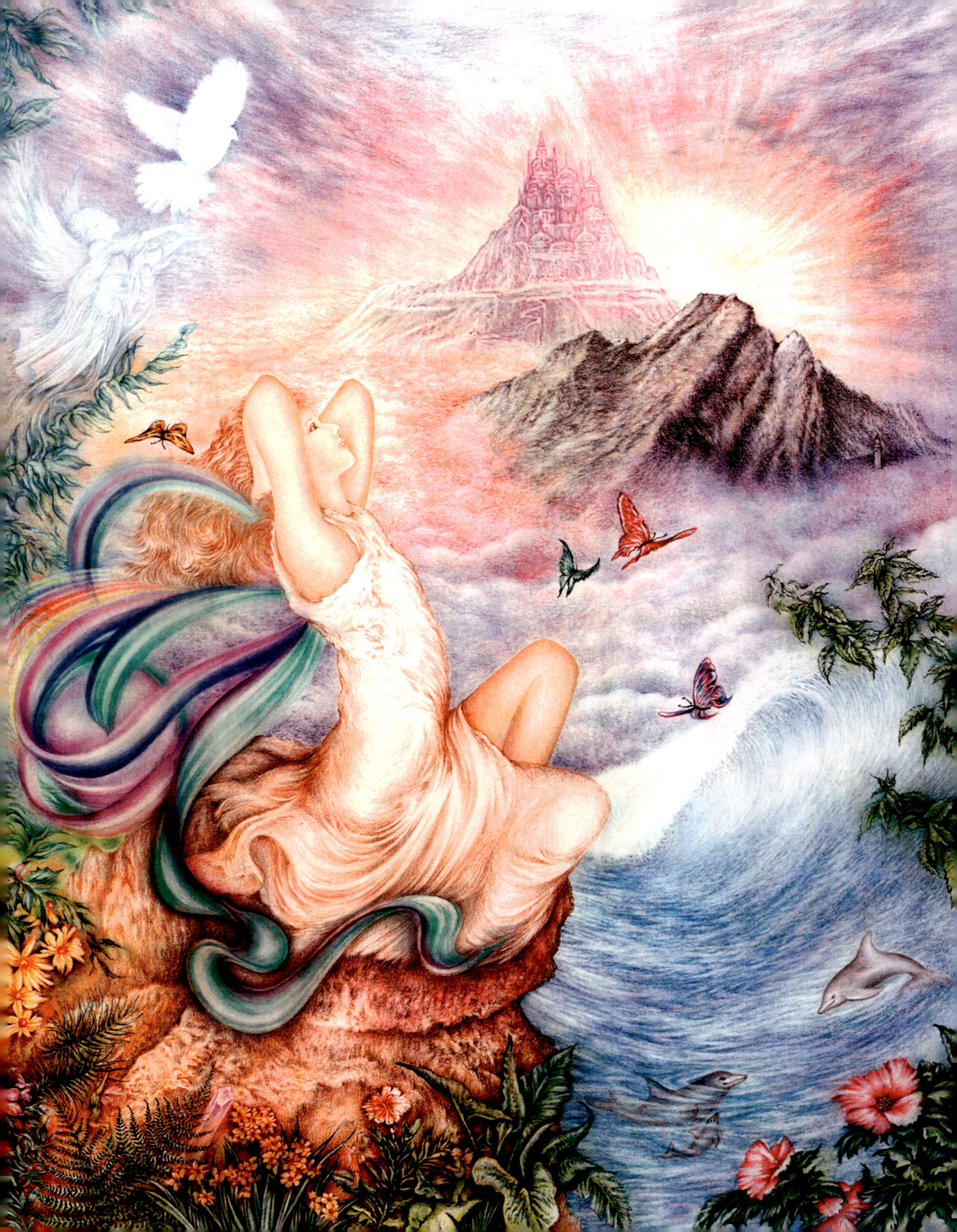

Star Seeker

Do what you LOVE!

Take this in a positive way… There are truly no guarantees in life, and people will have opinions and judgements toward anything you choose to do, so why not do what you love?

All you have is NOW.

Enjoy now. Be what you believe in now.
Live with No Regrets.

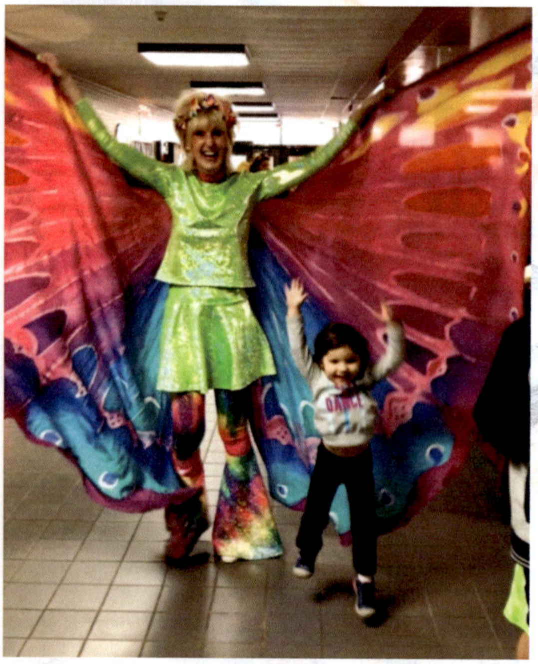

Do what you Love and LOVE doing it. Do it now!

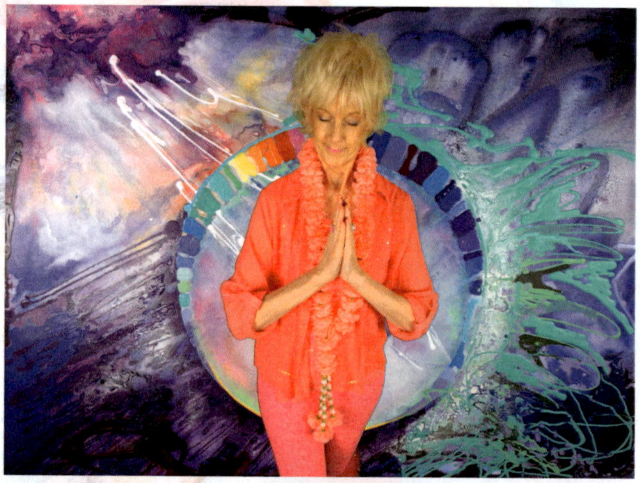

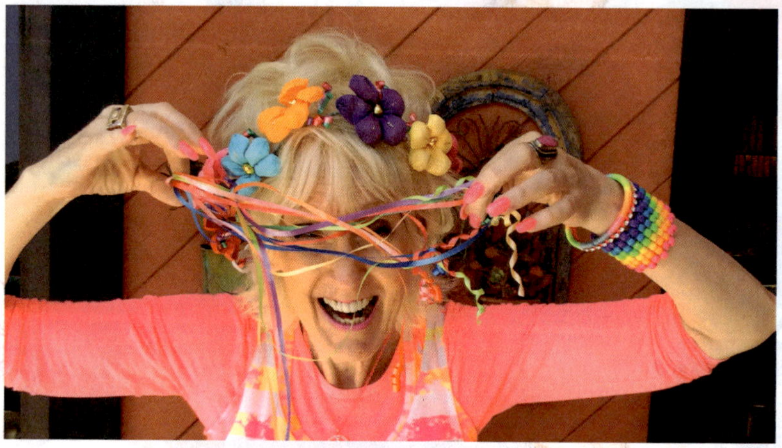

Opposite page: *Star Seeker*

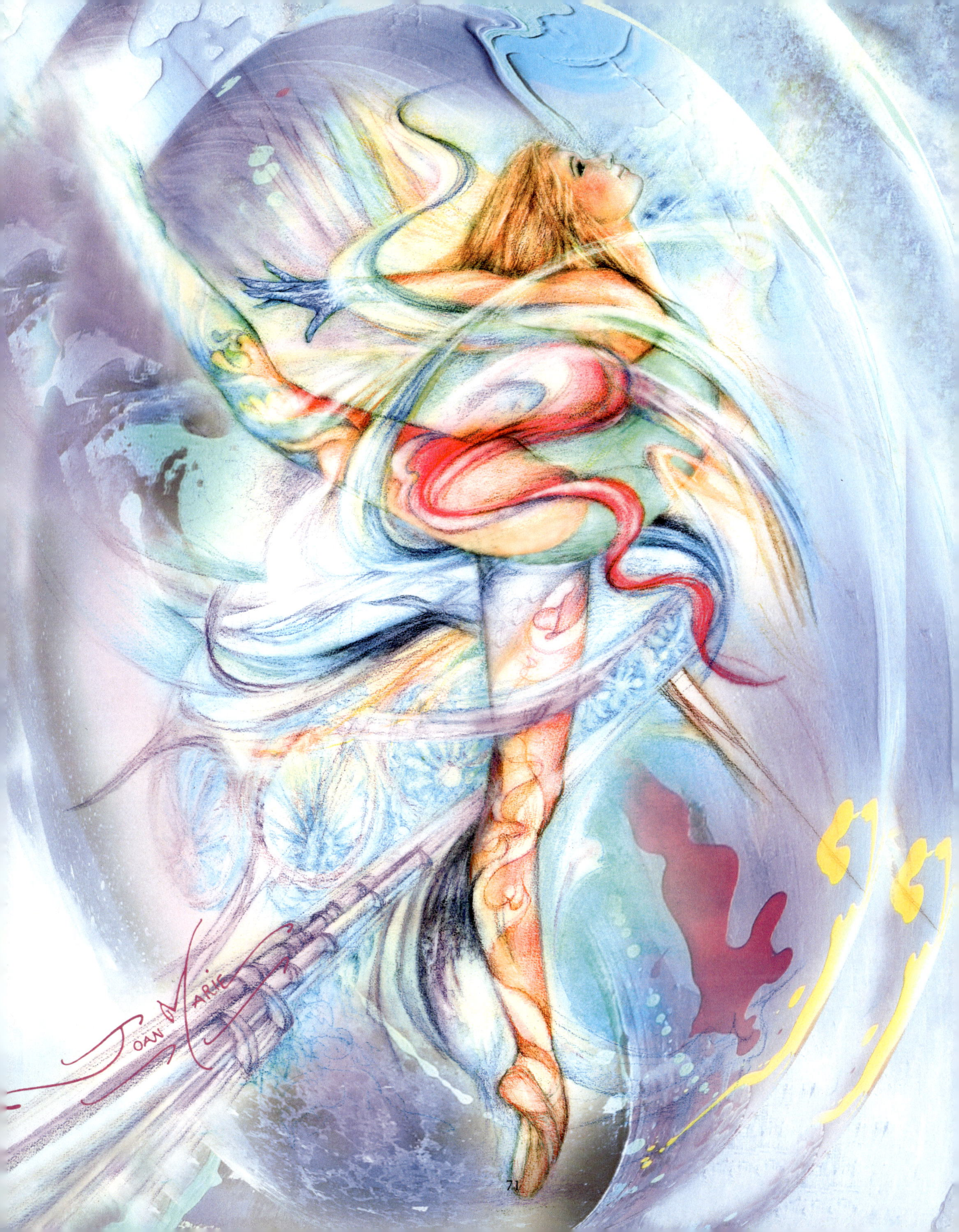
Joan Marie

Raphaella

Feel Your Power

Our Greatest Fear —Marianne Williamson
"Our deepest fear is not that we are inadequate.

Our deepest fear is that we are
powerful beyond measure.
It is our light not our darkness that
most frightens us.
We ask ourselves,
who am I to be brilliant, gorgeous,
talented and fabulous?
Actually, who are you not to be?
You are a child of God.
You playing small does
not serve the world.
There's nothing enlightened about
shrinking so that other
people won't feel insecure
around you.

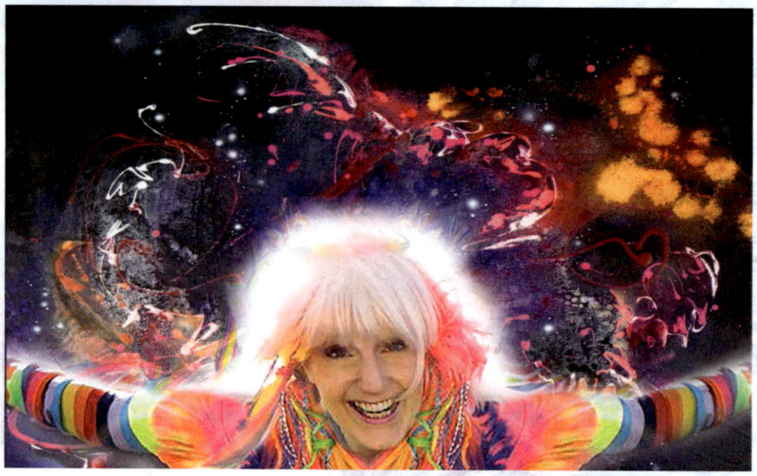

We were born to make manifest the glory of
God that is within us.

It's not just in some of us; it's in everyone.
And as we let our own light shine,
we unconsciously give other people
permission to do the same.

I created the Archangel, Raphaella, for my daughter as she went through a challenge during her college years. Raphaella has the most awesome and powerful wings of protection. You can see in her eyes her focus on helping hearts heal from the past, helping open your eyes to the present, and feeling much peace for the future.

Her grand wings represent the awesome potentiality of love.

Opposite page: *Raphaella*

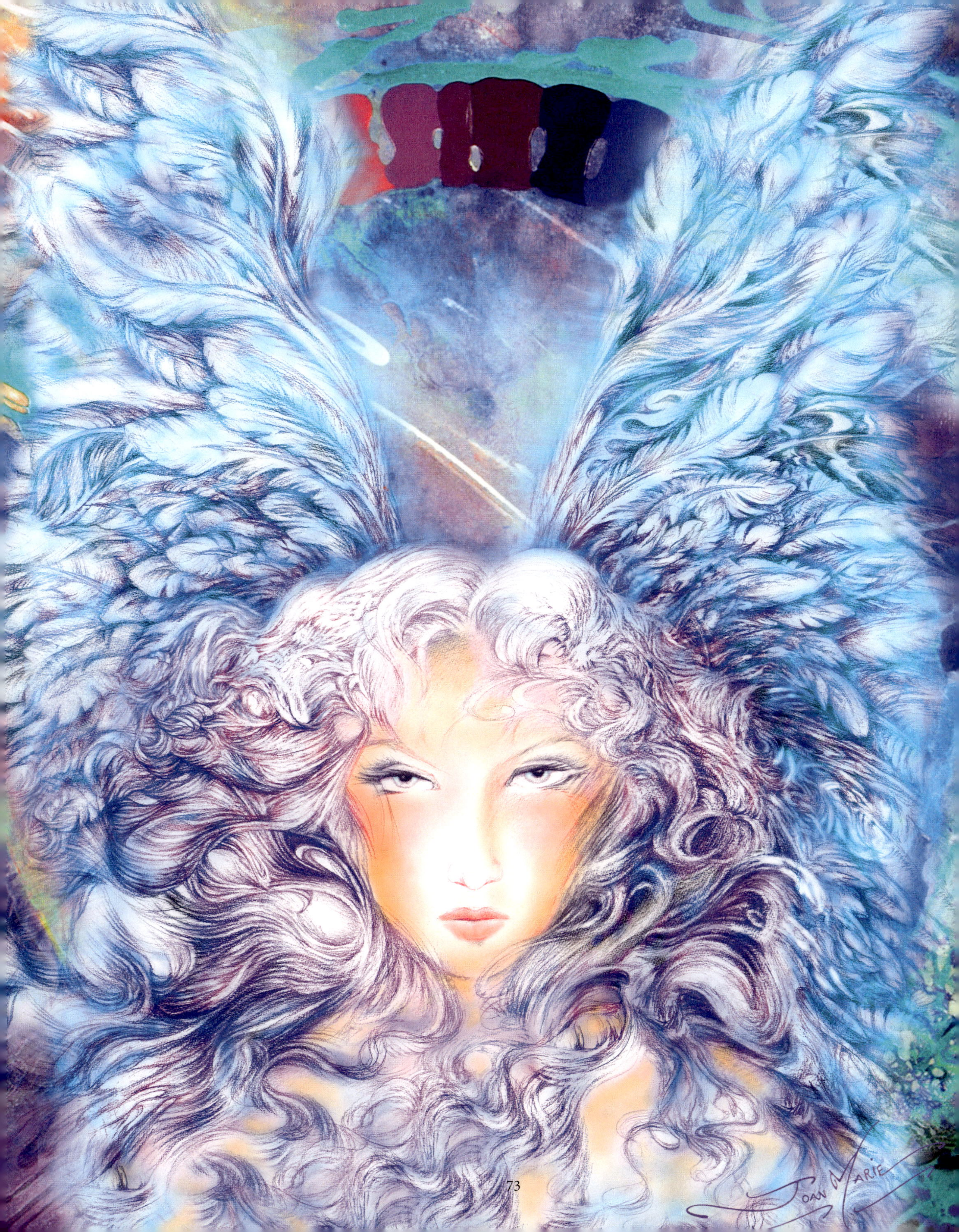
Joan Marie

Fairies Just Gotta have FUN

BE Who You Feel Inside!

We are each here to fulfill the purpose no one else can fill.

Step out!

Express your unique self...allow your inner wings to fly. Feel the fun and contentment when you are being what you feel inside!

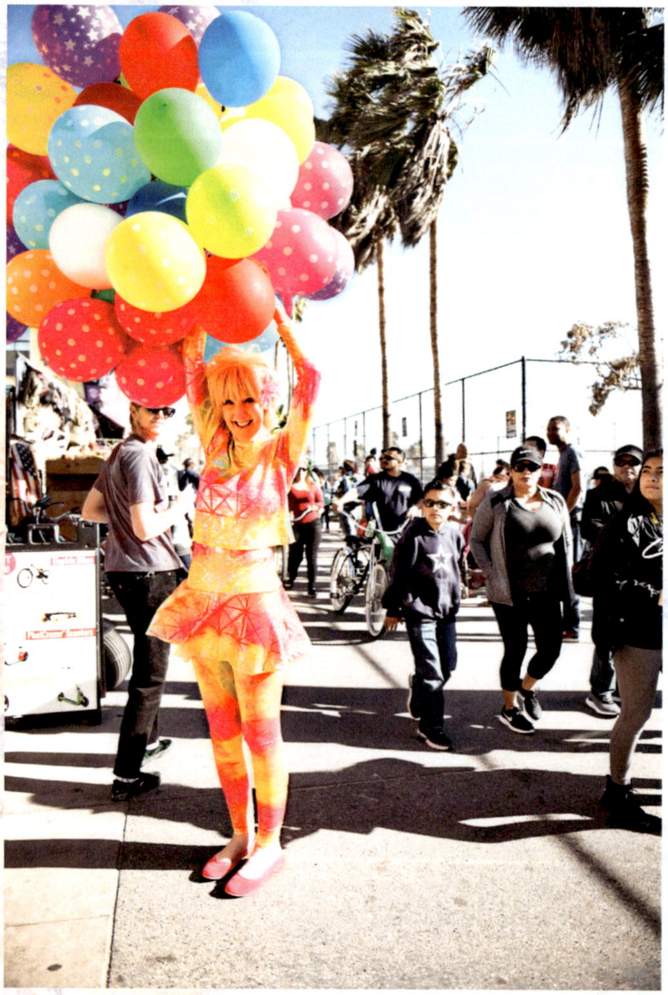

Believe. The classic movie the *Wizard of Oz*, is a reminder of **the power of the heart**. A memorable scene to me is when Dorothy, her dog Toto, The Cowardly Lion (courage), Scarecrow (brains) and the Tin Man (heart) are skipping down the yellow brick road to the radiant Emerald City. Our lives can mirror the symbolism in Dorothy's experiences. First, she was jolted by the intense battle with demon winged monkeys and the Wicked Witch of the East, then she danced with high expectations through the emerald gates, only to face the crushing false illusions of the wizard.

After all these challenges and disappointments in life, she finally realized who her friends really were (heart, courage, and brains). This led to the grand discovery when Dorothy said, *"if I ever go looking for my heart's desire again, I won't look any further than my own back yard (my heart)."* Then she clicked the heels of her red glitter slippers together to instantly go home. This tremendous power lies within all of us.

We have the power to create happiness in every moment, no matter what the challenge. *The Wizard of Oz* is a reminder of **the power of your heart**, ***"There's no place like home."***

Opposite page: *Post Modern Freedom*

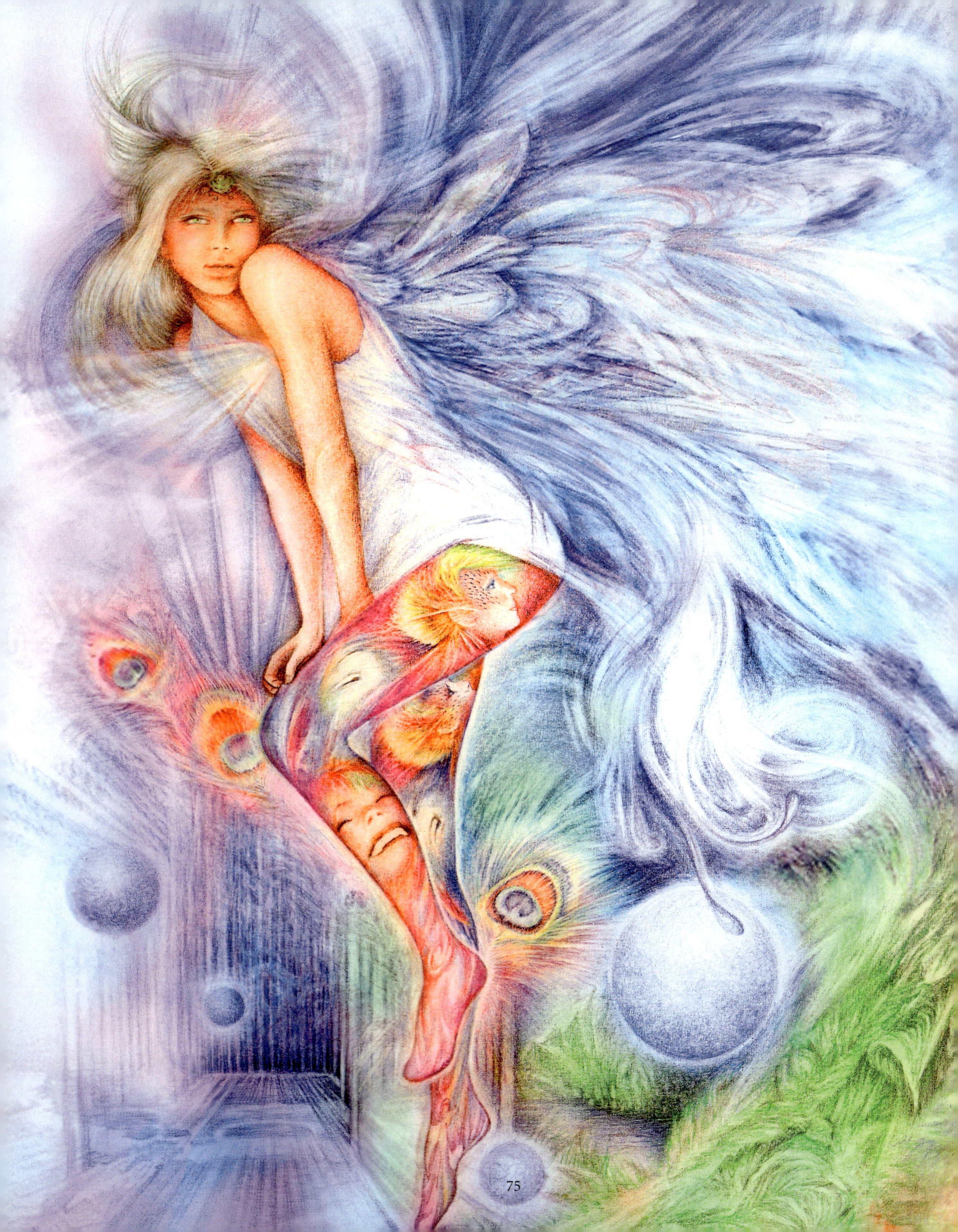

Abstract Music Paintings ... Celebrating Life

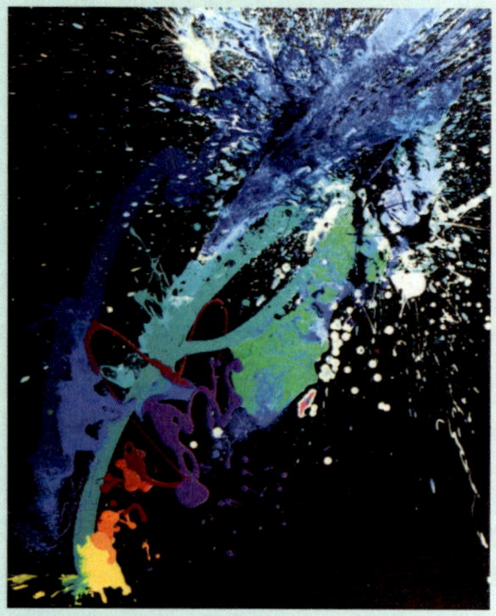
Painted to the song "Magic Carpet Ride", by Steppenwolf

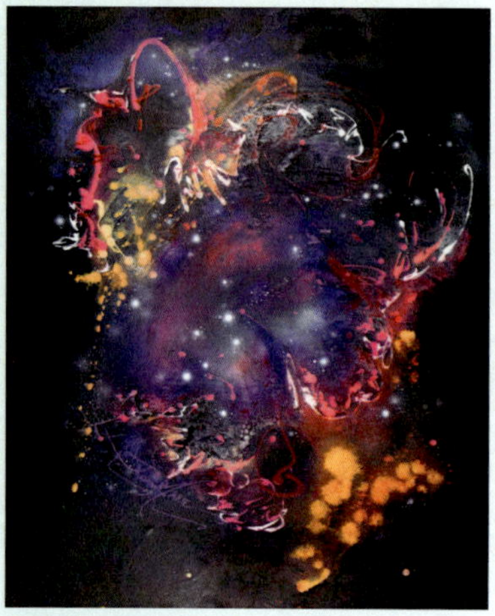
Inspired by Hubble outer space photos

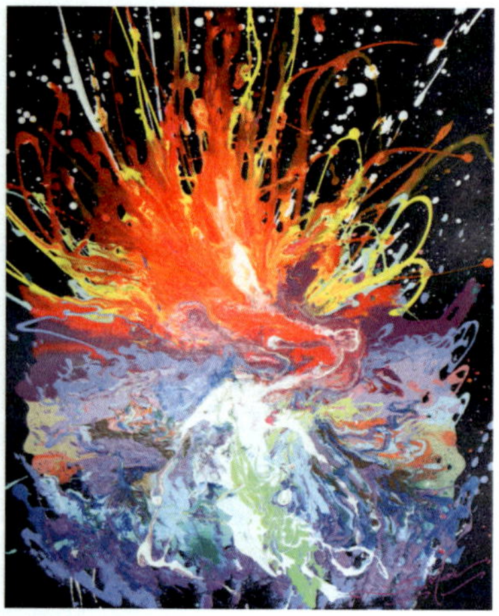
Painted to the song "I Gotta Feeling. . . Tonight's gonna be. . ." by Black Eyed Peas

For three years, I went wild. I threw, poured, and tipped paint.

I created Abstract Music Paintings.

I transformed the energy of favorite songs intuitively into colors and energy on canvas. I opened the doors to fearless adventure. The paint had a life of its' own. It came alive while trusting my intuition. My senses lead me to the right technique or tool to make the next move. **It felt like magic.** This exciting experience expanded my awareness of the flow of energy. Suddenly, I felt compelled to revisit the passion I had for expressing eyes, often referred to as "the windows of the soul".

In the last 20 paintings in this book, you will see how I found a new voice **combining the two worlds of wild abstraction and classically trained drawing skills.**

I have created a magical mix of ecstatic energy and passionate detail capturing the celebration of life!

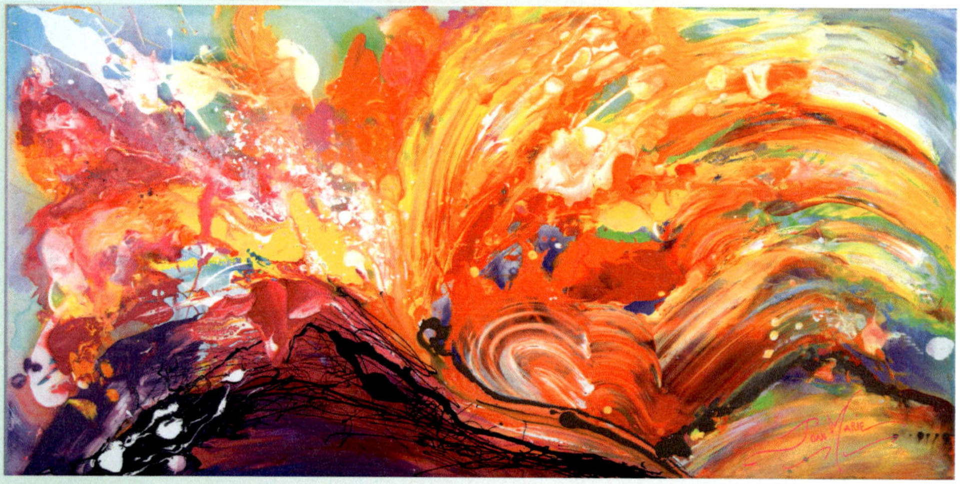
"Morning has Broken", by Cat Stevens"

OOGENISIS

The birth of a new moment!

Every moment is a new opportunity to start anew.

No regrets, no worries, only new vision for a new moment, now.

Feel the infinite circle of life from one vibrant-colorful moment to the next.
Everything you experience creates who you are.
Every moment is a gift to experience something new.

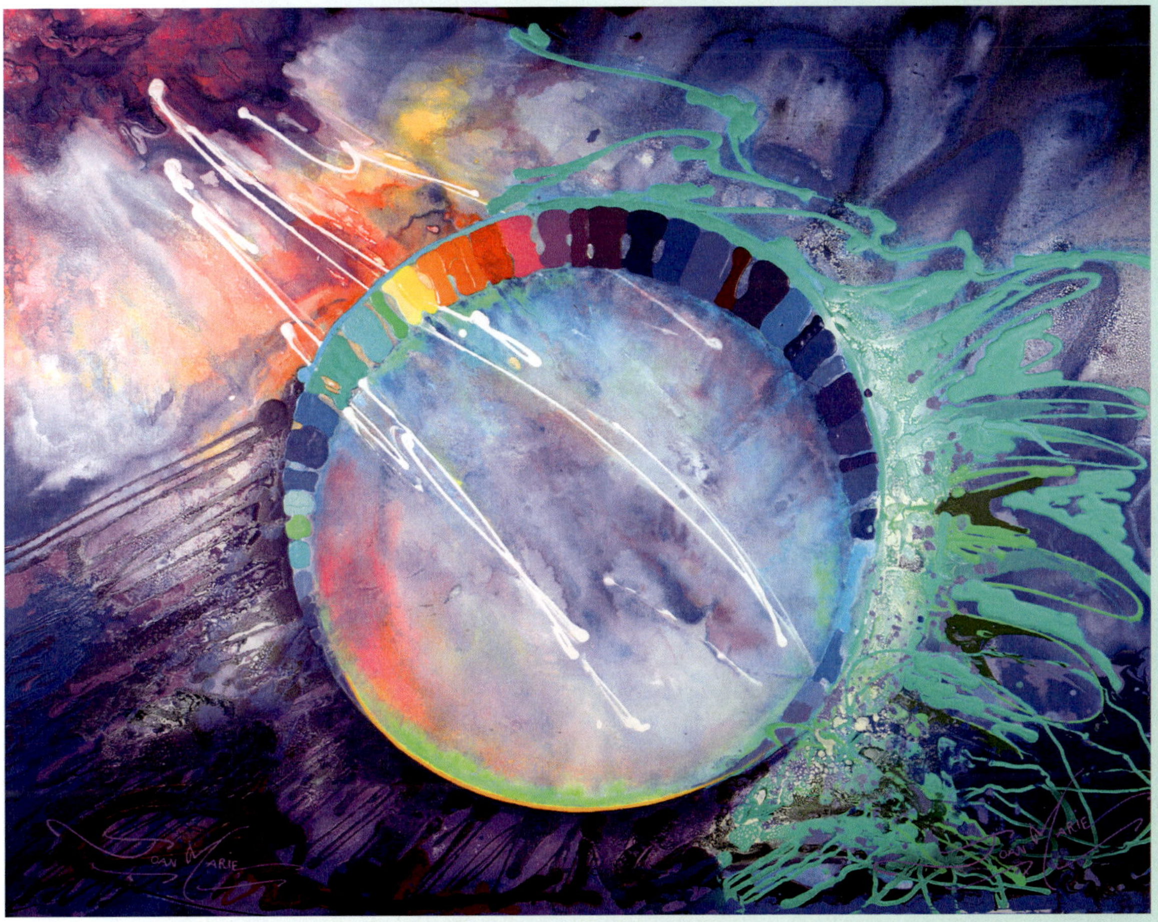

OOGENISIS

Magical UniKitty

Unikitty is pure magic. She inspires imagination and the desire to play. When Unikitty love is in your heart, don't you agree,

everything is always okay.

We are in this TOGETHER! What a peaceful state of mind to trust and believe that everything has always worked out. Everything is always OK.

Everything WILL always work out.

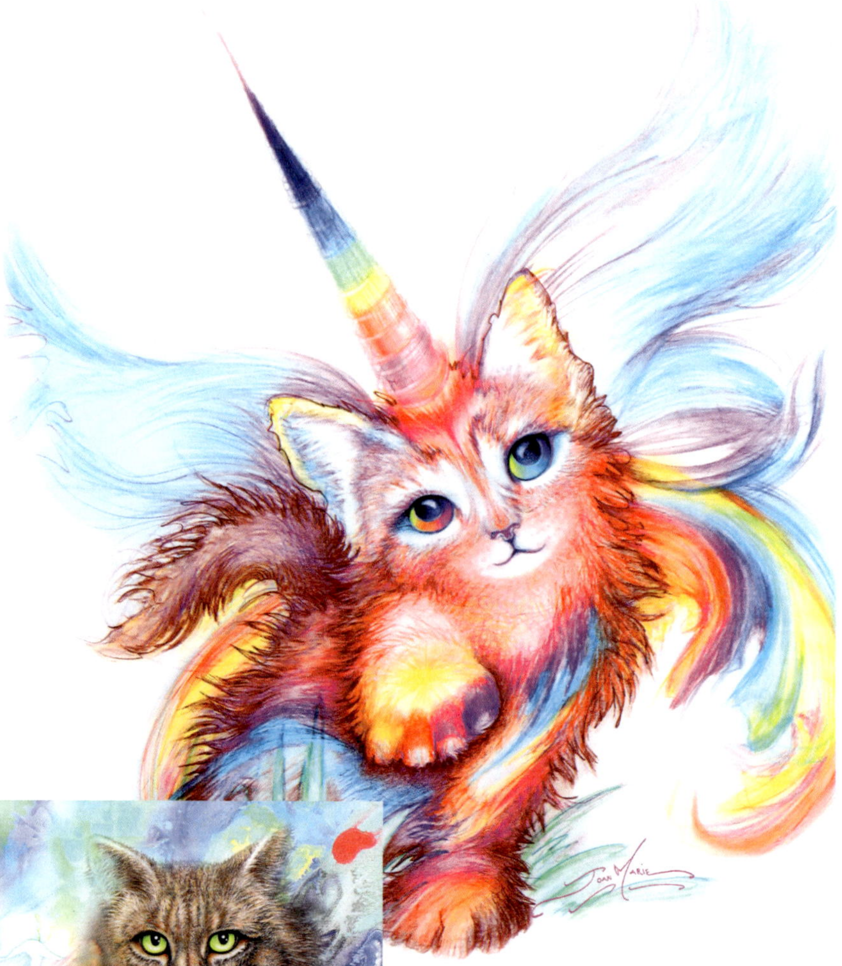

Precious Unikitty

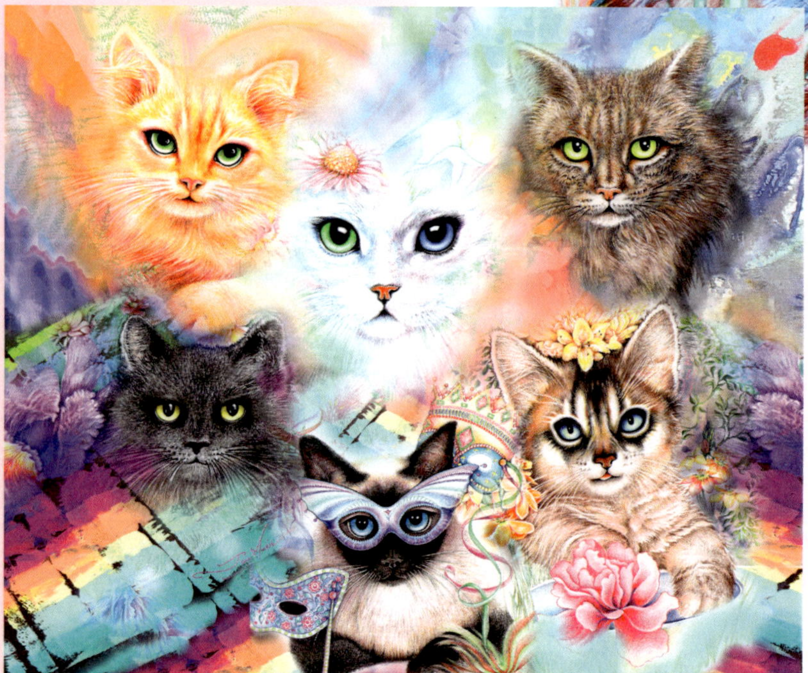

Crazy Cat Lovers

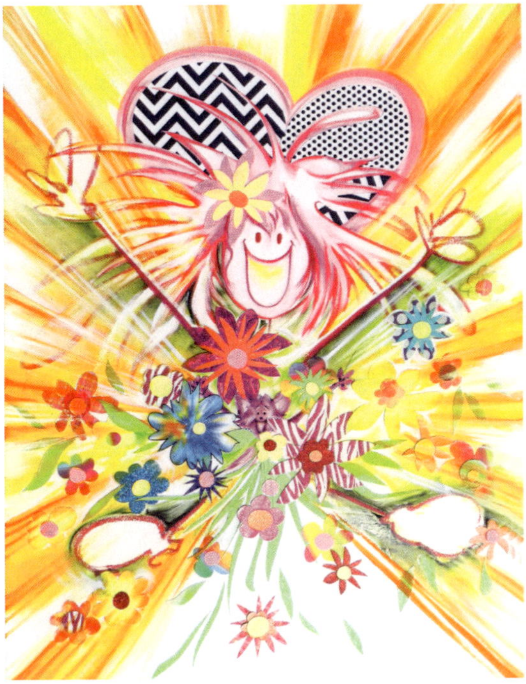

Sunburst

Pet your favorite pet. Feel the love all around you. This energy of love spreads and vibrates around the world.

Introducing…**HAPPEEE GIRL!** Yes, it's true! Life is meant to be fun! It's about choosing your viewpoint and shifting your perception.
It's about having Happeee-Girl-love in your heart…**It's time to beam your HAPPEEE GIRL energy!!!** Sing those negative thoughts and feelings right out of your head! A favorite weapon when repeatedly hearing a negative thought is to replace it with a favorite song. What song lifts the corners of your mouth? What are your favorite happeee songs? This works! It takes practice to think of a positive way to reword a negative thought. Instead jump right into a bouncy happeee song. My favorite is a Girl Scout campfire song. Does it work for you, too?

What is your favorite song?

"I love the mountains. I love the rolling hills. I love the flowers. I love the daffodils. Boom dee ah dah. Boom dee ah dah. Boom dee ah dah. Boom dee ah dah. Boom dee ah dah. Boom dee ah dah. Boom dee ah dah. Boom dee ah dah."

OR

Zip-a-dee-doo-dah,
zip-a-dee-day
My, oh my,
what a Wonderful Day
Plenty of sunshine
heading' my way!
Zip-a-dee-doo-dah,
zip-a-dee-day

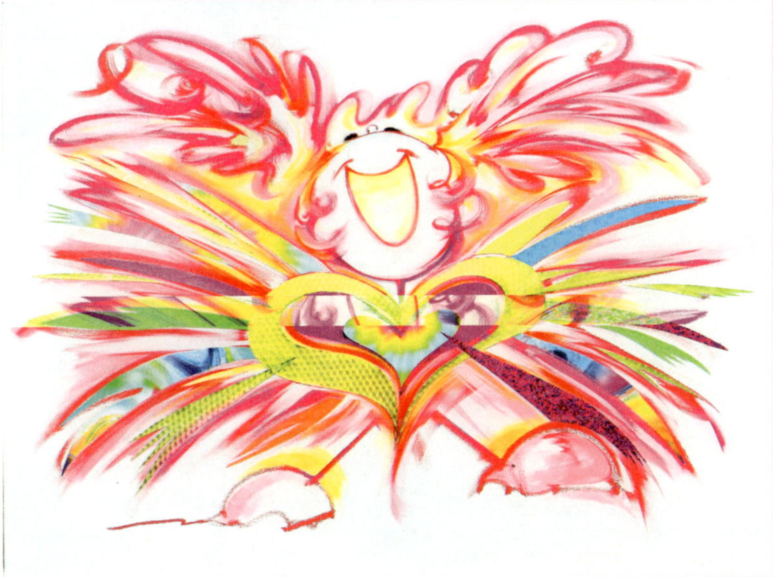

Heartburst

Know it with total certainty

Yes, life is meant to be fun!

It's not about getting exactly what you want. It's about getting happeee with what's here, right now.

Try picturing Happeee Girl in your mind, or if you're facing a challenge, try a new way to look at your situation.

You could relax, breathe, then shift your energy by saying "I trust that this too will pass." **Try seven new ways to view the same situation.** It's amazing to look back on life and discover what felt like disappointment or failure had directed life to a better place.

Most of the time you realize you wouldn't want your life to be any other way. If feeling tense, shift what you are thinking and feeling completely, or throw rainbow balls around the yard! Suddenly you are beaming.

Yep...It's time for you to SHINE!
LIFE is MEANT to be FUN!!!!

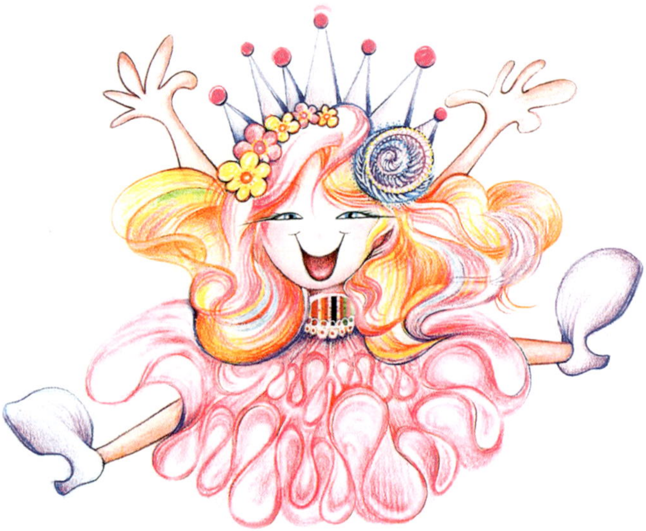

Bouncy Flouncy

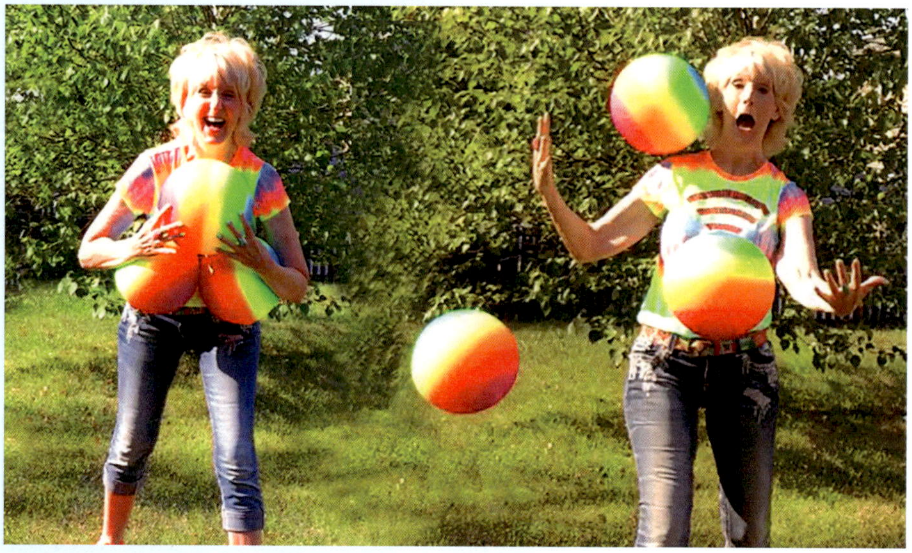

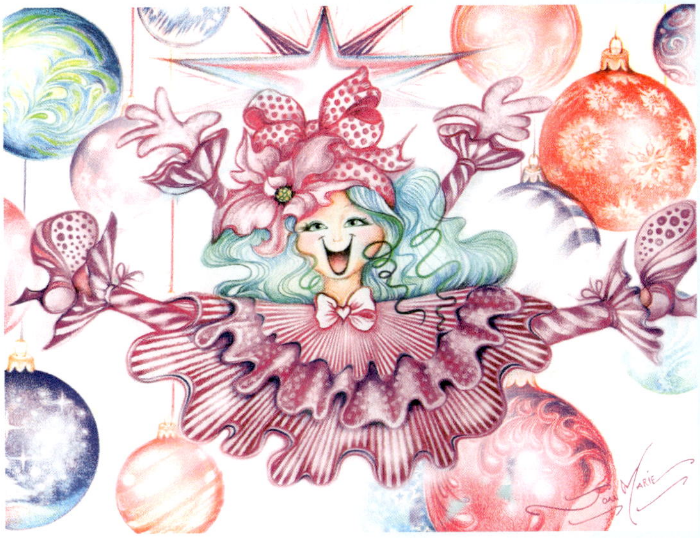

HAPPEEE GIRL !!!

HAVE FUN!

Not tomorrow…
Not later…
Not maybe…
but RIGHT NOW, with your family…
with your friends…
with yourself!
The time to
Celebrate is Now!
Share the love!

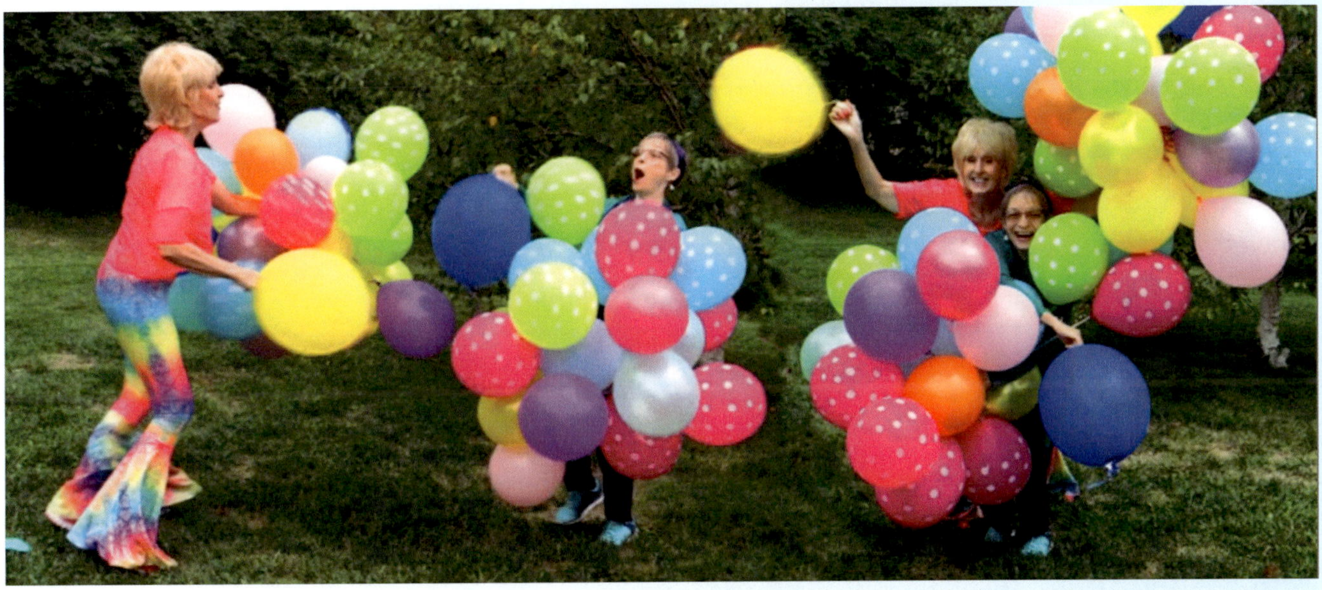

Crazy backyard balloon FUN with Chris Collins and me.

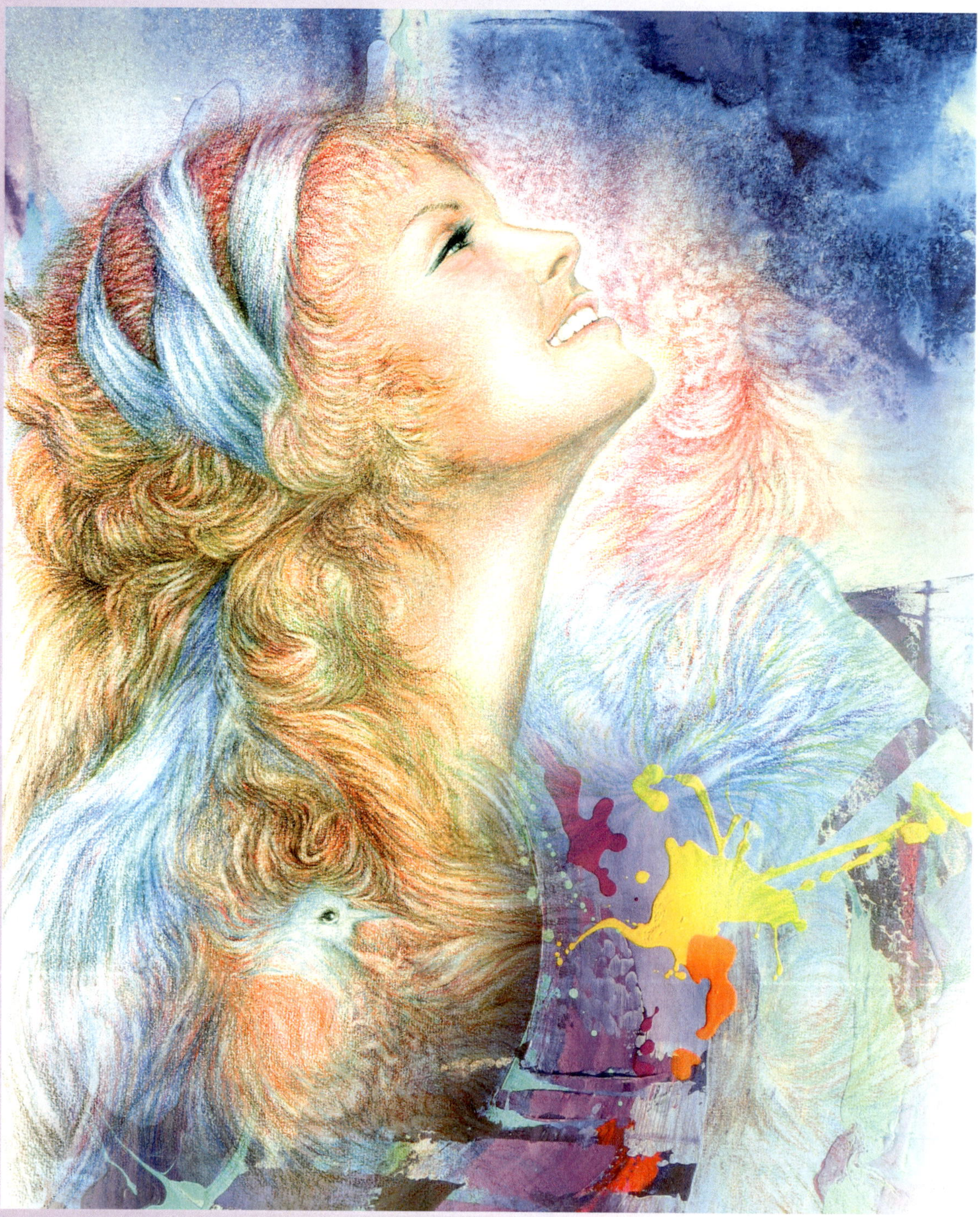
Blissful Happiness

Blissful Happiness

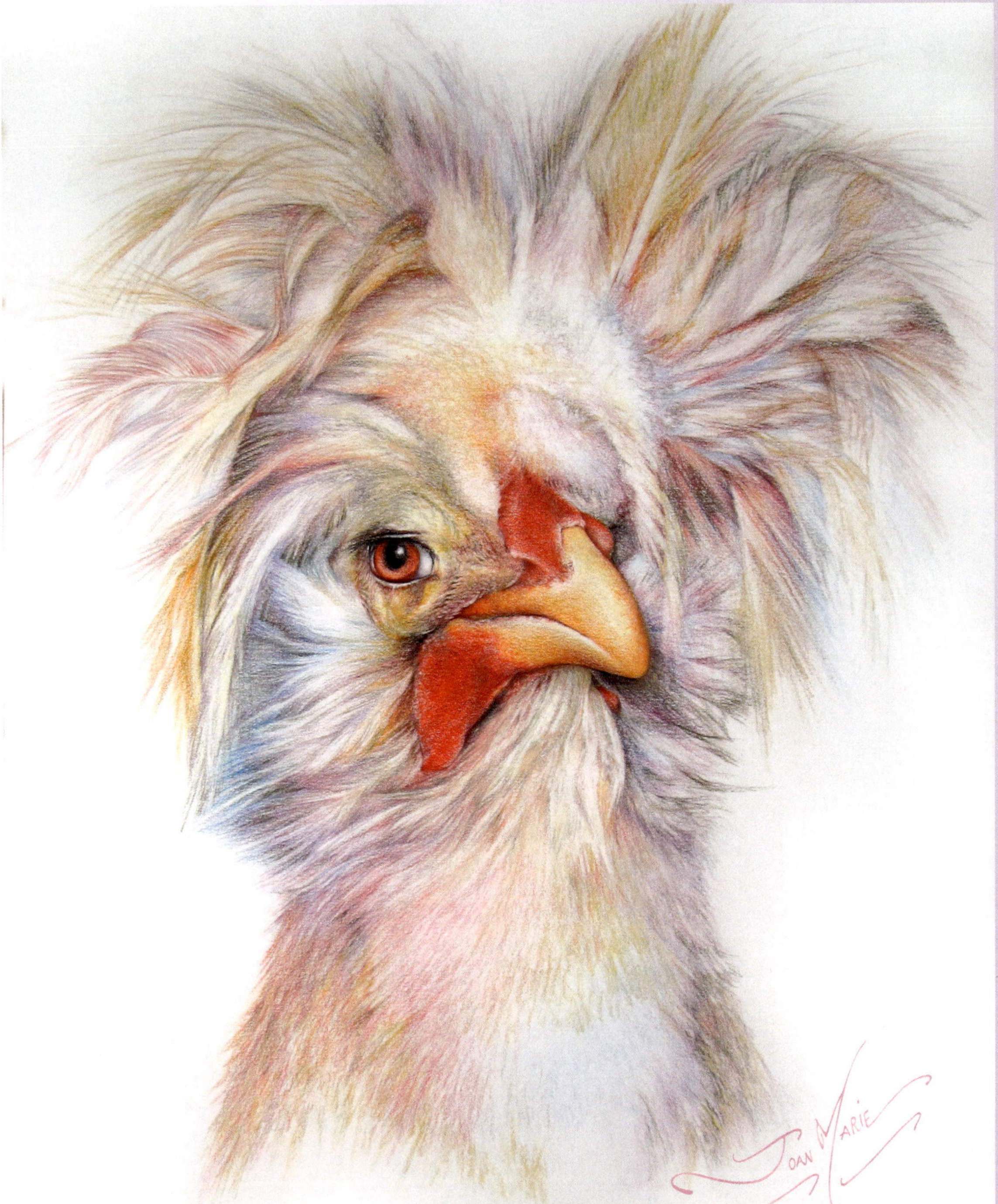

Goldie

GOLDIE

Jimmie Crack Corn, and I don't care!

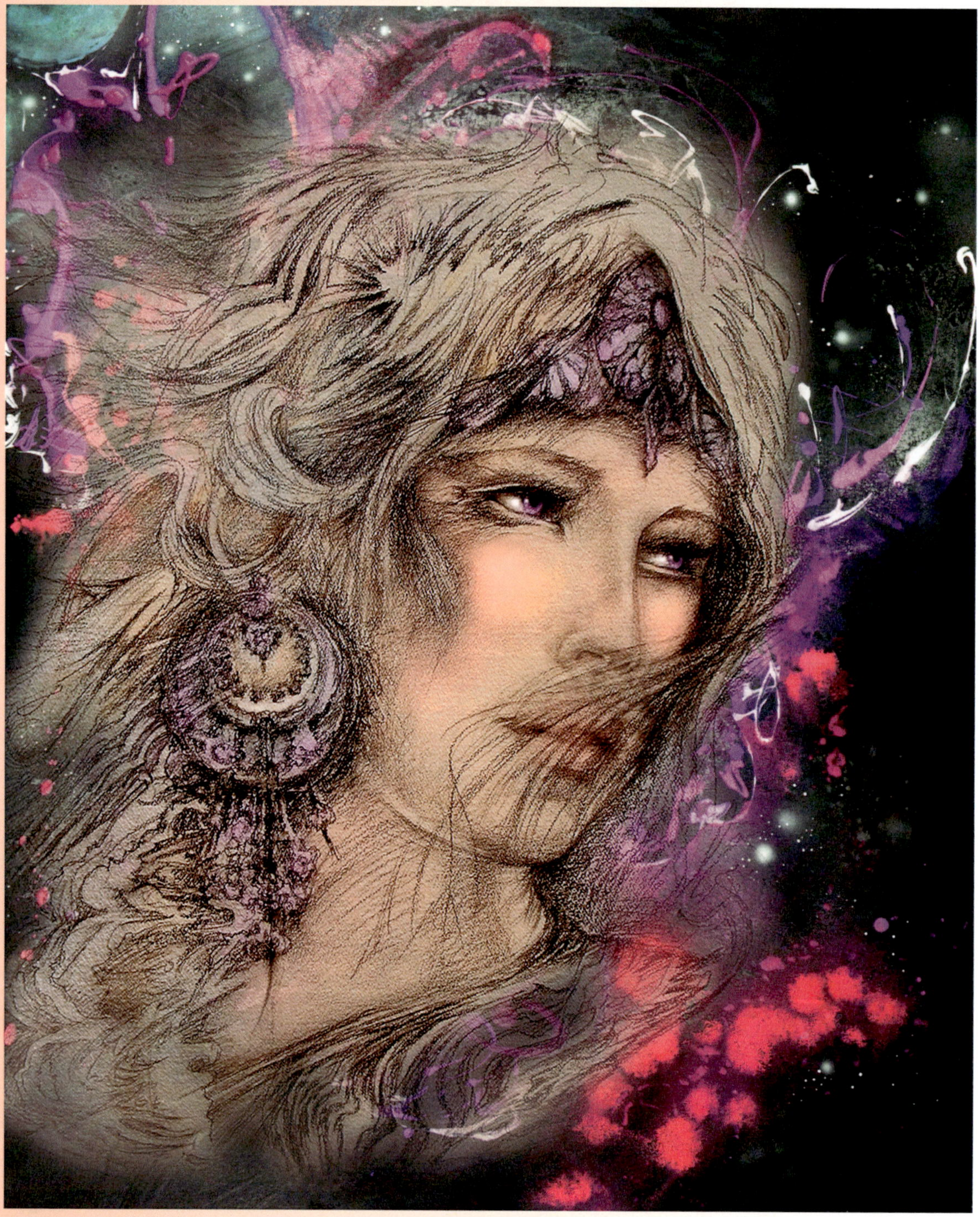

Nikita

Nikita

Free-spirited, wild and strong.
A gypsy spirit follows her heart.

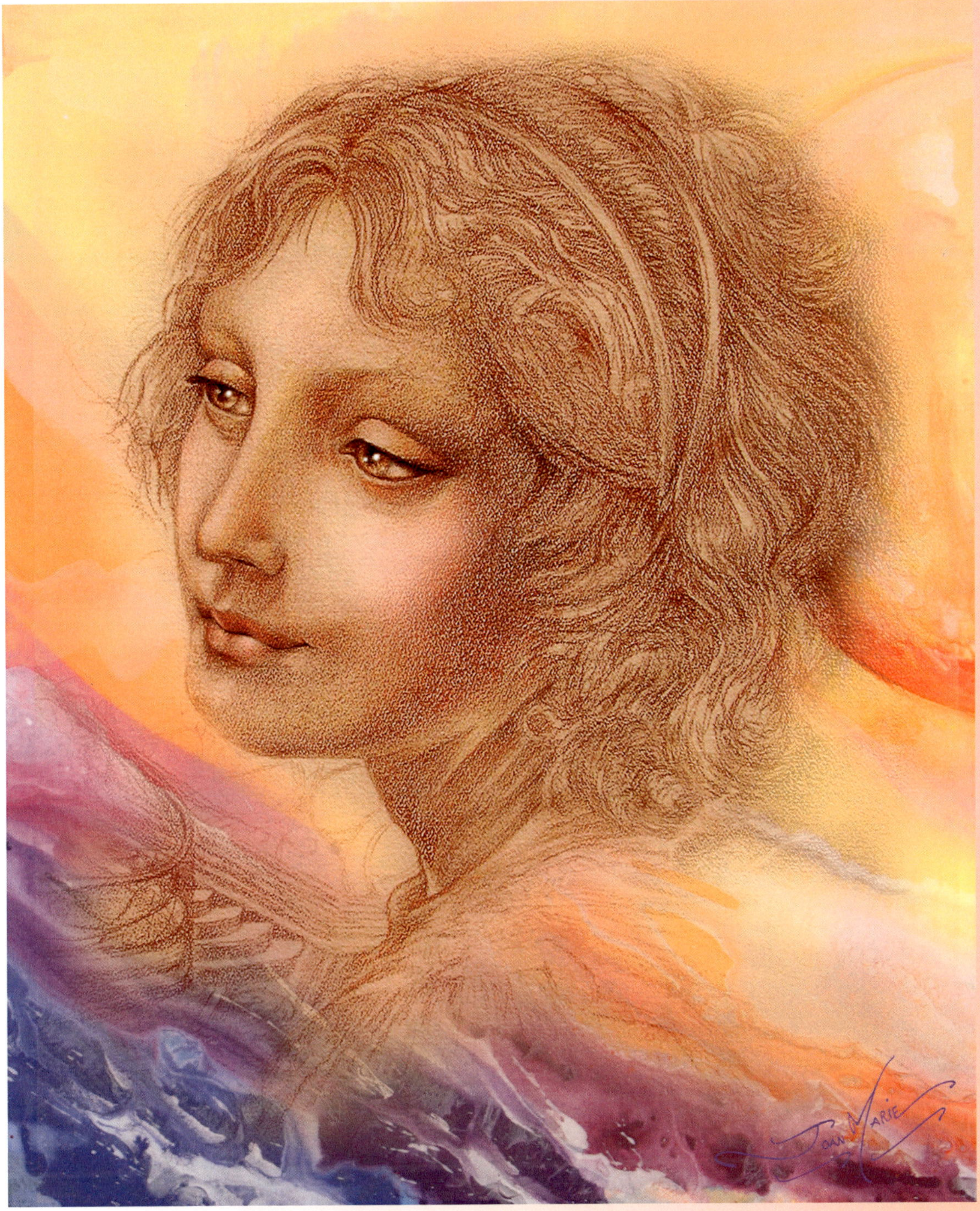

Guinevere

Guinevere

Blissful peace and beautiful inner confidence.
Deeply connected to the flow of life.

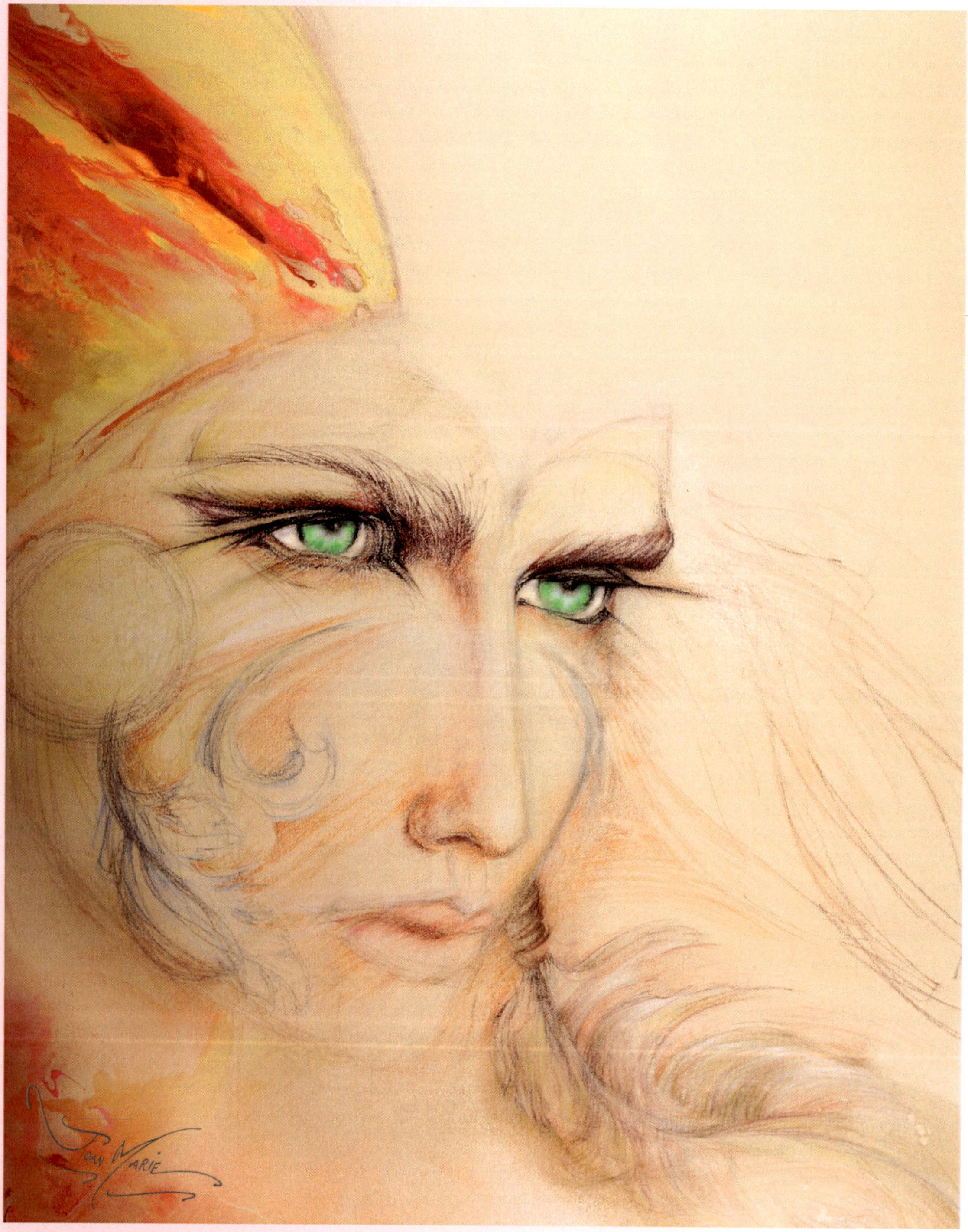

Indian River

One Heart

Within One Heart lives enough fire to warm the entire world.

Inspired by Peter Buffet's incredibly moving song, "Auglaize River,"
from the album, *1830-Spirit, The Seventh Fire*
Words for the painting, by Kate Miller

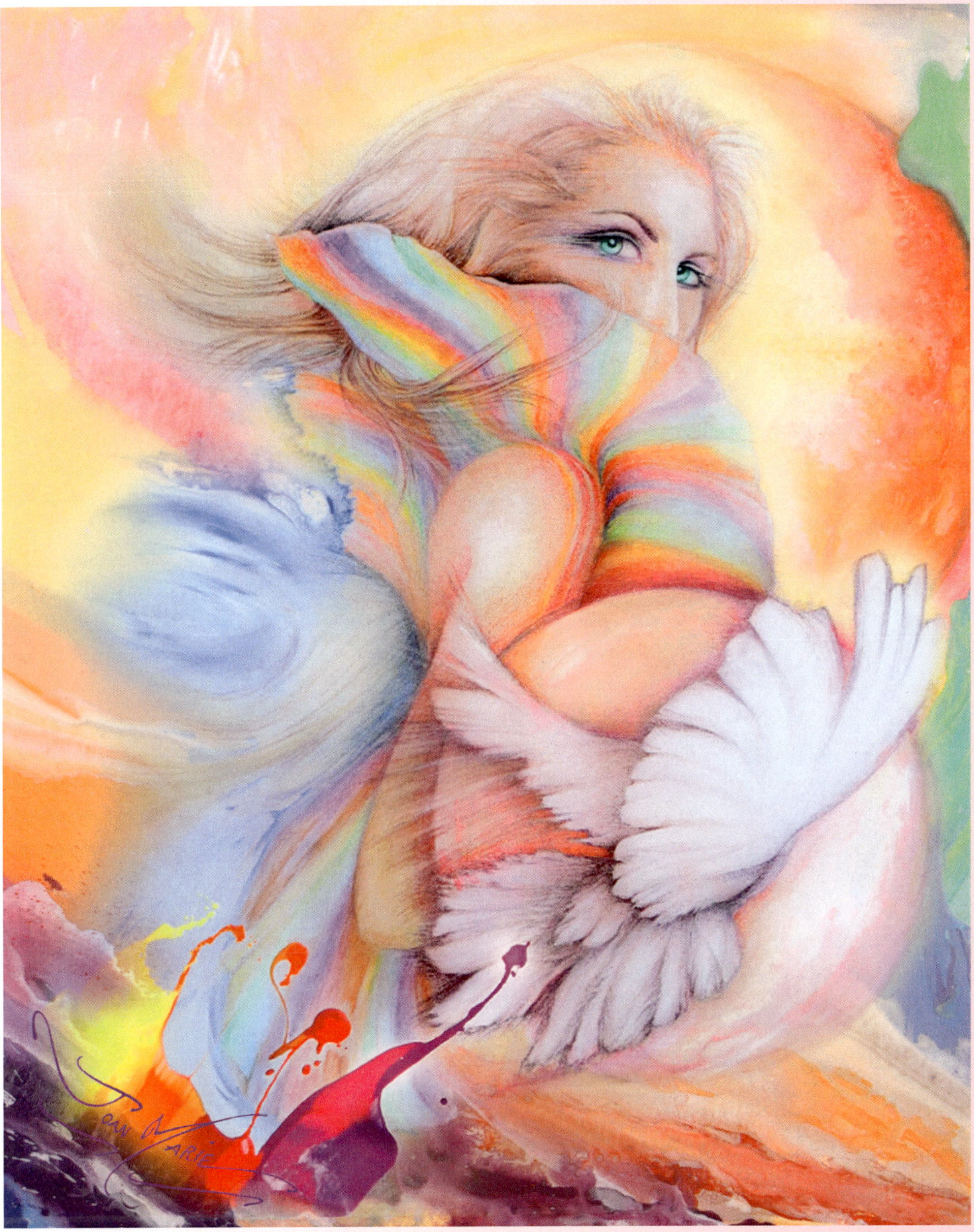

Mysterious Worlds

The Mysteries of Life

The m ysteries of life surround you! Let mysteries intrigue and engage you.
It could be easy to allow the surprises of life to send you into a whirl of negativity.
Instead thrive on change...on mystery...on discovery!
Is this what heaven on earth feels like?

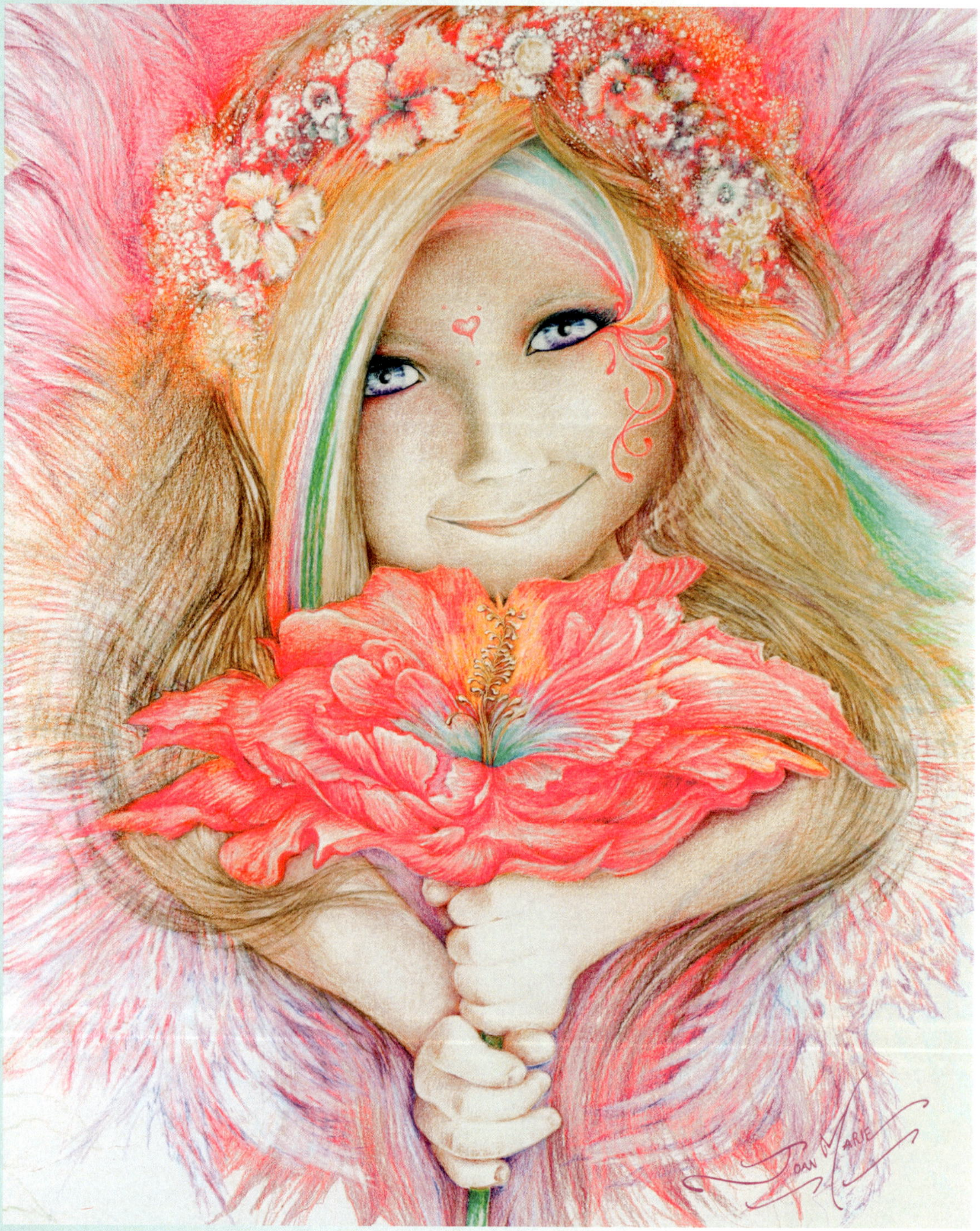

Gracie

Gracie

Offering God her glorious flower,
saying the most powerful and perfect prayer.
"Thank You, God! Thank You!"

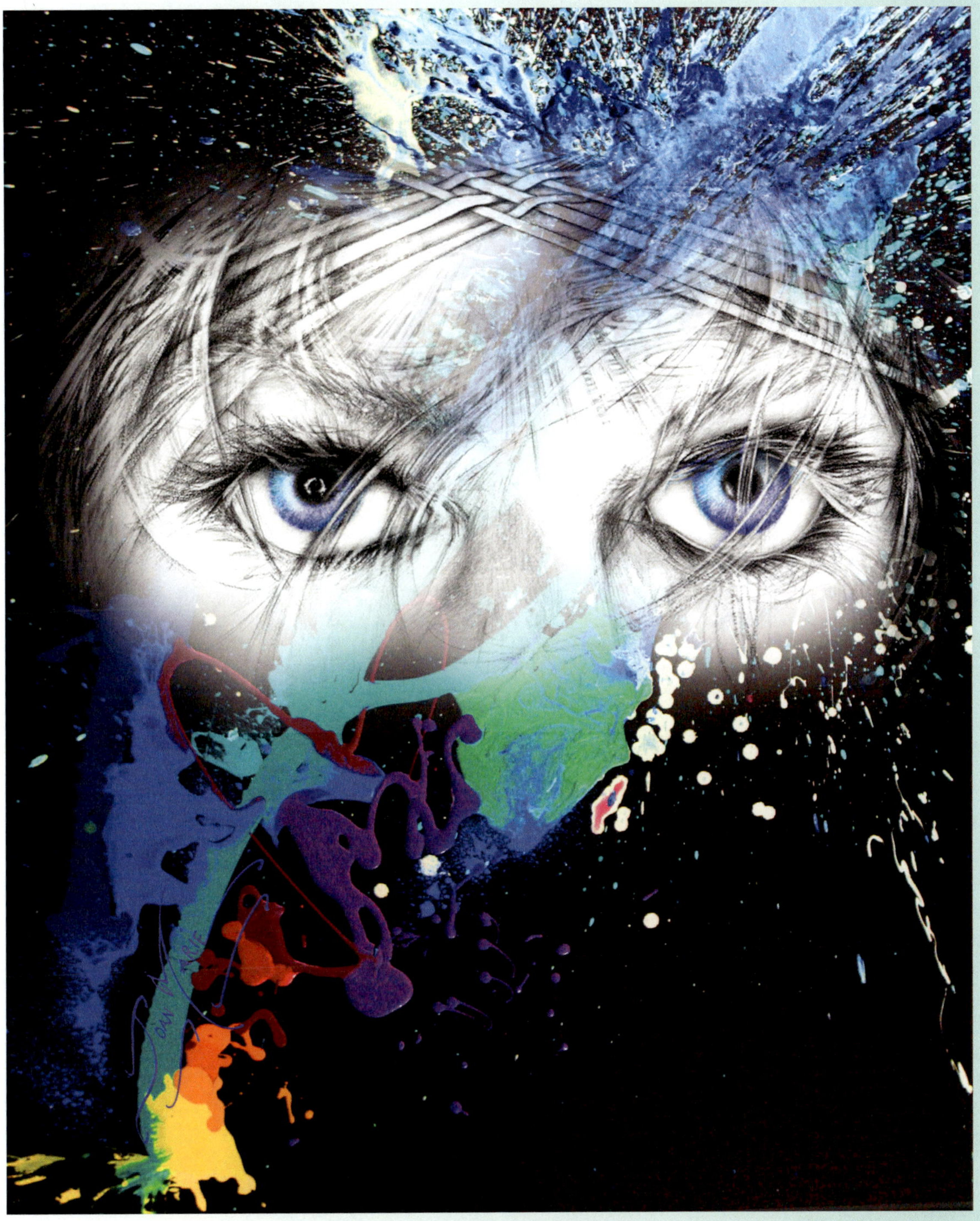

North Star

North Star

Stay focused on your goals

Fire and light shine from her eyes. She is colorful, creative and musical. She listens to messages from both heaven and earth passing through her third eye. Vibrant with intensity she shares her wisdom.

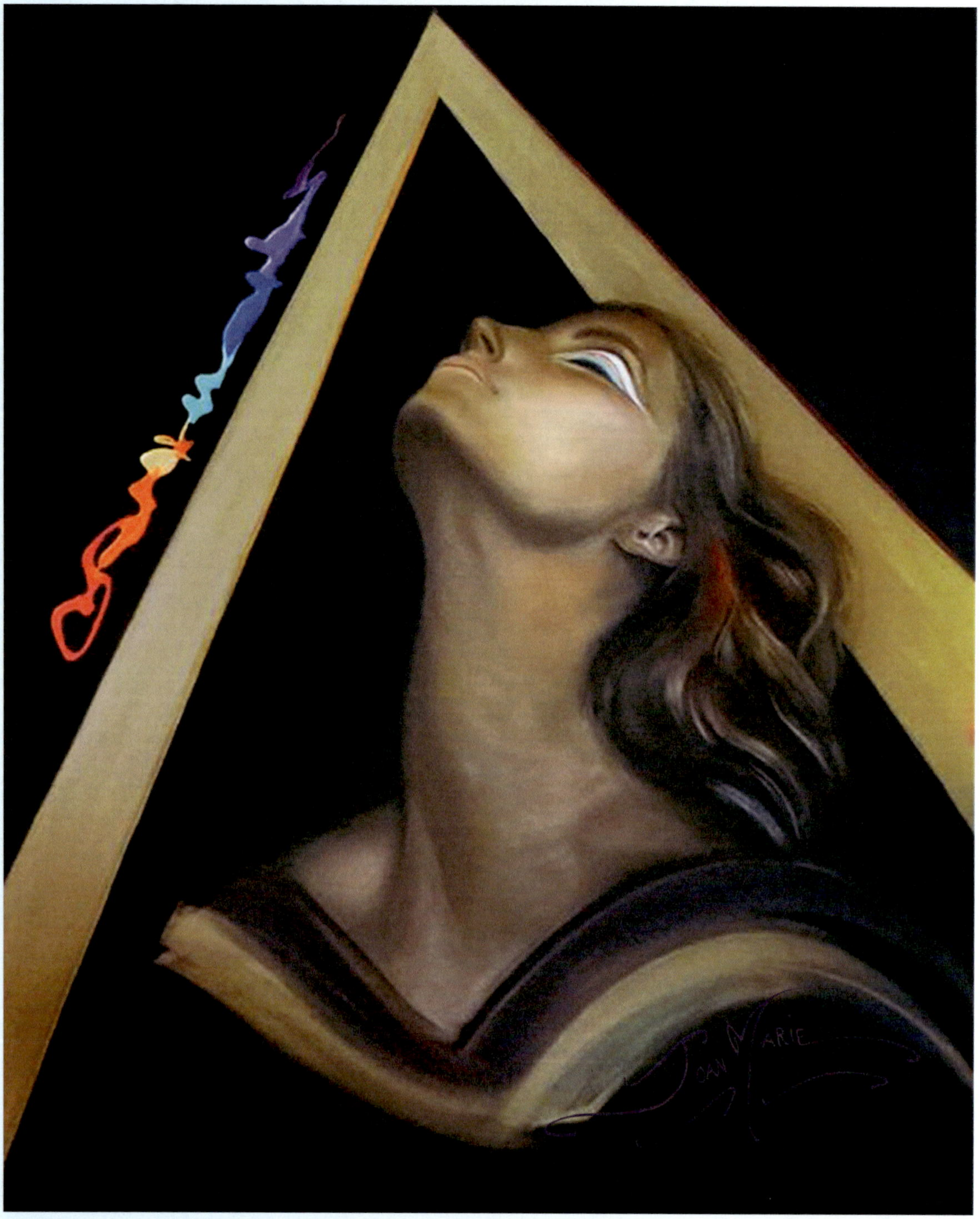

Open Compassion

Compassion

The world is healing from your compassion.
Feel your heart beaming love 'round the world.

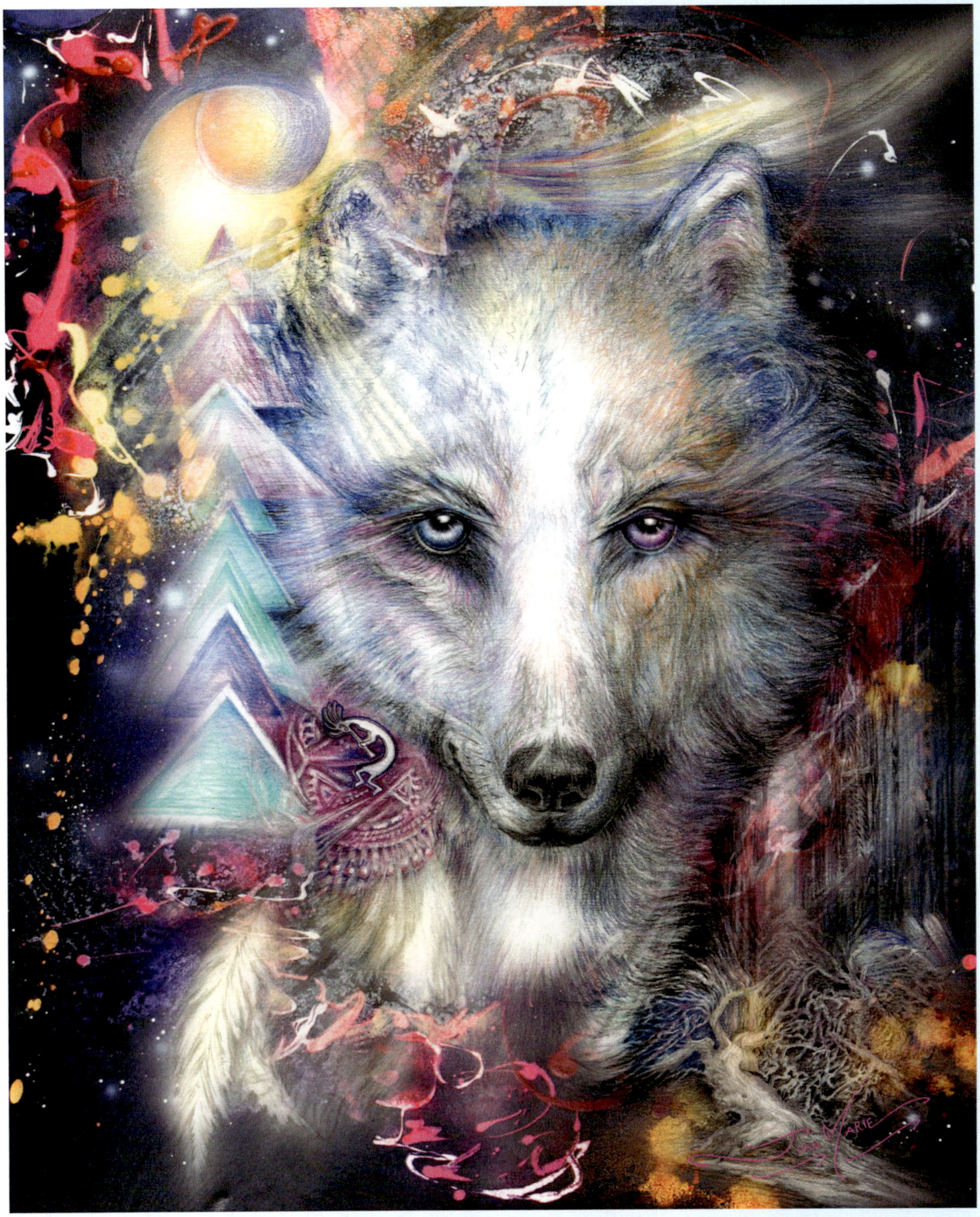

Spirit Protector

Spirit Protector

Escape the darkness, move into the light.
Kokopelli's flute dance fills the air with mystery
We are mesmerized by the presence of wisdom.

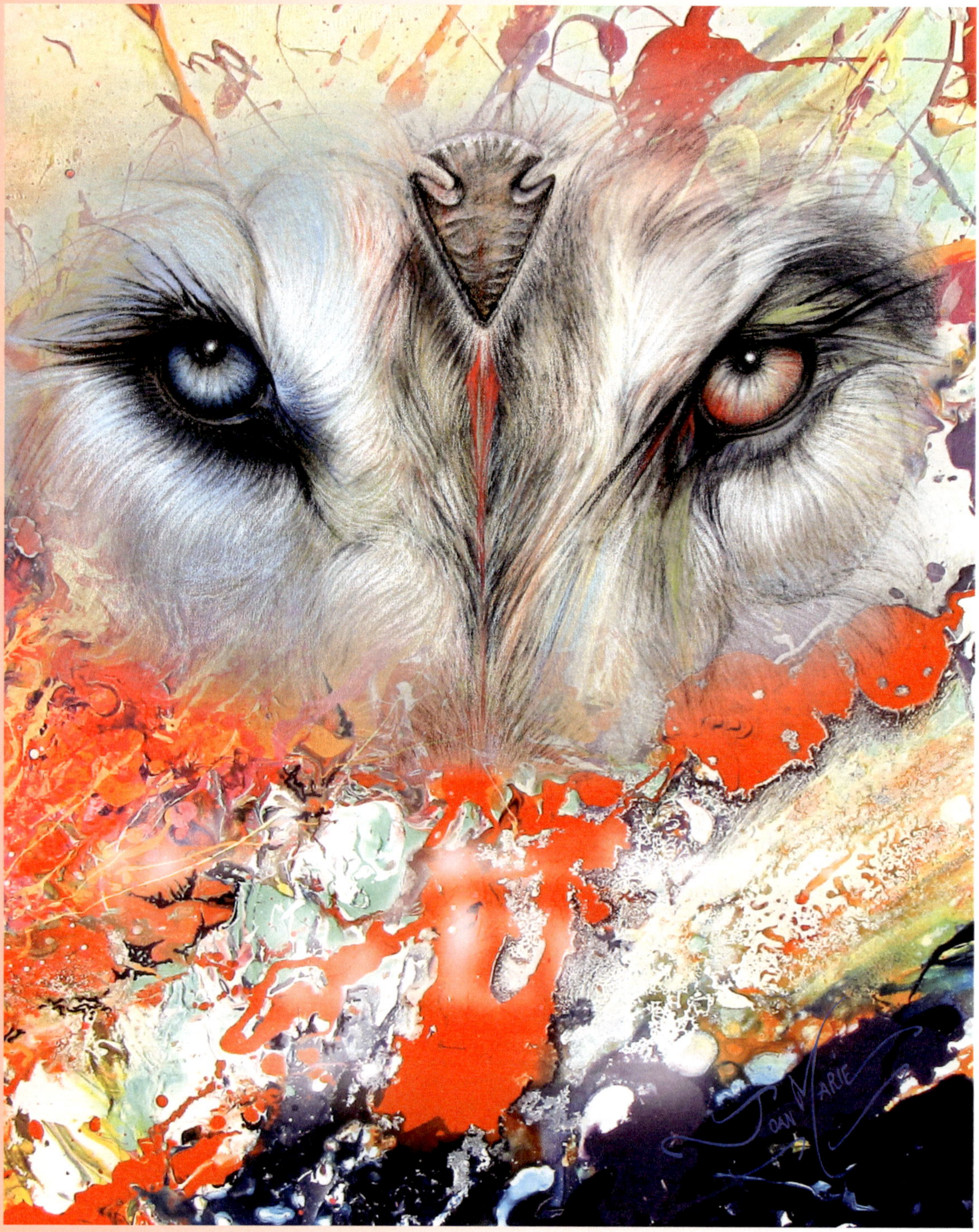

Protector

'Meet your Inner Goddess…She's Intense'

Words for painting by Kate Miller

Create the focus and determination to succeed.

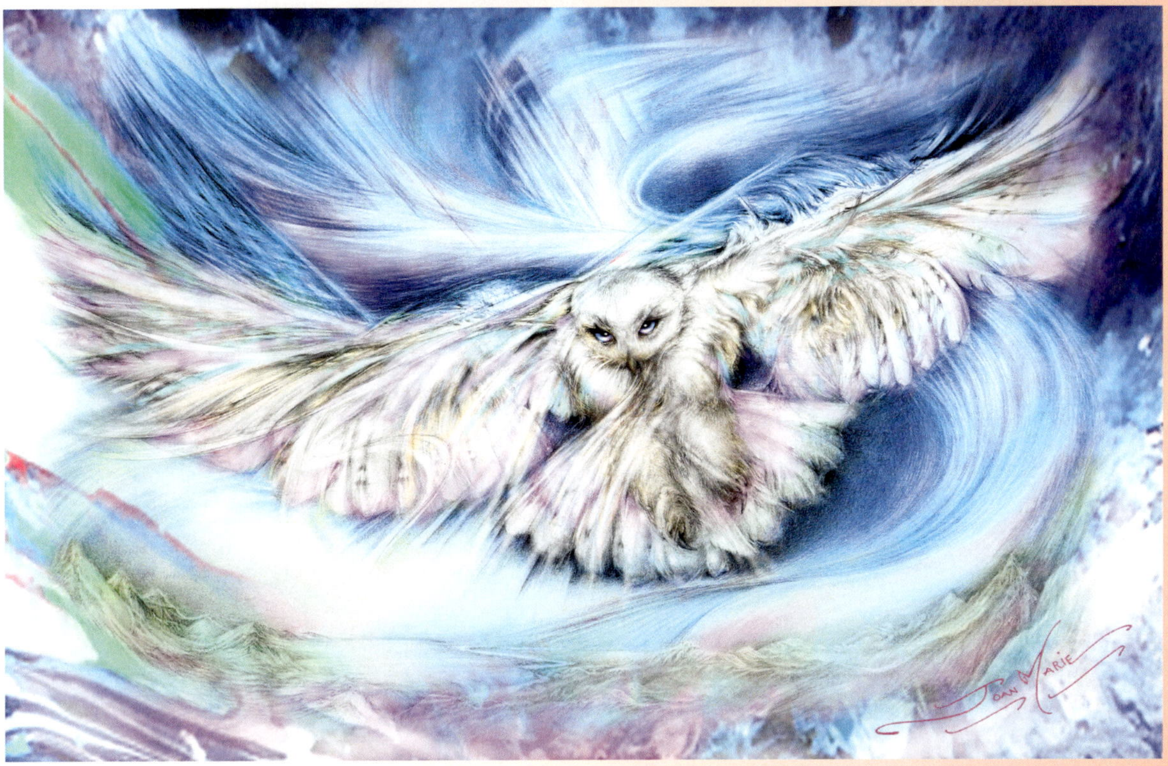

Destiny

Success begins with belief. It starts with believing inside that you are who you want to be. Once you believe that you are that person, FEEL how it feels to be that person, it will then feel natural to take steps toward that dream.

Enjoy the journey every minute, every day. As you develop the ability to see the world with compassion and trust, life takes on a glow: the glow of love. Stay on your path and practice viewing life through the eyes of love. You also might consider defining success differently.

What is success to you? Success can be feeling peace.

Success can be yours today and every day, accepting what is in this moment.

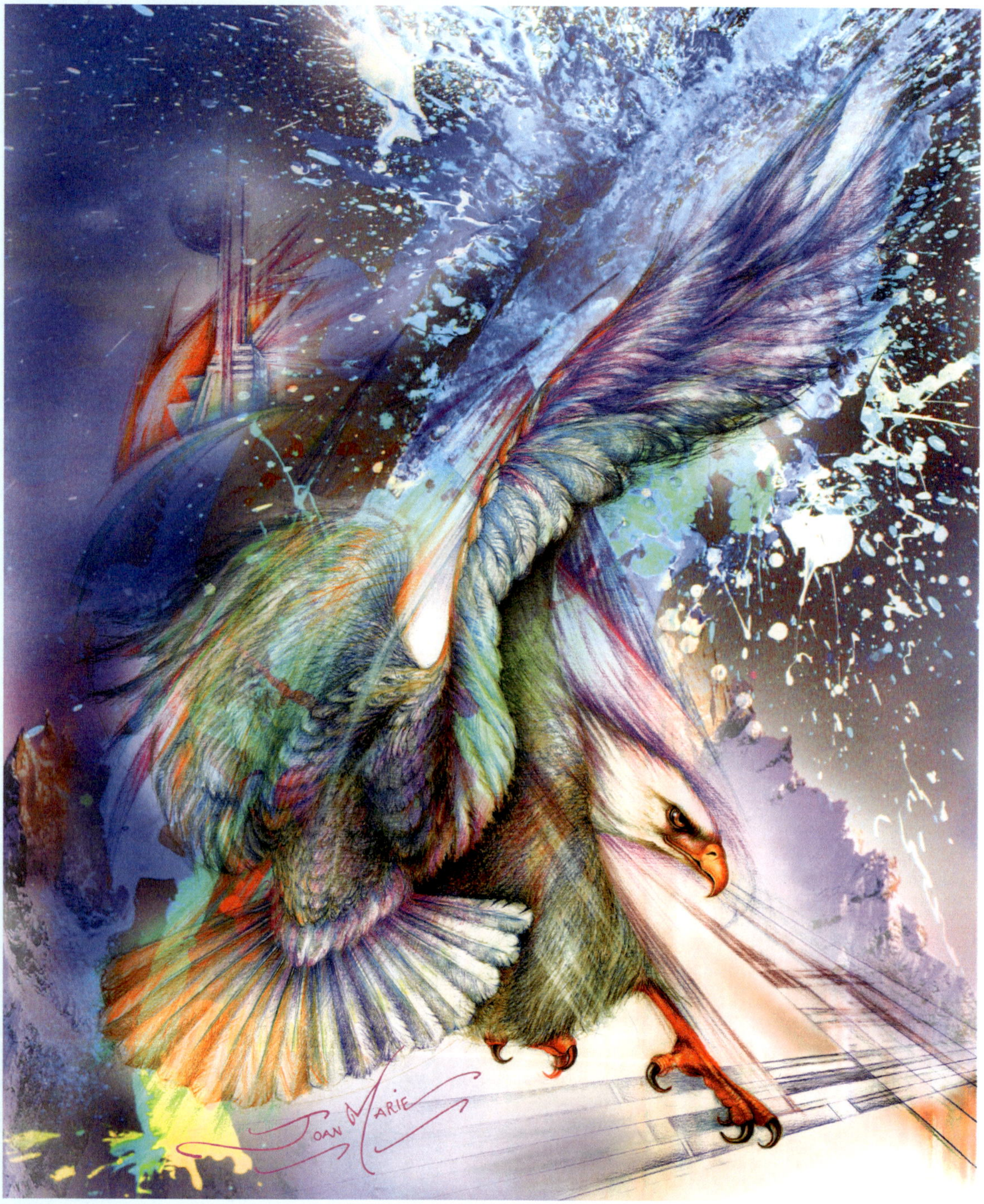

The Quest

The Quest

Reach high. Stretch more than you think you are capable of. Look at things with a greater perspective. Be patient with the present as you shift your vision to the skies. The eagle flies higher than any other bird.

Soar with him as he communicates with the heavens.

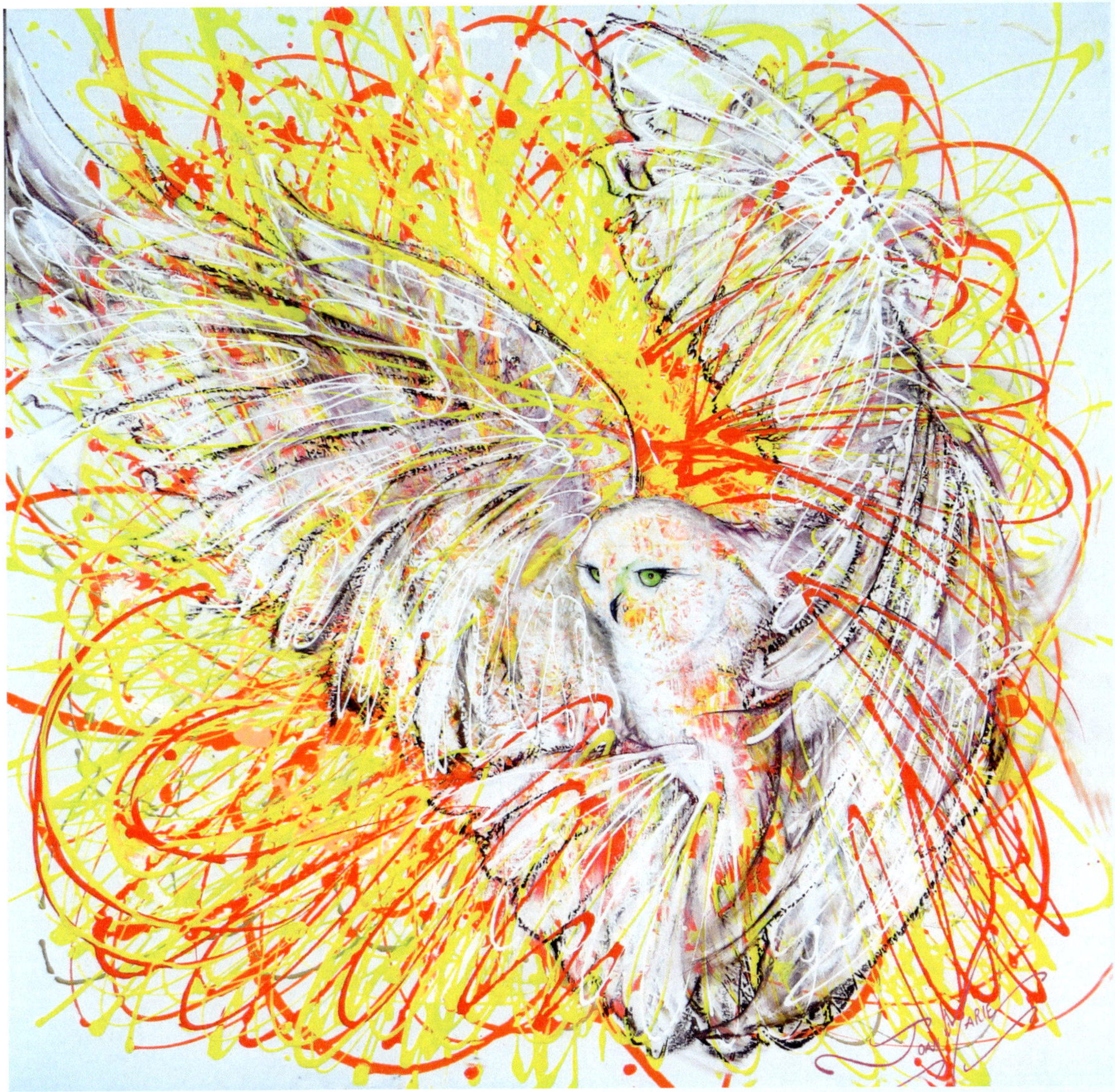

Out of the Chaos

Out of the Chaos

Out of chaos comes calm wisdom.
Glowing in the power of the sun,
the wise owl emerges from her challenges.
She has renewed confidence, power and grace.

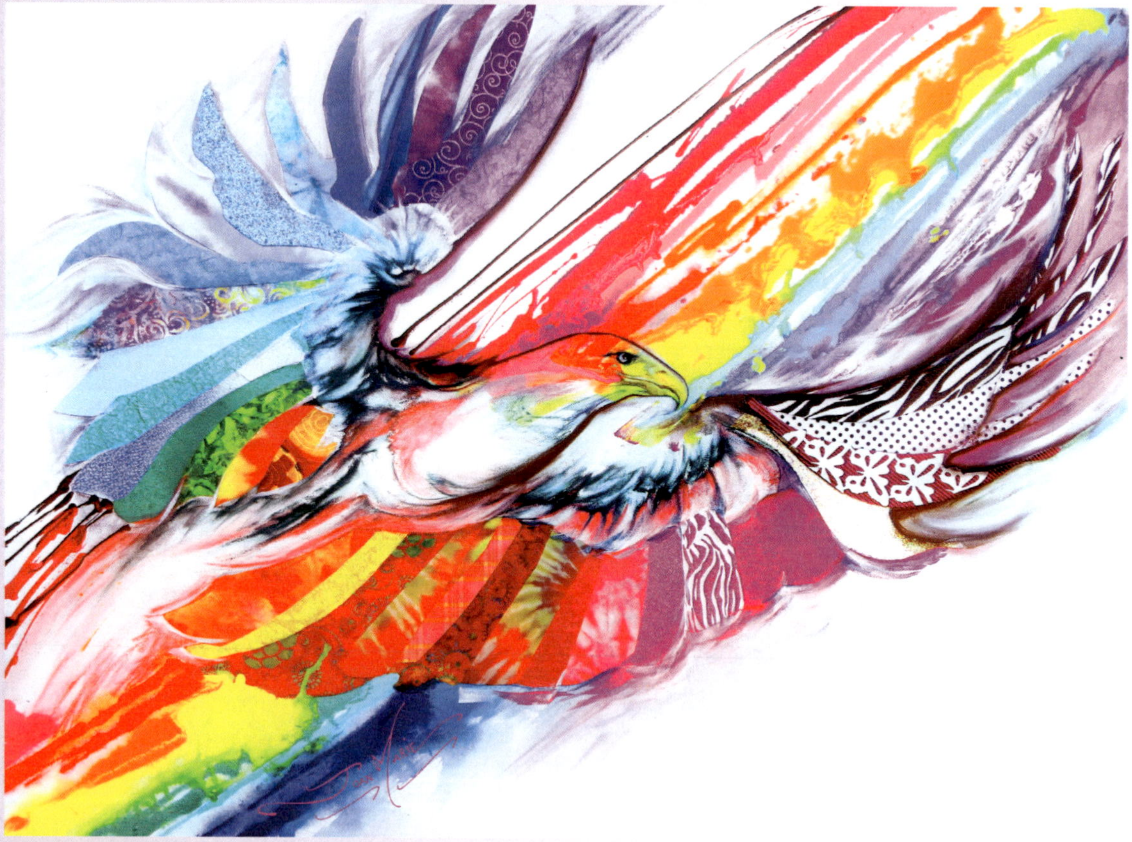

The Way

Uniting Together, and Flying HIGH

We are each represented by a feather on the wings of an eagle.
We are each unique, amazing, *flying and united as we experience this miraculous thing called life!*

"Looking for Space"

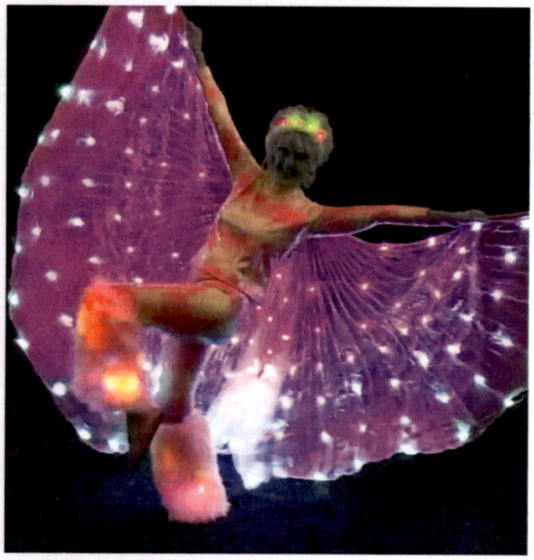

"It's a sweet, sweet dream
Sometimes I'm almost there
Sometimes I fly like an eagle
And sometimes I'm deep in despair…
Then I look in the center,
Suddenly everything's clear
I find myself in the sunshine and my dreams…
Sometimes I fly like an eagle
Like an eagle
I go flying High."
—John Denver

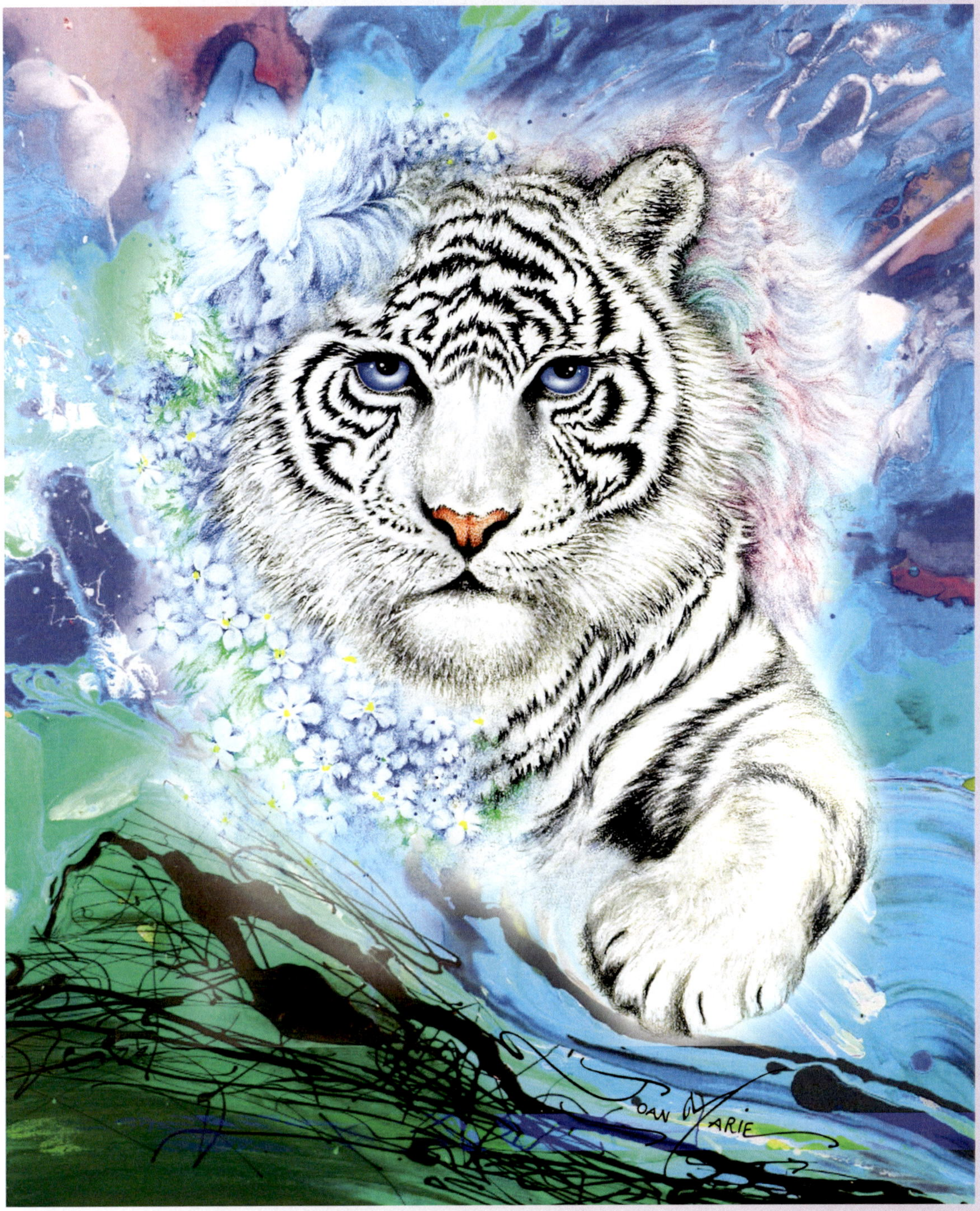

Bengal Magic

Vision and Courage

Fierce, protective and mysterious, she is both beautiful and strong. She is your guardian with magical, majestic energy. Full of vision and courage, she emits pure peace and power. Unite with the strength of her calmness.
Peace is the most powerful energy.

And the Tiger flew beside the Swans,
And the Swans said, "You cannot fly, you have no wings."
"Thank you for this information" said the Tiger
And on he Flew
–Kate Miller

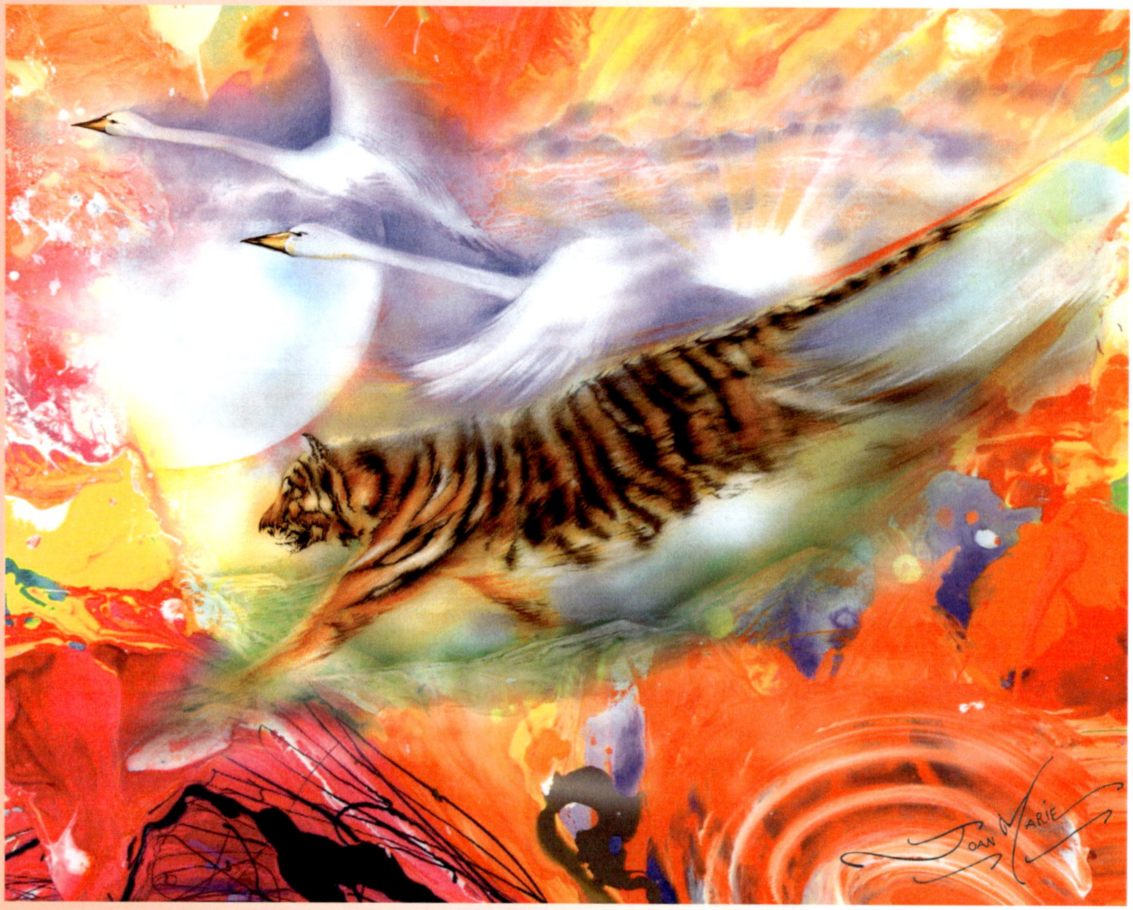

Victorious Flight

Victorious Flight

When first entering the business of art, I needed to be more grounded. Feeling more in touch with the spiritual world, I needed a way to flow with, embrace, and connect with the business world. Creating this painting helped me to connect with the grounded masculine energy (tiger) balanced with heavenly feminine energy (swans).

When you balance the two energies,
You feel the power to GO FOR IT!

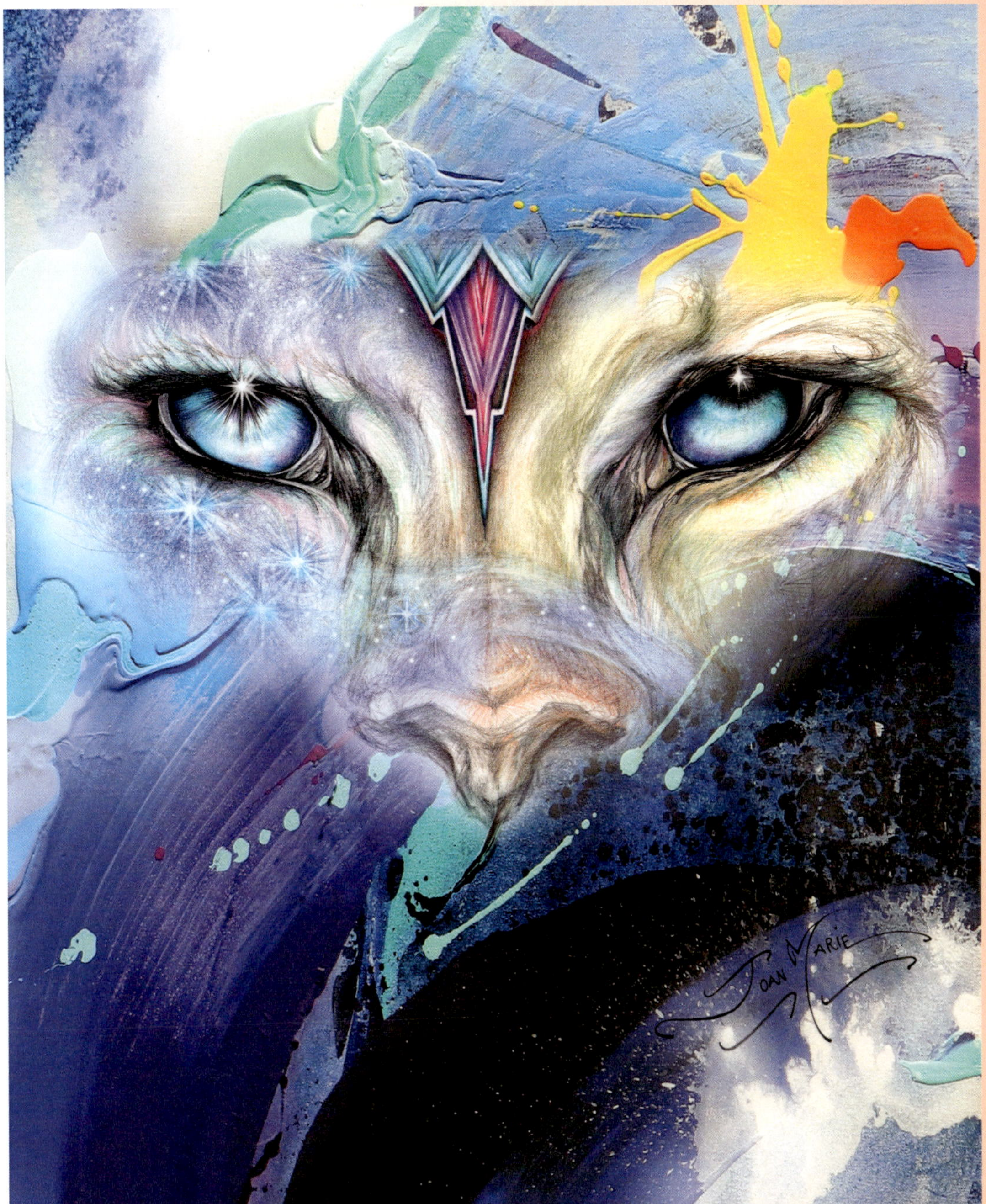

Mysterian

Mysterian

Feel the wisdom gained from passing through every storm. Connect to the gift of his calm majestic presence. Allow his strength to fill you with energy to stand in your power.

Inspired by the lion, Aslan, from the movie,
The Lion, the Witch and the Wardrobe

Magical Peace

Who are you in this circle of energy?
Unicorn, Dove, and Cathedral Spire are uniting,
beaming love to all the world.

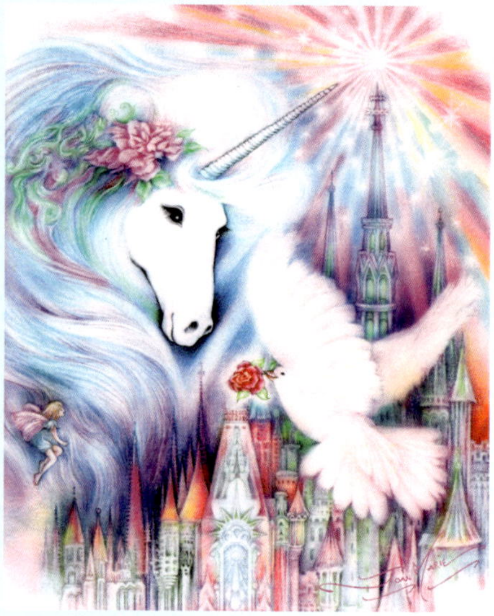

Magical Peace

God's Ride

Riding on life's rainbow of vibrant
swirling color, magic fills the air.

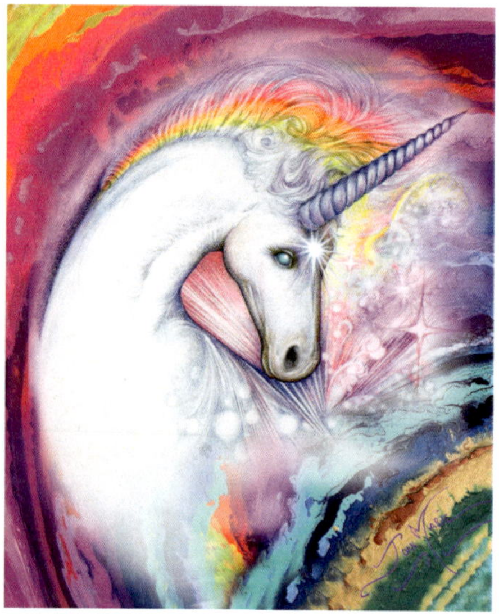

God's Ride

Unicorn Mist

Moonbeam enchantment
radiates her luminous soul.

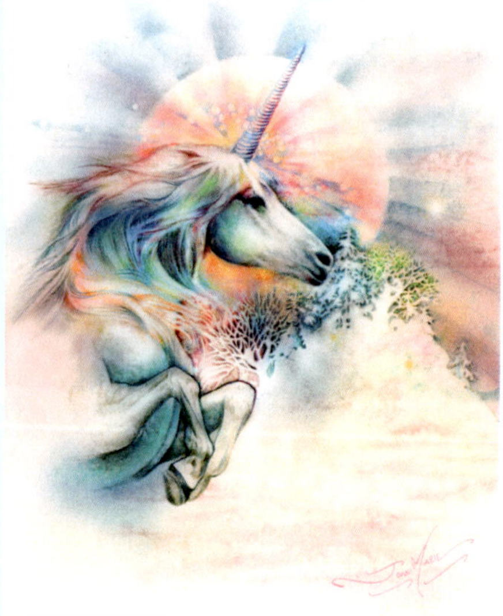

Unicorn Mist

Innocence

Purity and innocence at peace in this magical world.
Three precious fairies frolicking in her presence.

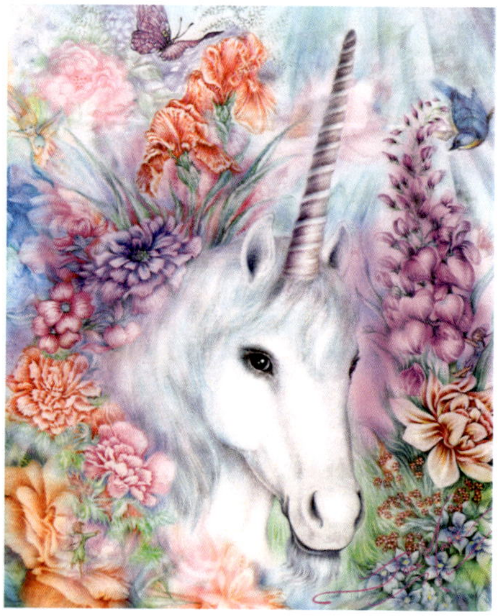

Innocence

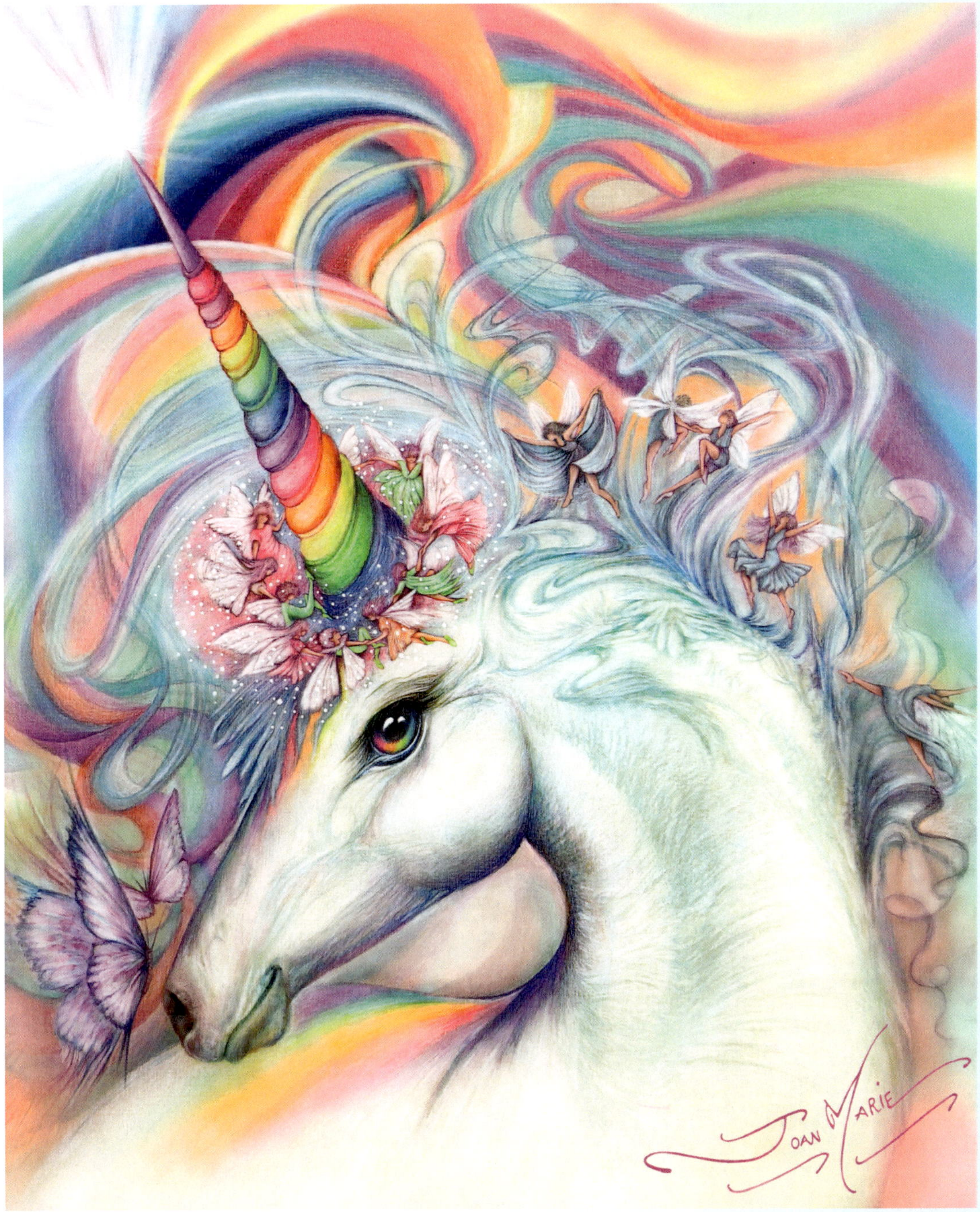

Magical Unicorn Fairy Parade

The Magical Unicorn Fairy Parade

Follow the Magical Unicorn Parade. Dance your way to Joy. Prance. Dance. Be Magical, Fantasize, and Dream BIG!

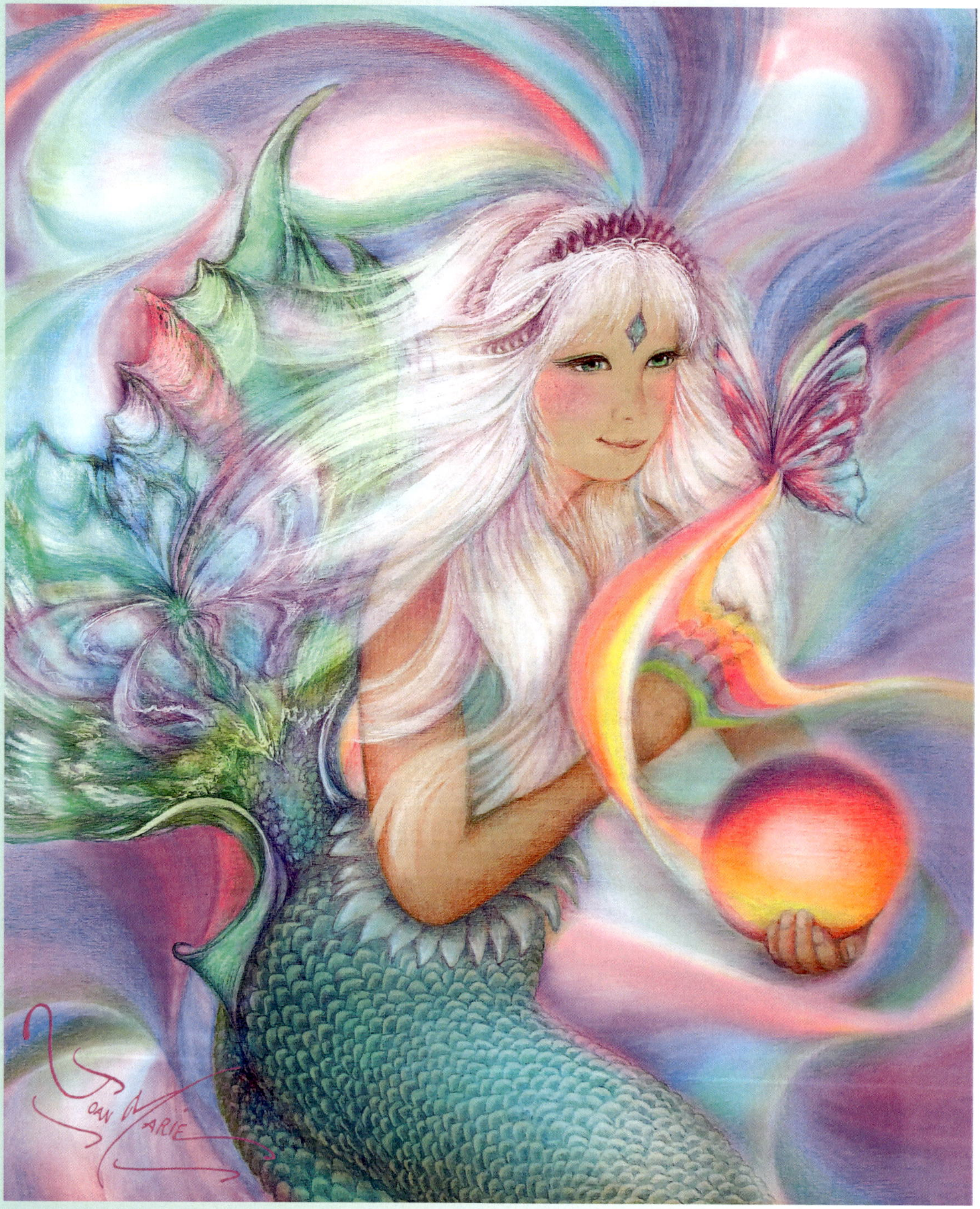

Mermaid Magic

Mermaid Magic

Serena's purity magically swirls love out into the world. Having the mermaid's power over nature, her innocent vision inspires peace.

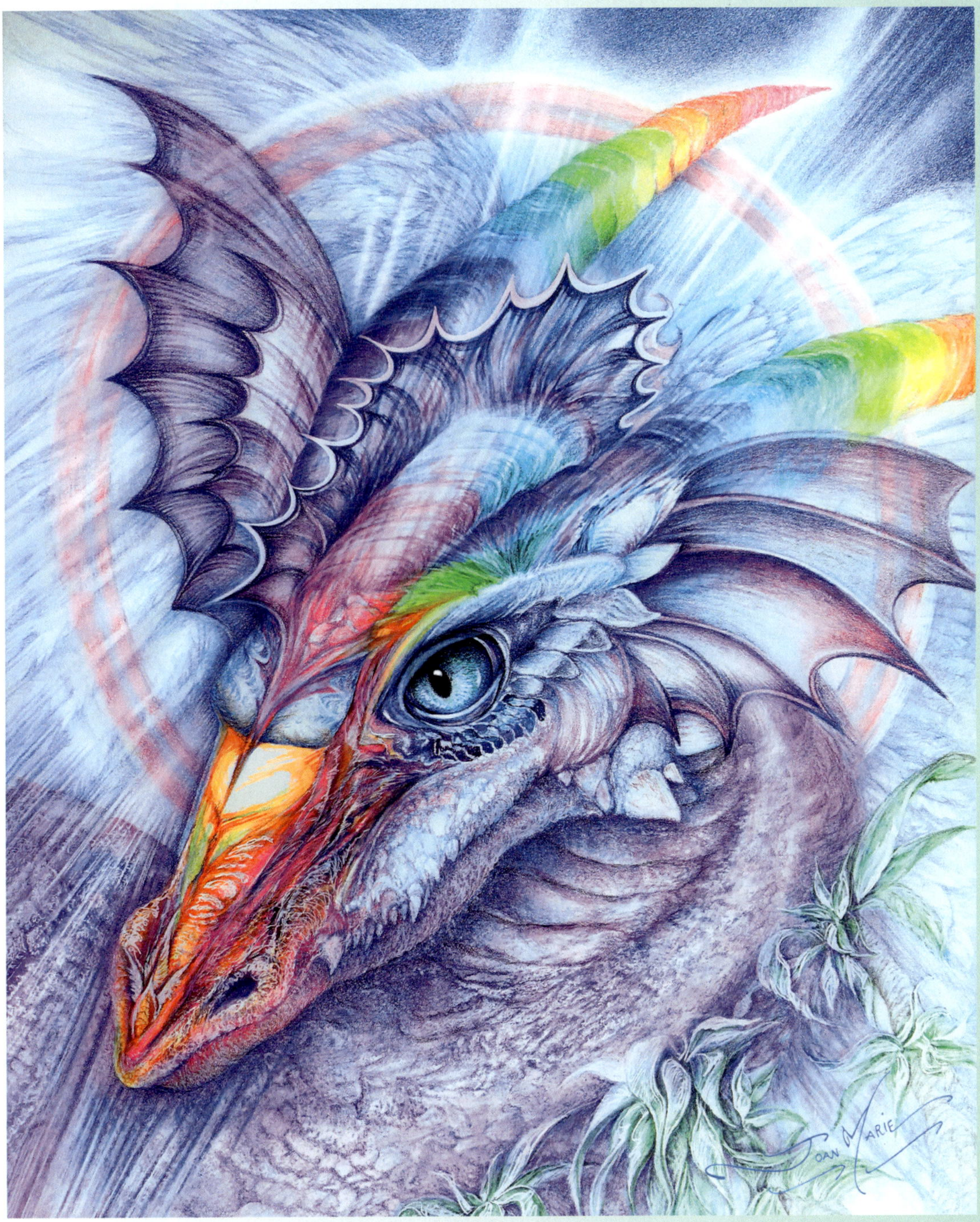

The Guardian of Peace

The Guardian of Peace

Hold on, everything's gonna be alright.
We are blessed with her magical protection and massive presence.
Relax in her optimism and bold energy. She is indeed our Guardian of Peace.

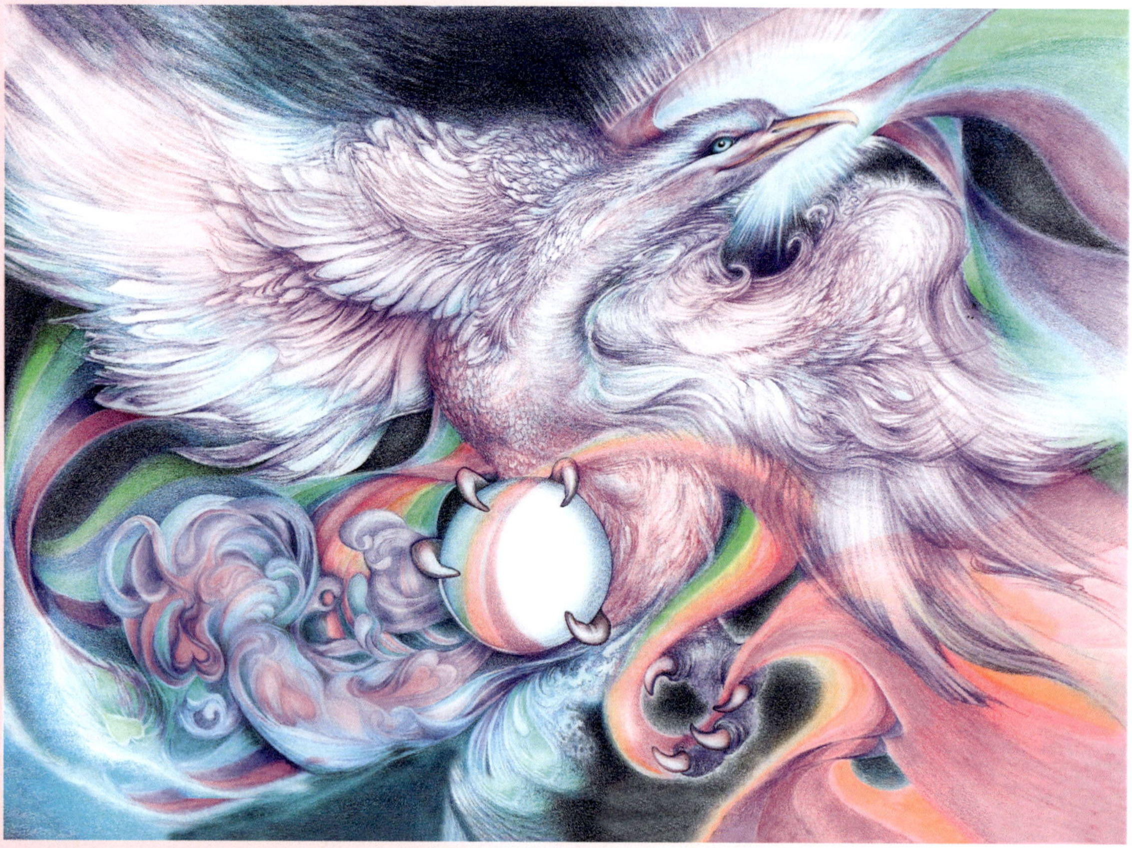

Deliverance of Expansion

PHOENIX

She is on a mission,
exhilarated with the victory of overcoming challenges.
It is now time to encircle the world with the power of healing love.
The world needs rejuvenation wrapped in swirls of love.

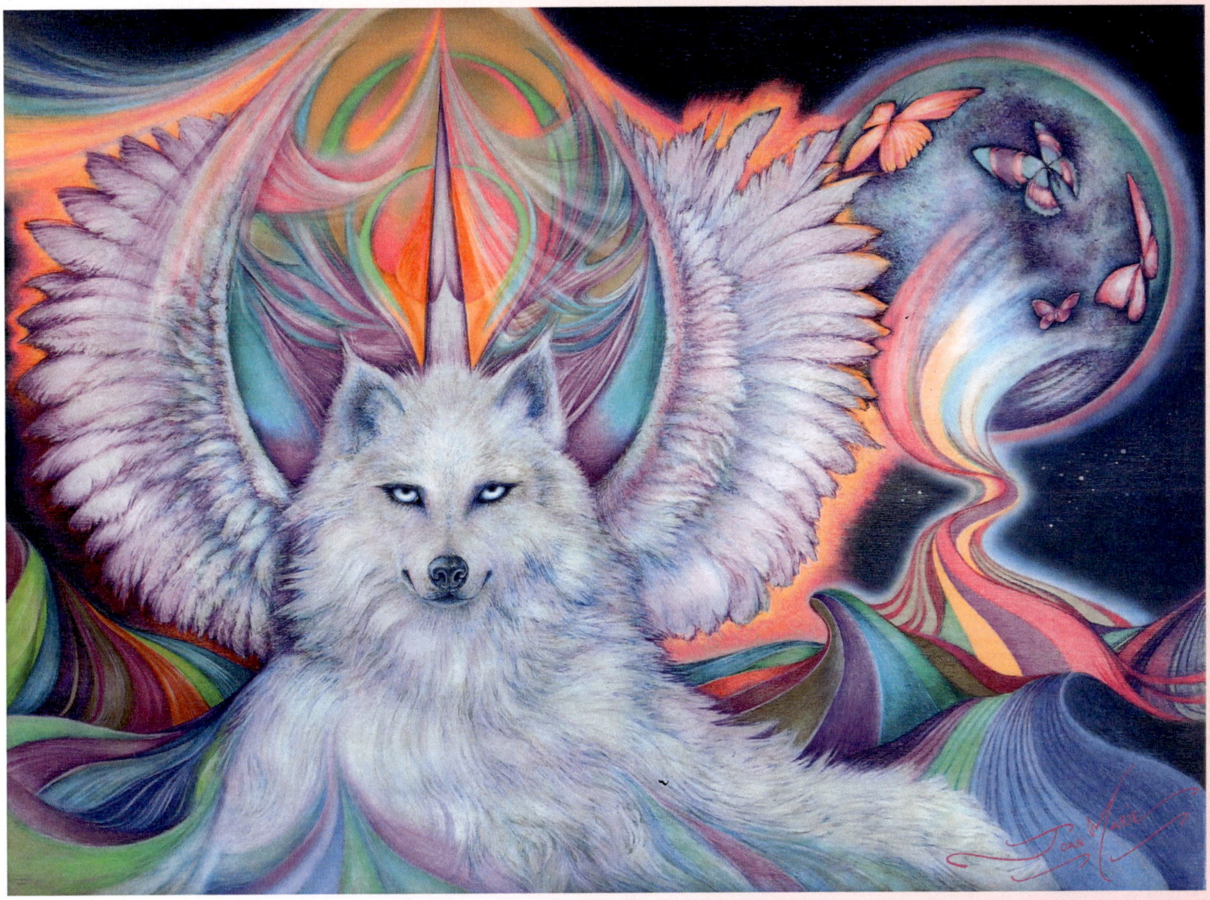

Majestic White Spirit

Majestic White Spirit

The ultimate symbol of believing in your potential.

Believing in herself, she is aware of her incredible potential. Energized by the swirling land of opportunity, she feels rooted in this magical world of possibilities. Her powerful horn beams endless creative ideas for the earth's new consciousness.

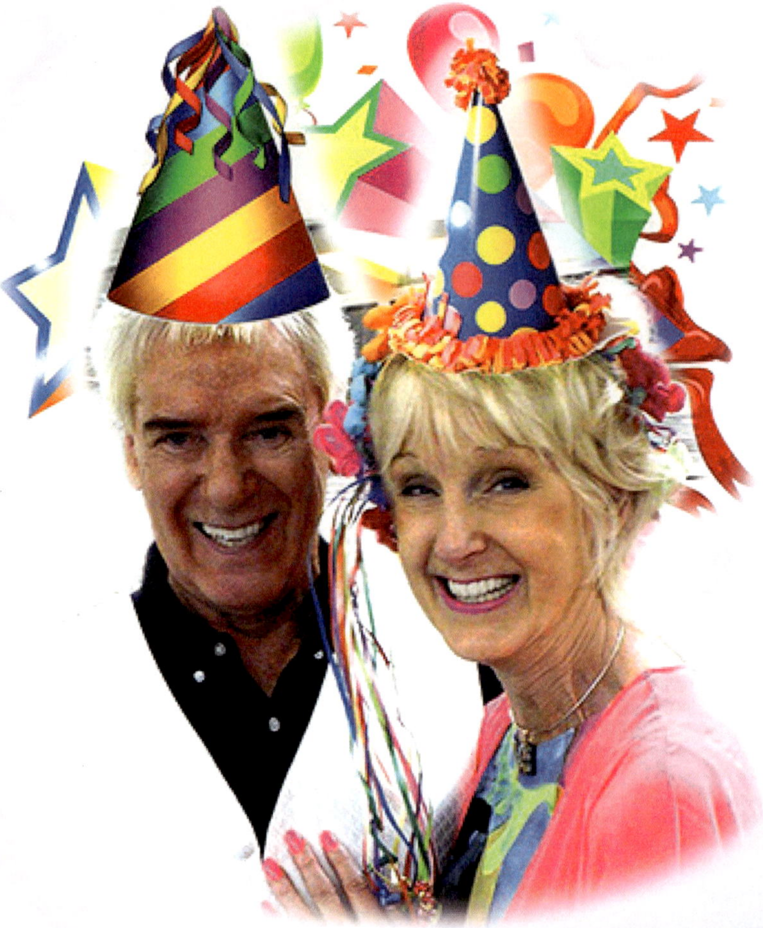

Acknowledgements

First and foremost, I bless my sweetie, George Hinds, for his endless support, humor, talent, and our love. He is my very own Renaissance man—an incredible musician, singer, writer, and artist. Thank you from the bottom of my heart for always being there for me, helping me spell every word correctly and pushing me as he suggests I need more darks in my painting. I know he's always right, darn it.

I have such a wonderful family! Thank you to my beautiful, fabulous daughter and my heart, Brittany Bishop, whom I forever bond with and get to share every feeling and thought even when she is miles away in California. I feel so blessed to have my best friends, sister Donna DeVoto and brother Paul Gast living near. Our weekly walks and talks are so healing, enlightening, and fun. Thank you, Paul, for my favorite line in the second paragraph of this book. Thank you to my Floridian big sister, Diane Becker, a fabulous artist with a heart of pure gold. No matter where we live, we are all a constant support for each other, such a blessing.

Oh, to be blessed with friends! Thank you, Brooke Harker, artist extraordinaire, and amazing fun friend, for your radiant linguistic coaching in the editing process! I endlessly Thank You!!!

My past student, forever friend and amazing artist, Lexi Zepp, edited with great suggestions and additions. I had no idea you had such great writing skills! Followed by my new best friend cutie-pie neighbor, Chris Collins, who was so enthusiastically willing to read and critique every moment I requested it. How fun is that? A huge thank you to Nancy Hightshoe, I originally sought her expertise on public speaking. However, it quickly turned into her giving me the perfect guidance and direction for this book. Thank you so much! And to my awesome friends Kate Miller and Marian Rein, so much love and fun thankfulness to you for the amazing contributions to this book, for your friendship and for so many ways you have enriched my life.

I am eternally grateful to Erin Duffy-Burke and Rhonda Mills for weekly providing Soul dancing, free-form movement, which has freed my body and heart endlessly to twirl and jump in response to music like Peter Pan. "I don't wanna Grow Up!"

Sending billows of gratitude to Laura Hollick. Her inspiring Soul Art Certification and Nu Icon programs set my artistic soul free! Laura, you are fabulous!

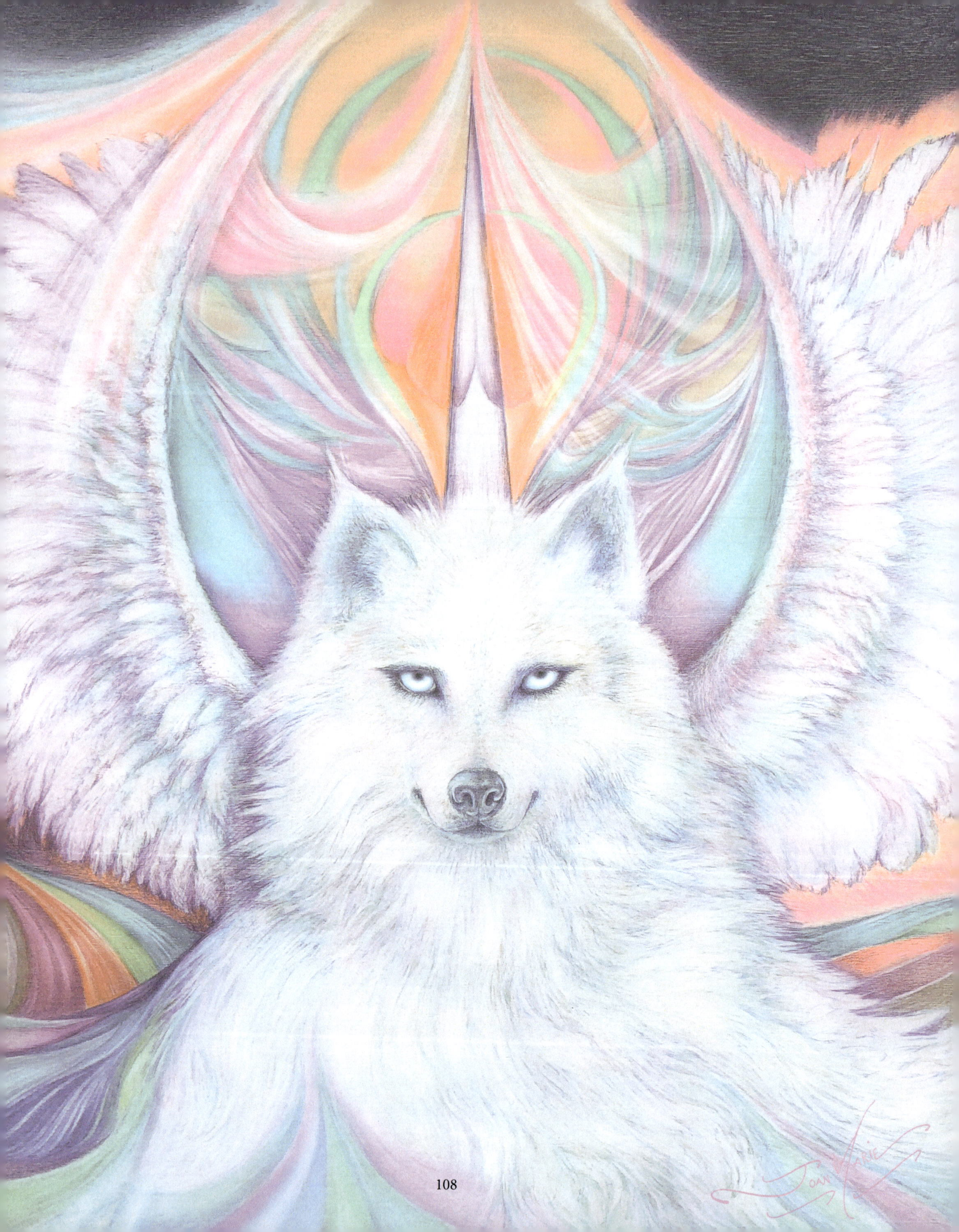

Contributors

I so deeply thank **Jim Fortin's** course TCP, The Transformational Coaching Program for inspiring major transformations I have made. I will start by saying that so much of what I have written in this book is thanks to his course. I am thankful for his incredible step by step clarity and constant personal guidance for everyone in the group. His pure heart of caring has helped everyone in the class experience major life changes! I have taken many spiritual classes over the years, (with some of the biggest names), but none have had his depth of wisdom or purity of intention and heart. You may also love checking out his fabulous Instagram feed: iamjimfortin. Please feel free to contact me with any questions about this inspiring life changing experience, or anything else of course.

A HUGE THANK YOU to my amazing FaceBook friends for always inspiring me, and who took the time to write their beautiful interpretations of my artwork! My original plan was to post them all in this book. I can't tell you how I tried to create a way to include all 10 pages, 5,000 words of them! To hear the different ways they interpreted my art with inspiring feelings filled my heart endlessly! I have saved them all and am planning a new way to share them. One plan may be to share them in my blog! With all my heart I Thank You so very very very much for your love and support!!

Adrienne Hoffman , Allison Lux Nuovo, Amanda Dowel, Amber Blandford, Amber Segura, Anisah Shu , Anna Clare Allen, Anne Moeckel, Annie Peters, Barb Zipperer, Beth Ann Thater Boesel, Betty MacConachie, Betty. L. Asher , Bob Allingham, Bonnie K Oliver, Bridgette Kossor, Burcu BB Beba, Cathy Lumsden, Cheri Chamberlin Weyermann, Cheri Layton, Chris Collins, Christine Richers, Christine Von Lossberg, Clare Fitzgerald , Debbie Wallace-Inman, Diane Price, Diane Weber, Donna Carroll, Donna M. Freeman, Donna Meyer Solomon, Dora Ficher, Doreen Flint, Dorey Searle Duncan, Dorothea Christel Maria LeBlanc, Eden Fasano, Elaine C. Tillinger, Elizabeth Wissbaum, Erin Duffy-Burke, Eveleen Murphy Fasano , Evelyn Whitson Brown , Gloria Corona-Prophet, Heather Starr, Janet Brandt, Janice Hovis, Jeanette Helton, Jeanette Lee, Jessica DeVoto, Jodie Jessmon, Karen Luke Goosic, Karen MacDonald , Karen White, Karla Blanco, Kate Miller, Katherine Riley, Kathy Fehr Cool, Kathy Granzeier Azzara, Katie Soy, Kay Moody Losciuto, Kymm Gaines Fehrs, Laura Hart Roberts, Laura Jaeger, Laura Lynne Dyer, Laura Montani, Leah Ashley, LeAnna Nicholson, Lisa DiPasquale Horner, Lisa R. DeGuzman, Lynne Dee Light Barrett, Margrieta Harma, Maria BonDurant, Marilyn Borgmann, Marla Goldberg , Mary Ellen Banks, Mary Francis Hoffman, Melissa Gordon, Meredith Ann Murray , Michelle Fink, Micki Hazz , Millie Hammer-Zelkowski , Mitzi MacDonald, Mitzi O'Keeffe, Nancy Hightshoe, Nancy Powell, Natalie Wanzel, Nina Lancia Walton, Norma Jean Terry, Pamela Burba, Parvin Nadimi, Pauline Nicols , Phyllis Thorpe, Raeeka Shehabi-Yaghmai , Rebecca May, Reina Cottier Artist , Sandra Kiefer Rothermich, Sarah Capps, Sarah Hodgkinson, Scotty Campbell, Sharon Burks Palas , Sharon Elaine Porter, Sue McClure, Sunne Bernt , Suzanne Gibbs, Suzanne Meindl-Lemley , Tamara Howard, Teresa Winston, Tina Harmon , Vicky Wilson-Hill, and Yoshi Arima .

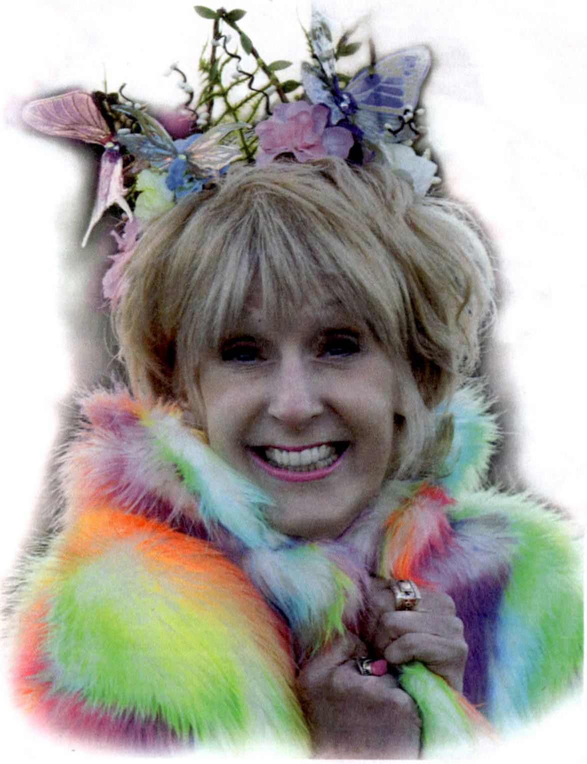

Joan Marie creates with exuberant joy! Whether capturing your heart through the eyes of an eagle, precious kitty, or dynamic women, her passion for life shines through. If you wonder why you feel better when her art is around you, you are receiving her subliminal messages. Life is meant to be fun. Love is the most important thing.

Her intense dedication as an artist began at age 19 when awestruck by Michelangelo's Sistine Ceiling.

Her captivating portraits, whether expressing the fascinating power of your spirit animal, or capturing your loved ones' face and heart, leave you feeling uplifted.

49 years of driven dedication to express the powerful joys of life have resulted in magical art that needs to be seen and felt.

During 28 years inspiring art in the public schools, her goal was to help students discover and love who they are, while developing their skills to express their unique voice.

As a drawing and painting major, receiving her BFA from Washington University in St. Louis, and her MFA from the University of South Florida in Tampa, and Lindenwood University in St. Louis, her focus was developing classical drawing skills.

With national and international agency representation, her art is licensed by multiple companies, selling millions of products such as collector plates, transfers, stationery, puzzles, etc., gracing dozens of books and magazine covers, and purchased by hundreds of private collections around the world. Shifting her focus, she was inspired by music, creating abstract music paintings. Throwing, pouring, and tipping paint, she intuitively transformed the energy of favorite songs into wild and mystical abstract paintings. Galleries in Miami, Chicago, Denver, and St. Louis enthusiastically displayed her radiant colors and explosive energy. Returning to her passion for romantic realism she created a new voice combining the two worlds of wild abstraction and her MFA classically trained drawing skills. She has created a magical mix of ecstatic energy and passionate detail capturing life's passion!

Join her magical world of believing in the joys of life
www.JoanMarieArt.com!
JoanMarieArt@charter.net

NCCN Guidelines for Patients®

La guía esencial para las personas que se enfrentan al cáncer.

Basada en las recomendaciones para la atención de destacados expertos en oncología.

Explica la atención oncológica de alta calidad que se brinda en centros oncológicos de vanguardia.

Revisada y corregida todos los años.

¿Sabía que los principales centros oncológicos de los Estados Unidos colaboran para mejorar la atención oncológica? Esta alianza de los principales centros oncológicos se denomina National Comprehensive Cancer Network® (NCCN®).

Como la atención oncológica está en constante evolución, NCCN elabora y actualiza con frecuencia recomendaciones basadas en pruebas que utilizan los profesionales de atención médica de todo el mundo. Estas recomendaciones se conocen como NCCN Clinical Practice Guidelines in Oncology (NCCN Guidelines®).

En NCCN Guidelines for Patients, se explican de manera sencilla estas recomendaciones de los expertos, para que pueda hablar con su equipo de atención médica sobre la mejor atención para usted.

NCCN Guidelines for Patients se basa en NCCN Guidelines® para la leucemia mieloide aguda (versión 3.2026, 24 de noviembre de 2025).

Ver NCCN Guidelines for Patients gratis en Internet: NCCN.org/patientguidelines

Buscar un centro oncológico de NCCN cerca de usted: NCCN.org/cancercenters

Conocer cómo se preparan las NCCN Guidelines for Patients: NCCN.org/patient-guidelines-process

Comuníquese con nosotros

@NCCNorg @NCCNVideo NCCN @NCCNorg

Quiénes nos apoyan

NATIONAL COMPREHENSIVE CANCER NETWORK®
NCCN FOUNDATION
Guiding Treatment. Changing Lives.

NCCN Guidelines for Patients cuenta con el apoyo financiero de NCCN Foundation®

NCCN Foundation agradece profundamente a las siguientes empresas colaboradoras por hacer posible esta NCCN Guidelines for Patients: Kura Oncology.

NCCN adapta, actualiza y aloja de forma independiente la guía de NCCN Guidelines for Patients. Nuestras empresas colaboradoras no participan en la elaboración de esta NCCN Guidelines for Patients y no se responsabilizan del contenido ni las recomendaciones que se incluyen en la presente guía.

Para hacer una donación, visite NCCNFoundation.org/Donate

Para obtener más información, visite la página NCCN.org/patientguidelines o envíe un correo electrónico a PatientGuidelines@NCCN.org